LIGHT & Luscious

LIGHT & Luscious

Oxmoor House®

Copyright 1994 by Oxmoor House, Inc.
Book Division of Southern Progress Corporation
P.O. Box 2463, Birmingham, Alabama 35201

Library of Congress Catalog Card Number: 93-87339
ISBN: 0-8487-1150-5

Manufactured in the United States of America
First Printing 1994

Editor-in-Chief: Nancy J. Fitzpatrick
Senior Foods Editor: Susan Carlisle Payne
Senior Editor, Editorial Services: Olivia Kindig Wells
Director of Manufacturing: Jerry R. Higdon
Art Director: James Boone

Light & Luscious

Editor: Anne C. Chappell, M.S., M.P.H., R.D.
Foods Editor: Cathy A. Wesler, R.D.
Copy Editor: Holly Ensor
Editorial Assistant: Rebecca Meng Sommers
Director, Test Kitchens: Vanessa Taylor Johnson
Assistant Director, Test Kitchens: Gayle Hays Sadler
Test Kitchen Home Economists: Beth Floyd,
Michele Brown Fuller, Telia Johnson, Elizabeth Luckett,
Christina A. Pieroni, Kathleen Royal,
Angie Neskaug Sinclair, Jan A. Smith
Photographer: Ralph Anderson
Photo Stylist: Virginia R. Cravens
Designer: Carol Middleton
Production Manager: Rick Litton
Associate Production Manager: Theresa L. Beste
Production Assistant: Marianne Jordan
Recipe Developers: Susan S. Bradley,
Trish Leverett, Debby Maugans,
Jane Ingrassia Reinsel, Elizabeth J. Taliaferro

Cover and Title Page: *Chocolate Torte* (page 218)
Frontispiece: *Creamy Cantaloupe Dessert Soup* (page 206)
Back Cover: *Lobster with Creamy Curry Sauce* (page 123)

TABLE OF CONTENTS

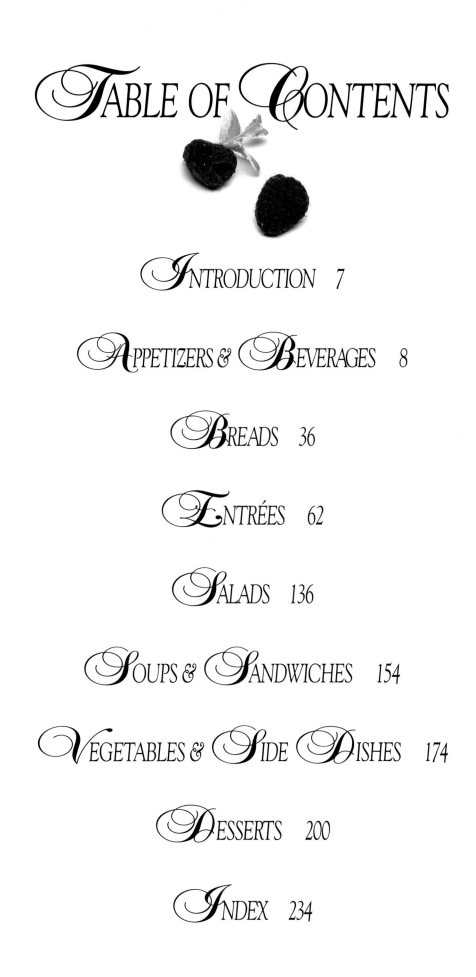

INTRODUCTION

Light & Luscious is essentially two cookbooks in one. You can choose between two versions of every recipe, using either the light version (left side of page) that is lower in fat and calories, or the more luscious version (right side of page) when fat and calories don't matter. The recipe titles will also help remind you of the difference in the recipes. The titles for the light recipes have a simpler-looking design; the luscious recipe titles are printed more decoratively.

The concept of each recipe is the same, but the light version incorporates low-fat ingredients and cooking techniques; some light recipes even offer an entirely different presentation of a traditionally high-fat food. The light recipes represent a moderate, commonsense approach to healthy eating; the luscious recipes were developed with indulgence in mind.

As you prepare the foods in this book, be sure to read the notes at the top of each page. This information highlights the differences between the two recipes on each page and explains the techniques used to decrease fat and calories. As you become familiar with the ways we have lightened our recipes, try the same techniques in some of your own recipes.

RECIPE MODIFICATIONS

You don't have to compromise flavor even though you're reducing fat and calories. The luscious quiche with its light counterpart pictured on the opposite page is an example of how we lightened a luscious recipe using the following principles:

Simple substitutions. Replace high-fat products with low-fat products. Add skim milk instead of whole milk, low-fat or nonfat cheeses in place of regular cheeses, and egg substitute or egg whites instead of whole eggs. Use reduced-calorie margarine, nonfat mayonnaise and salad dressings, nonfat yogurt, and nonfat sour cream regularly. Select lean meats and skinned poultry instead of high-fat meats.

Reduced amounts of high-fat ingredients. You can reduce the amounts of high-fat ingredients, especially strong-flavored ones such as sharp cheeses and nuts. For example, for a lightened muffin you can stir in 1/2 cup pecans instead of 1 1/2 cups. Frequently,

Left: *Light Spinach and Mushroom Quiche (top left) and Leek and Onion Quiche (page 134)*

you can replace some of the volume of a high-fat ingredient such as almonds with a low-fat ingredient such as blueberries.

Cooking methods. Use low-fat methods instead of high-fat methods. For example, bake, steam, or poach instead of deep-fat frying or pan-frying.

Healthy flavor enhancers. To limit fat and sodium but not flavor, infuse foods with high-flavor, low-fat, low-sodium ingredients such as vinegars, liqueurs, wines, extracts, herbs, spices, and fruit juices.

NUTRITIONAL ANALYSIS

Each recipe serving is analyzed for the following:

Calories	Fat
Percent calories from fat	Saturated fat
Carbohydrate	Cholesterol
Protein	Sodium

Over three-fourths of the light recipes derive no more than 30 percent of calories from fat.

Serving sizes for both versions are the same so that the nutritional analysis will offer a realistic comparison.

The nutrient breakdown for each recipe is derived from a computer analysis based on information from the U.S. Department of Agriculture. The nutrient values are based on the following guidelines:
- All nutrient breakdowns are listed per serving.
- When a range is given for an ingredient, the lesser amount is calculated.
- A reduction is calculated for the percentage of calories that evaporates when alcohol is heated.
- When a marinade is used, only the amount absorbed is calculated.
- Garnishes and other optional ingredients are not calculated.
- Fruits and vegetables are not peeled unless specified in the ingredient list.
- The fat that is used for greasing pans in luscious recipes is included in the analysis.
- If salt and/or fat are used in a luscious recipe to cook rice or pasta, the approximate amount of salt and fat absorbed is calculated.

We live in a world where we often choose a healthy eating style to feel better, have more energy, and live longer. But we also deserve to occasionally indulge and reward ourselves with our favorite foods. *Light & Luscious* offers the best of both worlds.

From left:
*Hot Spinach
Crabmeat Dip (page 11),
Chicken Nacho Dip (page 12),
Tropical Slush Punch (page 35)*

APPETIZERS & BEVERAGES

In Chunky Guacamole, some of the high-fat avocado is replaced with fat-free salad dressing and nonfat cream cheese, making the recipe as creamy as the luscious one but with one-fourth the fat.

CHUNKY GUACAMOLE

1	medium-size ripe avocado, peeled and mashed
¼	cup plus 3 tablespoons commercial fat-free Ranch-style dressing
¼	cup nonfat process cream cheese product
1	teaspoon lime juice
½	teaspoon ground cumin
1	cup seeded, diced tomato
½	cup diced sweet red pepper
½	cup diced green pepper
¼	cup diced purple onion
¼	cup minced fresh cilantro
2	tablespoons minced, seeded jalapeño pepper

Combine first 5 ingredients in a large bowl; stir until smooth. Add tomato and remaining ingredients; stir gently. Serve with cucumber and zucchini rounds. Yield: 3¼ cups.

Per tablespoon: Calories 12 (45% from fat)
Carbohydrate 1.2g Protein 0.3g Fat 0.6g (Sat. Fat 0.1g)
Cholesterol 0mg Sodium 29mg

Creamy Guacamole

2	medium-size ripe avocados, peeled and mashed
½	cup whipped cream cheese
1	teaspoon lemon juice
¼	cup minced green onions
2	tablespoons minced fresh cilantro
1	teaspoon Worcestershire sauce
½	teaspoon hot sauce
½	cup sour cream
½	cup (2 ounces) shredded Cheddar cheese
½	cup seeded, diced tomato
¼	cup sliced ripe olives
¼	cup drained sliced pickled jalapeño pepper

Combine first 3 ingredients in a large bowl; stir until smooth. Add green onions and remaining ingredients; stir gently. Serve with tortilla chips. Yield: 4 cups.

Per tablespoon: Calories 26 (83% from fat)
Carbohydrate 0.8g Protein 0.6g Fat 2.4g (Sat. Fat 1.0g)
Cholesterol 4mg Sodium 33mg

Either of these crabmeat dips is sure to please any crowd. Instead of high-fat bacon and pecans, crisp water chestnuts provide the crunch in Hot Spinach Crabmeat Dip.

HOT SPINACH CRABMEAT DIP

¾ cup nonfat ricotta cheese
¾ cup plus 2 tablespoons skim milk
½ cup nonfat mayonnaise
1 tablespoon dry sherry
1 (10-ounce) package frozen chopped spinach, thawed
1 (8-ounce) can sliced water chestnuts, drained and chopped
6 ounces fresh lump crabmeat, drained
¾ cup (3 ounces) shredded reduced-fat Monterey Jack cheese
½ cup drained finely diced roasted red pepper in water
¼ cup minced green onions
½ teaspoon hot sauce
Vegetable cooking spray

Press ricotta cheese through a fine-mesh sieve into a large bowl. Add skim milk, mayonnaise, and sherry; stir well.

Drain spinach; press between paper towels to remove excess moisture. Add spinach and next 6 ingredients to cheese mixture; stir well. Spoon mixture into a 1½-quart casserole coated with cooking spray. Cover and bake at 350° for 30 minutes. Uncover and bake an additional 10 minutes or until hot and bubbly. Serve with toasted pita wedges. Yield: 4¾ cups.

Per tablespoon: Calories 12 (23% from fat)
Carbohydrate 1.1g Protein 1.4g Fat 0.3g (Sat. Fat 0.1g)
Cholesterol 3mg Sodium 62mg

Creamy Spinach Crabmeat Dip

2 (3-ounce) packages cream cheese, softened
½ cup sour cream
½ cup mayonnaise
2 tablespoons dry sherry
1 (10-ounce) package frozen chopped spinach, thawed
6 ounces fresh lump crabmeat, drained
1 (2-ounce) jar diced pimiento, drained
¼ cup minced green onions
1 teaspoon dried whole dillweed
4 slices bacon, cooked and crumbled
⅓ cup finely chopped pecans

Combine first 4 ingredients in a large mixing bowl. Beat at medium speed of an electric mixer until smooth.

Drain spinach; press between paper towels to remove excess moisture. Add spinach and next 4 ingredients to cheese mixture; stir well. Cover and chill. Stir in bacon and pecans just before serving. Serve with wheat crackers. Yield: 3½ cups.

Per tablespoon: Calories 42 (84% from fat)
Carbohydrate 0.7g Protein 1.3g Fat 3.9g (Sat. Fat 1.3g)
Cholesterol 9mg Sodium 43mg

These nacho dips offer similar Tex-Mex flavors, but the light Chicken Nacho Dip contains lean chicken breast instead of chili. Serve the dip with no-oil baked tortilla chips rather than regular tortilla chips for further fat reduction.

CHICKEN NACHO DIP

1   (1¼-ounce) package taco seasoning mix
2½ cups shredded cooked chicken breast (skinned before cooking and cooked without salt)
½   cup light beer
1   (4-ounce) can chopped green chiles, undrained
½   cup commercial no-salt-added salsa
1   (15-ounce) can black beans, drained
1   tablespoon crushed garlic
½   cup minced fresh cilantro
1½ cups (6 ounces) shredded fat-free Cheddar cheese
1   (16-ounce) carton nonfat sour cream alternative
1½ cups seeded, diced tomato
½   cup minced green onions
¼   cup sliced ripe olives

Reserve 1 teaspoon taco seasoning mix; set aside. Combine remaining taco seasoning mix, chicken, beer, and chiles in a large skillet; bring to a boil. Reduce heat, and simmer, uncovered, 5 minutes or until mixture is thickened. Remove from heat; stir in salsa.

Mash beans and garlic until smooth; stir in cilantro. Spread bean mixture in a 10-inch quiche dish. Spoon chicken mixture evenly over bean mixture; top with cheese. Bake, uncovered, at 375° for 15 minutes or until cheese melts and mixture is thoroughly heated.

Combine sour cream and reserved 1 teaspoon taco seasoning mix; spread over melted cheese. Top with tomato, green onions, and olives. Serve with no-oil baked tortilla chips. Yield: 30 appetizer servings.

Per serving: Calories 69 (18% from fat)
Carbohydrate 5.6g Protein 8.1g Fat 1.4g (Sat. Fat 0.3g)
Cholesterol 14mg Sodium 186mg

Chili Nacho Dip

1   (7⅜-ounce) carton chili without beans
2   tablespoons tomato paste
1   (15-ounce) can pinto beans, drained
1   (10-ounce) can tomatoes with green chiles, drained and chopped
½   cup minced fresh cilantro
2   cups (8 ounces) shredded Cheddar cheese
1   cup peeled, diced avocado
1   teaspoon lemon juice
1   (16-ounce) carton sour cream
1   cup seeded, diced tomato
½   cup minced green onions
½   cup sliced ripe olives

Combine chili and tomato paste; stir well. Add beans, chopped tomato with green chiles, and cilantro; stir well. Spread chili mixture in a 10-inch quiche dish; top with cheese. Bake, uncovered, at 375° for 15 minutes or until cheese melts and mixture is thoroughly heated.

Combine avocado and lemon juice; toss gently to coat. Spread sour cream over melted cheese. Top with avocado mixture, diced tomato, green onions, and olives. Serve with tortilla chips. Yield: 30 appetizer servings.

Per serving: Calories 100 (71% from fat)
Carbohydrate 3.8g Protein 3.7g Fat 7.9g (Sat. Fat 3.8g)
Cholesterol 16mg Sodium 167mg

Even if you're trimming fat and cholesterol from your diet, you can enjoy savory Basil Cheese Spread. It uses frozen egg substitute, so it has less than one-third the cholesterol of the luscious spread.

BASIL CHEESE SPREAD

Vegetable cooking spray
8 ounces goat cheese, softened
1 (8-ounce) carton light process cream cheese product, softened
1 cup light ricotta cheese
¼ cup grated Parmesan cheese
½ cup frozen egg substitute, thawed
¼ cup minced fresh basil
½ teaspoon ground white pepper
Oil-Free Chunky Tomato Salsa
72 Melba rounds

Coat a 9-inch springform pan with cooking spray; set aside.

Combine cheeses; beat at medium-high speed of an electric mixer until smooth. Add egg substitute, basil, and white pepper; beat until well blended. Pour into prepared pan. Bake at 350° for 40 minutes or until a knife inserted in center comes out clean. Cool completely on a wire rack.

Invert cheese mixture onto a serving platter, and top with Oil-Free Chunky Tomato Salsa. To serve, spread about 1 tablespoon cheese and salsa mixture on each Melba round. Yield: 72 appetizers.

Oil-Free Chunky Tomato Salsa

1½ cups seeded, chopped tomato
¼ cup minced onion
2 tablespoons minced fresh basil
½ teaspoon minced garlic
1½ teaspoons commercial oil-free Italian dressing
¼ teaspoon freshly ground pepper

Combine all ingredients in a small bowl; stir well. Cover and let stand at room temperature at least 1 hour. Yield: 1½ cups.

Per appetizer: Calories 36 (48% from fat)
Carbohydrate 2.7g Protein 2.1g Fat 1.9g (Sat. Fat 1.1g)
Cholesterol 5mg Sodium 72mg

Goat Cheese Spread

Vegetable cooking spray
11 ounces goat cheese, softened
1 (8-ounce) package cream cheese, softened
1 (3-ounce) package cream cheese, softened
2 eggs
1 egg yolk
¼ cup commercial pesto sauce
Chunky Tomato Salsa
72 Melba rounds

Coat a 9-inch springform pan with cooking spray; set aside.

Combine cheeses; beat at medium-high speed of an electric mixer until smooth. Add eggs, egg yolk, and pesto sauce; beat until well blended. Pour into prepared pan. Bake at 350° for 40 minutes or until a knife inserted in center comes out clean. Cool completely on a wire rack.

Invert cheese mixture onto a serving platter, and top with Chunky Tomato Salsa. To serve, spread about 1 tablespoon cheese and salsa mixture on each Melba round. Yield: 72 appetizers.

Chunky Tomato Salsa

1½ cups seeded, chopped tomato
¼ cup minced onion
2 tablespoons minced fresh basil
½ teaspoon minced garlic
1½ teaspoons olive oil
¼ teaspoon freshly ground pepper

Combine all ingredients in a small bowl; stir well. Cover and let stand at room temperature at least 1 hour. Yield: 1½ cups.

Per appetizer: Calories 52 (66% from fat)
Carbohydrate 2.7g Protein 2.1g Fat 3.8g (Sat. Fat 2.0g)
Cholesterol 17mg Sodium 73mg

These spreads make striking presentations, especially when prepared in pretty molds. The light spread has nonfat cream cheese, low-fat Cheddar, and juicy pineapple; the luscious spread is packed with Cheddar and cream cheeses and is adorned with honey-roasted peanuts.

PINEAPPLE APRICOT CHEESE SPREAD

1   (8-ounce) can crushed pineapple in juice, undrained
½   cup finely chopped dried apricot
¼   cup commercial chopped chutney
¼   cup brandy
½   teaspoon ground ginger
2   cups (8 ounces) 50% less-fat shredded Cheddar cheese
2   (8-ounce) packages nonfat process cream cheese product, softened
¼   cup reduced-calorie margarine, softened
2   tablespoons brandy
    Edible flowers (optional)
64 gingersnaps

Drain pineapple, reserving 3 tablespoons juice. Combine pineapple, reserved juice, apricot, and next 3 ingredients in a small saucepan. Bring to a boil; reduce heat, and simmer, uncovered, 5 to 7 minutes or until thickened, stirring frequently. Transfer to a bowl; chill thoroughly.

Position knife blade in food processor bowl. Add cheeses and margarine; process until smooth, scraping sides of processor bowl occasionally.

Line 2 (2½-cup) molds with cheesecloth dampened with 2 tablespoons brandy. Spread ½ cup cheese mixture in bottom of each mold. Spread ¼ cup pineapple mixture over cheese mixture in each. Repeat layers with ½ cup cheese mixture and half of remaining pineapple mixture in each mold. Spread remaining cheese mixture evenly over each. Cover and chill. Unmold onto serving plates; peel off cheesecloth. Garnish with edible flowers, if desired. To serve, spread 1 tablespoon cheese mixture on each gingersnap. Yield: 64 appetizers.

Per appetizer: Calories 55 (33% from fat)
Carbohydrate 7.2g Protein 2.1g Fat 2.8g (Sat. Fat 0.6g)
Cholesterol 5mg Sodium 86mg

Nutty Apricot Cheese Spread

¾   cup chopped dried apricot
¾   cup apricot nectar
⅓   cup raisins
⅓   cup commercial chopped chutney
¼   cup brandy
½   teaspoon ground ginger
2   cups (8 ounces) shredded sharp Cheddar cheese
2   (8-ounce) packages cream cheese, softened
½   cup margarine, softened
1⅓ cups finely chopped honey-roasted peanuts, divided
    Edible flowers (optional)
72 gingersnaps

Combine first 6 ingredients in a small saucepan. Bring to a boil; reduce heat, and simmer, uncovered, 12 minutes or until thickened, stirring frequently. Transfer to a bowl; chill thoroughly.

Position knife blade in food processor bowl. Add cheeses and margarine; process until smooth, scraping sides of processor bowl occasionally.

Line 2 (2½-cup) molds with heavy-duty plastic wrap. Spread ½ cup cheese mixture in bottom of each mold. Spread ¼ cup plus 2 tablespoons apricot mixture over cheese mixture in each. Repeat layers with ½ cup cheese mixture and half of remaining apricot mixture in each mold. Spread remaining cheese mixture evenly over each. Cover and chill. Unmold onto serving plates; peel off plastic wrap. Press ⅔ cup peanuts gently onto each cheese mold. Garnish with edible flowers, if desired. To serve, spread 1 tablespoon cheese mixture on each gingersnap. Yield: 72 appetizers.

Per appetizer: Calories 99 (61% from fat)
Carbohydrate 8.0g Protein 2.4g Fat 6.7g (Sat. Fat 2.7g)
Cholesterol 13mg Sodium 85mg

Right: *Nutty Apricot Cheese Spread*

These elegant stuffed mushroom recipes are very similar, but the one for Onion Parmesan Stuffed Mushrooms is lower in fat because it has proportionately more breadcrumbs and green onions and less cheese than the luscious one.

Onion Parmesan Stuffed Mushrooms

24 large fresh mushrooms
   Olive oil-flavored cooking spray
²/₃ cup minced green onions
1 cup soft breadcrumbs
2 tablespoons freshly grated Parmesan cheese
¼ teaspoon salt
1 ounce goat cheese
½ teaspoon freshly ground pepper

Clean mushrooms with damp paper towels. Remove stems. Set mushroom caps aside. Finely chop stems, and set aside.

Coat a large nonstick skillet with cooking spray; place over medium-high heat until hot. Add mushroom caps; sauté 5 minutes. Remove from skillet, and drain on paper towels. Coat skillet with cooking spray, and add reserved mushroom stems and green onions; sauté over medium heat 3 minutes or until tender. Remove from heat. Stir in breadcrumbs, Parmesan cheese, and salt. Set aside.

Crumble goat cheese evenly into mushroom caps. Spoon breadcrumb mixture evenly into mushroom caps over goat cheese, and sprinkle evenly with pepper. Arrange mushrooms on rack of a broiler pan coated with cooking spray. Broil 5½ inches from heat (with electric oven door partially opened) 2 to 3 minutes or until lightly browned. Yield: 2 dozen.

Per mushroom: Calories 24 (30% from fat)
Carbohydrate 3.3g Protein 1.5g Fat 0.8g (Sat. Fat 0.4g)
Cholesterol 1mg Sodium 57mg

Goat Cheese Stuffed Mushrooms

24 large fresh mushrooms
1 tablespoon olive oil
¹/₃ cup minced green onions
½ cup freshly grated Parmesan cheese, divided
½ cup soft breadcrumbs
¹/₃ cup minced pecans, toasted
2 tablespoons minced fresh thyme
½ teaspoon freshly ground pepper
2 ounces goat cheese
   Vegetable cooking spray

Clean mushrooms with damp paper towels. Remove stems, reserving stems for another use.

Sauté mushroom caps in 1 tablespoon hot olive oil in a large skillet over medium-high heat 5 minutes. Remove from skillet, and drain on paper towels. Add green onions to skillet; sauté over medium-high heat until tender. Remove from heat; stir in ¹/₃ cup Parmesan cheese and next 4 ingredients. Set aside.

Crumble goat cheese evenly into mushroom caps. Spoon breadcrumb mixture evenly into mushroom caps over goat cheese, and sprinkle evenly with remaining Parmesan cheese. Arrange mushrooms on rack of a broiler pan coated with cooking spray. Broil 5½ inches from heat (with electric oven door partially opened) 2 to 3 minutes or until lightly browned. Yield: 2 dozen.

Per mushroom: Calories 44 (63% from fat)
Carbohydrate 2.5g Protein 2.2g Fat 3.1g (Sat. Fat 1.1g)
Cholesterol 4mg Sodium 59mg

The light potato skins are baked, stuffed with a spicy corn filling, and generously sprinkled with low-fat Cheddar cheese. The luscious version features crispy-fried potato skins, a creamy corn filling, and a heaping measure of Cheddar cheese.

MEXICAN BAKED POTATO SKINS

4 large baking potatoes
Vegetable cooking spray
1 tablespoon reduced-calorie margarine
1 cup finely diced sweet red pepper
½ cup minced green onions
1½ cups fresh corn cut from cob (about 3 ears)
2 teaspoons chili powder
¼ teaspoon salt
¼ teaspoon pepper
½ cup nonfat sour cream alternative
¼ cup minced fresh cilantro
2 cups (8 ounces) 50% less-fat Cheddar cheese
Fresh cilantro sprigs (optional)

Scrub potatoes; prick each potato several times with a fork. Bake at 400° for 1 hour or until potatoes are done.

Coat a large nonstick skillet with cooking spray; add margarine. Place over medium-high heat until margarine melts. Add red pepper and green onions; sauté 3 minutes or until tender. Stir in corn, chili powder, salt, and pepper; sauté 3 minutes or until tender. Remove from heat, and let cool. Stir in sour cream and minced cilantro. Set aside.

Allow potatoes to cool to touch. Cut potatoes in half lengthwise. Carefully scoop out pulp, leaving about ⅛-inch-thick shells. Cut each shell in half lengthwise. Reserve potato pulp for another use.

Place shells, skin side down, on an ungreased baking sheet; spray shells lightly with cooking spray. Bake at 425° for 15 minutes or until crisp. Spoon corn mixture evenly into shells; sprinkle evenly with cheese. Broil 5½ inches from heat (with electric oven door partially opened) 2 to 3 minutes or until cheese melts. Garnish with cilantro sprigs, if desired. Serve immediately. Yield: 16 appetizers.

Per appetizer: Calories 86 (29% from fat)
Carbohydrate 10.4g Protein 5.8g Fat 2.8g (Sat. Fat 1.1g)
Cholesterol 8mg Sodium 167mg

Fried Potato Skins Olé

4 large baking potatoes
1 cup finely diced sweet red pepper
½ cup minced green onions
1 tablespoon margarine, melted
1½ cups fresh corn cut from cob (about 3 ears)
2 teaspoons chili powder
½ teaspoon salt
1 cup sour cream
¼ cup minced fresh cilantro
Vegetable oil
2 cups (8 ounces) shredded Cheddar cheese
Fresh cilantro sprigs (optional)

Scrub potatoes; prick each potato several times with a fork. Bake at 400° for 1 hour or until potatoes are done.

Sauté red pepper and green onions in margarine in a large skillet over medium-high heat 3 minutes or until tender. Stir in corn, chili powder, and salt; sauté 3 minutes or until tender. Remove from heat, and let cool. Stir in sour cream and minced cilantro. Set aside.

Allow potatoes to cool to touch. Cut potatoes in half lengthwise. Carefully scoop out pulp, leaving about ⅛-inch-thick shells. Cut each shell in half lengthwise. Reserve potato pulp for another use.

Pour oil to depth of 2 to 3 inches in a Dutch oven. Fry shells in hot oil (375°) for 1 to 2 minutes or until browned. Invert and drain on paper towels. Place shells, skin side down, on an ungreased baking sheet. Spoon corn mixture evenly into shells; sprinkle evenly with cheese. Broil 5½ inches from heat (with electric oven door partially opened) 2 to 3 minutes or until cheese melts. Garnish with cilantro sprigs, if desired. Serve immediately. Yield: 16 appetizers.

Per appetizer: Calories 256 (79% from fat)
Carbohydrate 10.2g Protein 5.2g Fat 22.4g (Sat. Fat 7.5g)
Cholesterol 21mg Sodium 185mg

The recipe for "oven-fried" Honey Dijon Chicken Nuggets calls for baking the chicken with a crispy pretzel coating and serving it with a sweet-and-spicy sauce. The nuggets in the Tex-Mex version are batter-dipped, fried, and served with a sour cream-salsa mixture.

HONEY DIJON CHICKEN NUGGETS

1½ cups no-sugar-added apricot spread
½ cup Dijon mustard
¼ cup plus 2 tablespoons honey
1¼ teaspoons ground red pepper
¾ teaspoon garlic powder
6 (4-ounce) skinned, boned chicken breast halves, cut into 1-inch pieces
2 cups crushed pretzels
1 cup water
1 tablespoon plus 1 teaspoon cornstarch
2 tablespoons water

Combine first 5 ingredients in a medium bowl; stir well. Measure 1 cup apricot mixture, and set aside.

Dip chicken pieces in remaining apricot mixture; dredge in crushed pretzels. Place on 2 large baking sheets. Bake at 400° for 15 minutes or until chicken is done.

Combine reserved 1 cup apricot mixture and 1 cup water in a medium saucepan. Bring to a boil; reduce heat, and simmer 3 minutes. Combine cornstarch and 2 tablespoons water; stir well. Add to hot apricot mixture. Cook, stirring constantly, until mixture is thickened. Serve sauce with chicken nuggets. Yield: 15 appetizer servings.

Per serving: Calories 171 (8% from fat)
Carbohydrate 26.8g Protein 11.7g Fat 1.5g (Sat. Fat 0.3g)
Cholesterol 26mg Sodium 420mg

Tex-Mex Chicken Nuggets

¾ cup sour cream
¾ cup commercial green salsa
½ cup mayonnaise
2 teaspoons lime juice
½ teaspoon ground red pepper
1 cup masa harina
1 tablespoon baking powder
1 teaspoon salt
1 tablespoon chili powder
¾ cup whole milk
¼ cup plus 2 tablespoons club soda
1 egg, beaten
1 egg white
⅓ cup minced pickled jalapeño pepper
6 (4-ounce) skinned, boned chicken breast halves, cut into 1-inch pieces
Vegetable oil

Combine first 5 ingredients in a small bowl; stir well. Cover and chill at least 1 hour.

Combine masa harina, baking powder, salt, and chili powder; stir well. Combine milk, club soda, egg, and egg white; add mixture to dry ingredients, stirring well. Stir in jalapeño pepper.

Dip chicken pieces in batter, coating well. Pour oil to depth of 2 inches in a Dutch oven; heat to 375°. Fry chicken, a few pieces at a time, 4 to 5 minutes or until golden. Drain on paper towels. Serve with sour cream mixture. Yield: 15 appetizer servings.

Per serving: Calories 303 (73% from fat)
Carbohydrate 7.5g Protein 12.8g Fat 24.5g (Sat. Fat 5.5g)
Cholesterol 52mg Sodium 379mg

Crisp phyllo pastry is lower in fat than regular pastry, and the phyllo pastry in the light version is coated with vegetable cooking spray instead of butter. Also, pineapple and water chestnuts lace the light chicken salad mixture instead of bacon and almonds.

PINEAPPLE CHICKEN SALAD IN PHYLLO CUPS

Butter-flavored vegetable cooking spray
5 sheets commercial frozen phyllo pastry, thawed
1 (8-ounce) can pineapple tidbits in juice
1¼ cups finely diced cooked chicken breast (skinned before cooking and cooked without salt)
2 tablespoons diced water chestnuts
2 tablespoons minced fresh chives
1 tablespoon diced pimiento
⅓ cup reduced-calorie mayonnaise
1½ teaspoons curry powder

Coat 2 miniature (1¾-inch) muffin pans with cooking spray; set aside.

Place 1 sheet of phyllo on a damp towel (keep remaining phyllo covered). Lightly coat phyllo with cooking spray. Layer remaining 4 sheets phyllo on first sheet, lightly coating each sheet with cooking spray. Cut phyllo stack into 24 circles using a 2½-inch biscuit cutter. Place phyllo circles into prepared muffin cups, pressing phyllo against bottom and up sides of cups. Bake at 350° for 8 to 10 minutes or until lightly browned. Let cool completely in pans on a wire rack; remove from pans.

Drain pineapple, reserving 2 tablespoons juice. Combine pineapple and next 4 ingredients in a medium bowl; stir well. Combine mayonnaise, curry powder, and reserved pineapple juice; stir into chicken mixture. Cover and chill at least 2 hours.

When ready to serve, spoon chicken mixture evenly into phyllo cups. Yield: 2 dozen.

Per phyllo cup: Calories 40 (36% from fat)
Carbohydrate 3.4g Protein 2.9g Fat 1.6g (Sat. Fat 0.2g)
Cholesterol 8mg Sodium 50mg

Crunchy Chicken Salad in Phyllo Cups

¼ cup butter, melted and divided
5 sheets commercial frozen phyllo pastry, thawed
1 cup finely diced cooked chicken breast
4 slices bacon, cooked and crumbled
1 hard-cooked egg, finely diced
⅓ cup slivered almonds, toasted
1 (2-ounce) jar diced pimiento, drained
3 tablespoons minced fresh chives
⅓ cup mayonnaise
1 tablespoon lemon juice
1 teaspoon curry powder

Brush 2 miniature (1¾-inch) muffin pans with 1 tablespoon melted butter; set aside.

Place 1 sheet of phyllo on a damp towel (keep remaining phyllo covered). Lightly brush phyllo with melted butter. Layer remaining 4 sheets phyllo on first sheet, brushing each sheet with melted butter. Cut phyllo stack into 24 circles using a 2½-inch biscuit cutter. Place phyllo circles into prepared muffin cups, pressing phyllo against bottom and up sides of cups. Bake at 350° for 8 to 10 minutes or until lightly browned. Let cool completely in pans on a wire rack; remove from pans.

Combine chicken and next 5 ingredients in a medium bowl; stir well. Combine mayonnaise, lemon juice, and curry powder; stir into chicken mixture. Cover and chill at least 2 hours.

When ready to serve, spoon chicken mixture evenly into phyllo cups. Yield: 2 dozen.

Per phyllo cup: Calories 81 (71% from fat)
Carbohydrate 2.8g Protein 3.3g Fat 6.4g (Sat. Fat 2.0g)
Cholesterol 22mg Sodium 81mg

Serve either of these Provençal pizzas as a hearty, unique appetizer. The light polenta pizza's rich flavor comes from the thick cornmeal crust and mixture of three cheeses. A rich pesto sauce and toasted walnuts give Crusty Provençal Pizza its luscious status.

POLENTA PROVENÇAL PIZZA

1⅓ cups stone ground cornmeal
1   cup all-purpose flour
¼   teaspoon salt
¾   cup warm water
2   tablespoons olive oil
    Vegetable cooking spray
1½ cups firmly packed fresh basil
    leaves
½   cup freshly grated Parmesan cheese
½   cup light ricotta cheese
2   tablespoons canned no-salt-added
    chicken broth, undiluted
2   cloves garlic, cut in half
¾   cup (3 ounces) shredded part-skim
    mozzarella cheese
1¼ cups cubed cooked chicken breast
    (skinned before cooking and cooked
    without salt)
1   cup diced sweet red pepper
¾   cup drained and chopped canned
    artichoke hearts

Combine cornmeal, flour, and salt in a medium bowl; stir well. Combine water and olive oil; stir with a wire whisk until blended. Add oil mixture to cornmeal mixture, stirring just until dry ingredients are moistened.

Press mixture into bottom and ½ inch up sides of a 13- x 9- x 2-inch pan coated with cooking spray. Bake at 425° for 5 minutes. Let cool completely on a wire rack.

Position knife blade in food processor bowl; add basil and next 4 ingredients. Process 1 minute or until smooth, scraping sides of processor bowl once. Spread basil mixture over cornmeal crust, leaving a ½-inch border on all sides. Sprinkle with mozzarella cheese, chicken, red pepper, and artichoke. Bake, uncovered, at 425° for 30 minutes or until crust is set. Cut into 18 rectangles. Yield: 18 appetizer servings.

Per serving: Calories 128 (30% from fat)
Carbohydrate 14.3g Protein 8.5g Fat 4.2g (Sat. Fat 1.5g)
Cholesterol 16mg Sodium 144mg

Crusty Provençal Pizza

1   (10-ounce) can refrigerated pizza dough
1½ cups firmly packed fresh basil leaves
¾   cup freshly grated Parmesan cheese,
    divided
⅔   cup chopped walnuts, toasted and
    divided
2   cloves garlic, cut in half
⅓   cup olive oil
1½ cups (6 ounces) shredded mozzarella
    cheese
½   pound smoked turkey, cubed
1   cup diced sweet red pepper
1   (6-ounce) jar marinated artichoke
    hearts, drained and chopped

Unroll pizza dough, and press into bottom of a greased 13- x 9- x 2-inch pan. Set aside.

Position knife blade in food processor bowl; add basil, ½ cup Parmesan cheese, ⅓ cup walnuts, and garlic. Process 1 minute or until smooth, scraping sides of processor bowl once. With processor running, pour olive oil through food chute in a slow, steady stream until combined.

Spread basil mixture over pizza dough, leaving a ½-inch border on all sides. Sprinkle with mozzarella cheese, turkey, red pepper, artichoke, remaining ¼ cup Parmesan cheese, and remaining ⅓ cup walnuts. Bake, uncovered, at 425° for 30 minutes or until crust is golden and cheese melts. Cut into 18 rectangles. Yield: 18 appetizer servings.

Per serving: Calories 188 (58% from fat)
Carbohydrate 11.5g Protein 9.0g Fat 12.2g (Sat. Fat 3.1g)
Cholesterol 18mg Sodium 362mg

Right: *Crusty Provençal Pizza*

Cut calories and fat with an oil-free marinade in Chicken Satay. In the luscious satay, infuse chicken and pork with flavor by using cream of coconut, lime juice, and teriyaki sauce.

Chicken Satay

7 (4-ounce) skinned, boned chicken breast halves, cut into $\frac{1}{4}$-inch-wide strips
$\frac{1}{4}$ cup unsweetened pineapple juice
$\frac{1}{4}$ cup low-sodium soy sauce
2 tablespoons brown sugar
$\frac{1}{4}$ teaspoon ground red pepper
2 cloves garlic, crushed
$\frac{1}{4}$ cup plus 2 tablespoons low-sodium soy sauce
3 tablespoons creamy no-salt-added peanut butter
2 tablespoons rice wine vinegar
1 tablespoon water
$\frac{1}{4}$ teaspoon ground red pepper
1 large sweet red pepper, seeded
Vegetable cooking spray

Place chicken in a heavy-duty, zip-top plastic bag. Combine pineapple juice and next 4 ingredients; pour over chicken. Seal bag, and marinate chicken in refrigerator 1 hour, turning bag occasionally. Soak 24 (6-inch) bamboo skewers in water 30 minutes; set aside.

Combine soy sauce, peanut butter, vinegar, water, and $\frac{1}{4}$ teaspoon ground red pepper in container of an electric blender; cover and process until smooth. Set aside.

Drain chicken; discard marinade. Thread chicken evenly onto skewers. Cut sweet red pepper into 12 ($1\frac{1}{2}$-inch) squares. Cut each square diagonally in half, forming 24 triangles. Place 1 triangle on the end of each skewer. Place half of skewers on rack of a broiler pan coated with cooking spray. Broil $5\frac{1}{2}$ inches from heat (with electric oven door partially opened) 4 minutes on each side or until chicken is done. Transfer to a serving platter. Repeat procedure with remaining skewers. Serve satay warm with peanut sauce. Yield: 2 dozen appetizers.

Per appetizer: Calories 62 (29% from fat)
Carbohydrate 1.9g Protein 8.4g Fat 2.0g (Sat. Fat 0.4g)
Cholesterol 21mg Sodium 149mg

Chicken-Pork Satay

4 (4-ounce) skinned, boned chicken breast halves, cut into $\frac{1}{4}$-inch-wide strips
1 pound lean boneless center-cut loin pork chops, cut into $\frac{1}{4}$-inch-wide strips
$\frac{1}{2}$ cup cream of coconut
3 tablespoons lime juice
1 tablespoon vegetable oil
1 tablespoon teriyaki sauce
$\frac{1}{4}$ teaspoon ground coriander
$\frac{1}{8}$ teaspoon ground red pepper
2 cloves garlic, crushed
$\frac{2}{3}$ cup chunky peanut butter
$\frac{2}{3}$ cup water
$\frac{1}{4}$ cup teriyaki sauce
2 tablespoons rice wine vinegar
$\frac{1}{4}$ teaspoon ground red pepper
3 cloves garlic, crushed
1 large sweet red pepper, seeded

Place chicken and pork in a heavy-duty, zip-top plastic bag. Combine cream of coconut and next 6 ingredients; pour over meat. Seal bag, and marinate meat in refrigerator 4 hours, turning bag occasionally. Soak 24 (6-inch) bamboo skewers in water 30 minutes; set aside.

Combine peanut butter and next 5 ingredients in container of an electric blender; cover and process until smooth. Set aside.

Drain meat; discard marinade. Thread chicken and pork evenly onto skewers. Cut sweet red pepper into 12 ($1\frac{1}{2}$-inch) squares. Cut each square diagonally in half, forming 24 triangles. Place 1 triangle on the end of each skewer. Place half of skewers on rack of a lightly-greased broiler pan. Broil $5\frac{1}{2}$ inches from heat (with electric oven door partially opened) 4 minutes on each side or until chicken and pork are done. Transfer to a serving platter. Repeat procedure with remaining skewers. Serve satay warm with peanut sauce. Yield: 2 dozen appetizers.

Per appetizer: Calories 113 (55% from fat)
Carbohydrate 2.5g Protein 10.4g Fat 6.9g (Sat. Fat 2.2g)
Cholesterol 24mg Sodium 182mg

When you brown the pot stickers and then cook them in water, they have only a fraction of the calories and fat of the deep fat-fried Thai Wontons.

Thai Pot Stickers

Vegetable cooking spray
½ teaspoon vegetable oil
1 tablespoon peeled, minced gingerroot
1 tablespoon minced garlic
¾ cup finely shredded cooked chicken breast (skinned before cooking and cooked without salt)
¼ cup minced water chestnuts
2 tablespoons minced fresh cilantro
1 tablespoon minced fresh mint
1 teaspoon sesame seeds, lightly toasted
½ teaspoon ground cumin
⅛ teaspoon salt
8 egg roll wrappers
1 tablespoon water
1 tablespoon vegetable oil
⅔ cup water
¼ cup no-sugar-added apricot spread
⅓ cup reduced-sodium teriyaki sauce
1 tablespoon hot sauce
1 tablespoon lime juice

Coat a large nonstick skillet with cooking spray; add ½ teaspoon oil. Place over medium-high heat until hot. Add gingerroot and garlic; cook, stirring constantly, until tender. Remove from heat, and stir in chicken and next 6 ingredients.

Cut egg roll wrappers in half lengthwise. Lightly brush edges with 1 tablespoon water. Place about 1 tablespoon chicken mixture at base of a wrapper half; fold the right bottom corner over to form a triangle. Continue folding back and forth into a triangle to end of wrapper half. Repeat procedure with remaining wrapper halves and chicken mixture.

Coat skillet with cooking spray; add 1 tablespoon oil. Add filled egg roll wrappers; cook 1 minute on each side or until golden. Add ⅔ cup water; cook 5 minutes or until water evaporates, turning once.

Combine apricot spread and remaining ingredients; stir well. Serve pot stickers with apricot sauce. Yield: 16 appetizers.

Per appetizer: Calories 53 (29% from fat)
Carbohydrate 5.4g Protein 3.7g Fat 1.7g (Sat. Fat 0.4g)
Cholesterol 19mg Sodium 158mg

Thai Wontons

½ pound lean ground lamb
1 tablespoon peeled, minced gingerroot
1 tablespoon minced garlic
2 tablespoons minced fresh cilantro
2 tablespoons minced fresh mint
1 tablespoon sesame seeds, lightly toasted
½ teaspoon ground cumin
⅛ teaspoon salt
8 egg roll wrappers
1 tablespoon water
Vegetable oil
3 tablespoons teriyaki sauce
3 tablespoons honey
3 tablespoons creamy peanut butter
2 tablespoons hot sauce
1 tablespoon lime juice
2 teaspoons dark sesame oil

Cook ground lamb, gingerroot, and garlic in a large skillet over medium heat until browned, stirring until meat crumbles; drain.

Combine lamb mixture, cilantro, mint, sesame seeds, cumin, and salt in a bowl; stir well, and set aside.

Cut egg roll wrappers in half lengthwise. Lightly brush edges with 1 tablespoon water. Place about 1 tablespoon lamb mixture at base of a wrapper half; fold the right bottom corner over to form a triangle. Continue folding back and forth into a triangle to end of wrapper half. Repeat procedure with remaining wrapper halves and lamb mixture.

Pour vegetable oil to depth of 2 inches in a Dutch oven; heat to 375°. Fry filled egg roll wrappers 1 to 2 minutes or until golden, turning once. Drain well.

Combine teriyaki sauce and remaining ingredients; stir well. Serve wontons with peanut sauce. Yield: 16 appetizers.

Per appetizer: Calories 317 (87% from fat)
Carbohydrate 6.7g Protein 4.9g Fat 30.7g (Sat. Fat 5.7g)
Cholesterol 21mg Sodium 212mg

Keep calories to a minimum by using a marinade that forgoes oil in Sherry Pepper Shrimp.

SHERRY PEPPER SHRIMP

48 unpeeled large fresh shrimp (2 pounds)
⅔ cup plus 1 tablespoon dry sherry, divided
2 teaspoons crushed red pepper
1 teaspoon fennel seeds, crushed
3 cloves garlic, crushed
2½ cups finely chopped sweet red pepper
1 (14½-ounce) can no-salt-added whole tomatoes, drained and chopped
¼ cup minced shallots
1 teaspoon Hungarian paprika
2 teaspoons hot sauce
1 teaspoon lemon juice
2½ tablespoons capers, drained
¼ cup reduced-calorie mayonnaise
Vegetable cooking spray

Peel and devein shrimp, leaving tails intact; place shrimp in a shallow dish. Combine ⅓ cup sherry, crushed red pepper, fennel, and garlic; pour over shrimp. Cover; marinate in refrigerator 4 hours.

Combine sweet red pepper, tomato, shallots, and ⅓ cup sherry in a saucepan. Bring to a boil; cover, reduce heat, and simmer 15 minutes. Uncover and cook over high heat 10 minutes or until liquid evaporates, stirring frequently. Cool completely. Transfer mixture to container of an electric blender; add paprika, hot sauce, and lemon juice. Cover and process 2 minutes or until smooth. Transfer to a bowl; stir in capers. Combine mayonnaise and remaining 1 tablespoon sherry; stir well.

Remove shrimp from marinade; discard marinade. Thread shrimp onto 8 (12-inch) metal skewers. Coat grill rack with cooking spray, and place on grill over medium-hot coals (350° to 400°). Place kabobs on rack; grill, uncovered, 4 to 5 minutes on each side or until shrimp turn pink.

Spoon ¼ cup pepper puree into each dish. Drizzle mayonnaise mixture over puree. Arrange 6 shrimp in each dish. Yield: 8 appetizer servings.

Per serving: Calories 114 (24% from fat)
Carbohydrate 6.9g Protein 13.1g Fat 3.1g (Sat. Fat 0.3g)
Cholesterol 113mg Sodium 424mg

Left: *Sherry Pepper Shrimp*

Tartar Sauce Shrimp

48 unpeeled large fresh shrimp (2 pounds)
⅔ cup olive oil
1 tablespoon ground turmeric
2 teaspoons crushed red pepper
3 cloves garlic, crushed
2 large sweet red peppers
3 tablespoons minced shallots
1 teaspoon Hungarian paprika
2 to 3 teaspoons hot sauce
2 teaspoons lemon juice
⅓ cup olive oil
½ cup mayonnaise
3 tablespoons diced sweet gherkin pickle
1½ tablespoons capers, drained
24 large bay leaves, halved crosswise
3 lemons, each cut into 8 wedges

Peel and devein shrimp, leaving tails intact; place shrimp in a shallow dish. Combine ⅔ cup olive oil and next 3 ingredients; pour over shrimp. Cover; marinate in refrigerator 4 hours.

Cut peppers in half lengthwise; remove and discard seeds and membrane. Place peppers, skin side up, on a baking sheet; flatten with palm of hand. Broil 4 inches from heat (with electric oven door partially opened) 10 minutes or until charred. Place in ice water 5 minutes. Remove from water; peel and discard skins. Combine roasted pepper, shallots, and next 3 ingredients in container of an electric blender. Cover and process on high speed 1 minute or until smooth. With machine running, add ⅓ cup olive oil in a slow steady stream, processing until blended. Transfer to a bowl; stir in mayonnaise, pickle, and capers. Cover and chill.

Soak 24 (6-inch) bamboo skewers in water 30 minutes. Remove shrimp from marinade; discard marinade. Thread 2 shrimp, 2 bay leaf halves, and 1 lemon wedge alternately onto each skewer. Place kabobs on rack; grill, uncovered, over medium-hot coals (350° to 400°), 4 to 5 minutes on each side or until shrimp turn pink. Discard bay leaves. Serve shrimp with tartar sauce. Yield: 8 appetizer servings.

Per serving: Calories 405 (84% from fat)
Carbohydrate 4.5g Protein 12.8g Fat 37.9g (Sat. Fat 5.4g)
Cholesterol 119mg Sodium 448mg

Shrimp rémoulade is a classy appetizer that involves little preparation. The light version contains reduced-calorie mayonnaise and nonfat sour cream and is served in artichoke bottoms. The luscious rémoulade, made with mayonnaise and sour cream, is arranged on French bread.

SHRIMP RÉMOULADE IN ARTICHOKE BOTTOMS

¼ cup diced celery
¼ cup diced sweet red pepper
¼ cup minced fresh parsley
¼ cup reduced-calorie mayonnaise
2 tablespoons nonfat sour cream
   alternative
2 tablespoons tangy steak sauce
1 tablespoon coarse-grained mustard
½ teaspoon dried whole tarragon
½ teaspoon ground red pepper
2 cups cooked peeled baby shrimp
16 canned artichoke bottoms, rinsed,
   drained, and patted dry

Combine first 9 ingredients in a medium bowl; stir well. Stir in shrimp. Cover and chill thoroughly.

To serve, spoon shrimp mixture evenly into artichoke bottoms. Yield: 16 appetizers.

Per appetizer: Calories 47 (25% from fat)
Carbohydrate 4.6g Protein 4.6g Fat 1.3g (Sat. Fat 0.1g)
Cholesterol 34mg Sodium 138mg

Shrimp Rémoulade Croustades

1¾ pounds unpeeled large fresh shrimp
3 tablespoons tequila, divided
1 tablespoon lime juice
½ cup mayonnaise
½ cup sour cream
2 tablespoons minced celery
2 tablespoons minced fresh chives
2 tablespoons minced fresh cilantro
2 tablespoons diced dill pickle
2 tablespoons capers, drained
2 tablespoons coarse-grained mustard
1 teaspoon ground red pepper
   Vegetable cooking spray
1 tablespoon peanut oil
16 (½-inch-thick) slices French bread,
   toasted

Peel and devein shrimp, leaving tails intact. Combine 2 tablespoons tequila and lime juice in a glass bowl; add shrimp, and toss well. Cover and chill 20 minutes.

Combine remaining 1 tablespoon tequila, mayonnaise, and next 8 ingredients; stir well, and set mixture aside.

Remove shrimp from marinade; discard marinade. Coat a large nonstick skillet with cooking spray; add peanut oil. Place over medium-high heat until hot. Add shrimp, and sauté 2 minutes or until shrimp turn pink.

To serve, arrange shrimp evenly on toasted bread slices; top each with 1½ tablespoons mayonnaise mixture. Serve immediately. Yield: 16 appetizers.

Per appetizer: Calories 160 (51% from fat)
Carbohydrate 10.9g Protein 7.2g Fat 9.0g (Sat. Fat 2.1g)
Cholesterol 46mg Sodium 345mg

Almonds and Brie cheese add distinctive flavor to Crabmeat and Almond Quesadillas. Fat is reduced in the light quesadillas when you add corn, sweet red pepper, and onions instead of almonds and when you substitute reduced-fat Monterey Jack cheese for the Brie.

CRABMEAT AND CORN QUESADILLAS

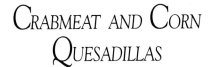

  8 ounces fresh lump crabmeat, drained
  ½ cup fresh or frozen corn kernels, thawed
  ½ cup diced sweet red pepper
  ½ cup minced fresh cilantro
  ⅓ cup chopped green onions
  ¼ cup plus 1 tablespoon nonfat sour cream alternative
  1 teaspoon hot sauce
  ½ teaspoon ground cumin
 10 (8-inch) flour tortillas
1¼ cups (5 ounces) shredded reduced-fat Monterey Jack cheese
     Vegetable cooking spray

Combine first 8 ingredients in a medium bowl; stir well. Spoon crabmeat mixture evenly over 5 tortillas; spread to within ½ inch of edge. Sprinkle evenly with cheese, and top with remaining tortillas.

  Coat a large nonstick skillet with cooking spray; place over medium-high heat until hot. Add quesadillas, one at a time, and cook 1 to 2 minutes on each side or until lightly browned and cheese melts. Cut each quesadilla into 4 wedges, and serve immediately. Yield: 20 wedges.

Per wedge: Calories 92 (27% from fat)
Carbohydrate 10.4g   Protein 6.2g   Fat 2.8g (Sat. Fat 1.0g)
Cholesterol 16mg   Sodium 158mg

Crabmeat and Almond Quesadillas

 10 ounces fresh lump crabmeat, drained
  ½ cup slivered almonds, toasted
  ⅓ cup minced green onions
  ¼ cup mayonnaise
  ½ teaspoon hot sauce
  ¼ teaspoon curry powder
  1 (2-ounce) jar diced pimiento, drained
  8 ounces Brie cheese
 10 (8-inch) flour tortillas
     Vegetable cooking spray

Combine first 7 ingredients in a medium bowl; stir well. Remove rind from cheese; cut cheese into thin slices, and arrange slices evenly on 5 tortillas. Spoon crabmeat mixture evenly over cheese, and top with remaining tortillas.

  Coat a large nonstick skillet with cooking spray; place over medium-high heat until hot. Add quesadillas, one at a time, and cook 1 to 2 minutes on each side or until lightly browned and cheese melts. Cut each quesadilla into 4 wedges, and serve immediately. Yield: 20 wedges.

Per wedge: Calories 148 (49% from fat)
Carbohydrate 13.5g   Protein 6.9g   Fat 8.0g (Sat. Fat 2.4g)
Cholesterol 25mg   Sodium 115mg

A cup of German Chocolate Espresso tastes as extravagant as it looks with its combination of milk chocolate, whipped cream, and coconut. Keep the flavor but cut the fat by replacing these rich ingredients with unsweetened cocoa, skim milk, and coconut extract.

GERMAN CHOCOLATE CAFÉ AU LAIT

¼ cup sugar
 2 tablespoons unsweetened cocoa
½ cup skim milk
2½ cups brewed chocolate almond-flavored coffee
½ teaspoon coconut extract
½ teaspoon almond extract

Combine sugar and cocoa in a small saucepan, and stir well. Gradually add milk, and stir well. Place over medium heat; cook until sugar dissolves, stirring frequently.

Remove from heat; stir in coffee and flavorings. Pour into individual cups. Serve immediately. Yield: 4 (¾-cup) servings.

Per serving: Calories 76 (5% from fat)
Carbohydrate 15.8g Protein 2.0g Fat 0.4g (Sat. Fat 0.3g)
Cholesterol 1mg Sodium 20mg

German Chocolate Espresso

1½ ounces premium quality milk chocolate, finely chopped
2⅔ cups hot brewed espresso
 3 tablespoons Coco Ribe or other coconut-flavored liqueur
 3 tablespoons Frangelico or other hazelnut liqueur
¼ cup whipping cream, whipped
¼ cup flaked coconut, toasted

Place chocolate in a medium bowl; pour espresso over chocolate, stirring until chocolate melts. Stir in liqueurs. Pour into individual cups. Top each serving evenly with whipped cream and coconut. Serve immediately. Yield: 4 (¾-cup) servings.

Per serving: Calories 190 (53% from fat)
Carbohydrate 22.1g Protein 1.5g Fat 11.1g (Sat. Fat 7.4g)
Cholesterol 21mg Sodium 36mg

Right: *German Chocolate Espresso*

If the dollop of whipped cream and sprinkle of shaved chocolate don't tell you that a cup of Rich and Creamy Hot Chocolate is luscious, one sip will. For the same rich flavor, the light version uses skim milk and unsweetened cocoa instead of whole milk and semisweet chocolate.

CINNAMON CREAM HOT COCOA

3 cups skim milk
2 (3-inch) sticks cinnamon
¼ cup unsweetened cocoa
3 tablespoons sugar
⅓ cup marshmallow cream
1½ teaspoons vanilla extract
¼ teaspoon almond extract
 Cinnamon sticks (optional)

Place milk and 2 cinnamon sticks in a medium saucepan. Bring to a boil over medium heat, stirring occasionally. Remove from heat, and let cool 10 minutes. Remove and discard cinnamon sticks.

Combine cocoa and sugar; stir well. Add to milk mixture, and stir well. Stir in marshmallow cream. Cook over medium heat, stirring constantly with a wire whisk, until thoroughly heated. Remove from heat; stir in flavorings. Pour into individual mugs. Garnish with cinnamon sticks, if desired. Yield: 4 (¾-cup) servings.

Per serving: Calories 171 (6% from fat)
Carbohydrate 31.3g Protein 7.9g Fat 1.1g (Sat. Fat 0.7g)
Cholesterol 4mg Sodium 101mg

Rich and Creamy Hot Chocolate

2¾ cups whole milk
2 (3-inch) sticks cinnamon
¾ cup marshmallow cream
2½ ounces semisweet chocolate, chopped
1 teaspoon vanilla extract
2 tablespoons whipping cream, whipped
2 tablespoons shaved semisweet
 chocolate

Place milk and cinnamon sticks in a medium saucepan. Bring to a boil over medium heat, stirring occasionally. Remove from heat, and let cool 10 minutes. Remove and discard cinnamon sticks.

Add marshmallow cream to milk mixture. Cook over medium heat, stirring constantly with a wire whisk, until thoroughly heated. Stir in chopped chocolate; cook, stirring constantly, until chocolate melts. Remove from heat; stir in vanilla. Pour into individual mugs, and top with whipped cream and shaved chocolate. Yield: 4 (¾-cup) servings.

Per serving: Calories 314 (42% from fat)
Carbohydrate 42.0g Protein 6.9g Fat 14.6g (Sat. Fat 9.1g)
Cholesterol 34mg Sodium 93mg

A half-cup serving of Marshmallow Cream Nog has only a fraction of the cholesterol of Rich Vanilla Eggnog because it contains frozen egg substitute. Skim milk and ice milk also create a slimming effect in this traditional holiday beverage.

MARSHMALLOW CREAM NOG

4   cups skim milk
½   cup marshmallow cream
3   tablespoons sugar
1   (4-inch) piece vanilla bean, split
      lengthwise
1⅔ cups frozen egg substitute, thawed
½   cup bourbon
½   teaspoon freshly grated nutmeg
2   cups vanilla ice milk, softened
      Freshly grated nutmeg (optional)

Combine first 4 ingredients in a large saucepan; stir well. Cook over medium-low heat until marshmallow cream melts. Gradually stir about one-fourth of hot mixture into egg substitute; add to remaining hot mixture, stirring constantly. Cook mixture over low heat, stirring constantly, 1 to 2 minutes or until mixture thickens.

Remove mixture from heat; stir in bourbon and ½ teaspoon nutmeg. Let cool. Cover and chill 3 hours. Remove and discard vanilla bean; stir in ice milk just before serving. Sprinkle with nutmeg, if desired. Yield: 16 (½-cup) servings.

Per serving: Calories 113 (7% from fat)
Carbohydrate 12.6g Protein 5.3g Fat 0.9g (Sat. Fat 0.5g)
Cholesterol 4mg Sodium 84mg

Rich Vanilla Eggnog

2½ cups plus 2 tablespoons whole milk
1   cup half-and-half
1   (4-inch) piece vanilla bean, split
      lengthwise
6   eggs, lightly beaten
½   cup sugar
½   cup bourbon
¼   teaspoon freshly grated nutmeg
1   quart French vanilla ice cream,
      softened
      Sweetened whipped cream (optional)
      Freshly grated nutmeg (optional)

Combine first 3 ingredients in a large saucepan; stir well. Cook over medium-low heat until thoroughly heated (do not boil). Combine eggs and sugar in a medium bowl; stir with a wire whisk until well blended. Gradually stir about one-fourth of hot mixture into egg mixture; add to remaining hot mixture, stirring constantly. Cook mixture over low heat, stirring constantly, 20 minutes or until mixture is slightly thickened and reaches 160°.

Remove mixture from heat; stir in bourbon and ¼ teaspoon nutmeg. Let cool. Cover and chill 3 hours. Remove and discard vanilla bean; stir in ice cream just before serving. If desired, top each serving with sweetened whipped cream and sprinkle with nutmeg. Yield: 18 (½-cup) servings.

Per serving: Calories 164 (42% from fat)
Carbohydrate 15.4g Protein 5.0g Fat 7.6g (Sat. Fat 4.2g)
Cholesterol 97mg Sodium 71mg

You won't think twice about treating yourself to a cool and creamy Strawberry Banana Shake. It uses nonfat frozen yogurt and skim milk instead of ice cream and whole milk. But when you want to splurge, indulge in a decadent White Chocolate Shake.

STRAWBERRY BANANA SHAKES

1   large banana, peeled and cut into
     $\frac{1}{2}$-inch-thick slices
1   teaspoon lemon juice
$1\frac{1}{2}$ cups strawberry nonfat frozen yogurt
1   cup frozen unsweetened strawberries
1   cup skim milk
1   teaspoon vanilla extract

Combine banana and lemon juice; toss gently to coat. Place banana slices on a baking sheet. Cover and freeze 1 hour or until firm.

Combine banana, yogurt, and remaining ingredients in container of an electric blender; cover and process until smooth, stopping twice to scrape down sides. Pour into glasses, and serve immediately. Yield: 4 (1-cup) servings.

Per serving: Calories 136 (2% from fat)
Carbohydrate 29.5g   Protein 5.2g   Fat 0.3g (Sat. Fat 0.2g)
Cholesterol 1mg   Sodium 78mg

White Chocolate Shakes

$1\frac{1}{2}$ cups whole milk
$\frac{1}{2}$ cup marshmallow cream
1   (4-inch) strip vanilla bean, split
     lengthwise
$3\frac{1}{2}$ ounces white chocolate, chopped
$2\frac{1}{2}$ cups vanilla ice cream
$\frac{1}{4}$ teaspoon freshly grated nutmeg

Combine first 3 ingredients in a small saucepan; stir with a wire whisk. Bring to a simmer over medium heat, stirring constantly. Add chocolate; reduce heat to low, and cook, stirring constantly, until chocolate melts. Let cool to room temperature, stirring occasionally. Remove and discard vanilla bean. Pour mixture into a freezer-proof container. Cover and freeze 3 hours or until slushy.

Combine milk mixture, ice cream, and nutmeg in container of an electric blender; cover and process until smooth, stopping twice to scrape down sides. Pour into glasses, and serve immediately. Yield: 4 (1-cup) servings.

Per serving: Calories 424 (41% from fat)
Carbohydrate 55.1g   Protein 8.3g   Fat 19.5g (Sat. Fat 11.8g)
Cholesterol 50mg   Sodium 143mg

Left: *Strawberry Banana Shakes and (in center) White Chocolate Shake*

A tall glass of cool Piña Colada Slush has less than one gram of fat per serving because it contains banana and nonfat dry milk powder instead of ice cream. Its tropical flavor comes from coconut extract instead of rich cream of coconut.

Piña Colada Slush

1   medium banana, peeled and sliced
1   tablespoon lemon juice
½   (12-ounce) can frozen pineapple juice concentrate, thawed and undiluted
¼   cup instant nonfat dry milk powder
¼   cup water
¼   cup light rum
2   tablespoons coconut liqueur
1   teaspoon coconut extract
    Crushed ice

Combine banana and lemon juice; toss gently to coat. Place banana slices on a baking sheet. Cover and freeze 1 hour or until firm.

Combine banana, pineapple juice concentrate, and next 5 ingredients in container of an electric blender; cover and process until smooth. Add enough crushed ice to reach 4 cups; cover and process until slushy. Pour into glasses, and serve immediately. Yield: 4 (1-cup) servings.

Per serving: Calories 194 (1% from fat)
Carbohydrate 28.8g   Protein 3.5g   Fat 0.2g (Sat. Fat 0.1g)
Cholesterol 1mg   Sodium 42mg

Creamy Piña Colada

1   (8-ounce) can crushed pineapple in light syrup, undrained
1   cup vanilla ice cream
⅓   cup light rum
¼   cup coconut liqueur
2   tablespoons cream of coconut
    Crushed ice

Combine first 5 ingredients in container of an electric blender; cover and process until smooth. Add enough crushed ice to reach 4 cups; cover and process until smooth. Pour into glasses, and serve immediately. Yield: 4 (1-cup) servings.

Per serving: Calories 230 (24% from fat)
Carbohydrate 17.5g   Protein 1.9g   Fat 6.2g (Sat. Fat 4.5g)
Cholesterol 15mg   Sodium 30mg

Punch up your next party with either of these beverages. Berries, banana, and sparkling mineral water make a fruity light selection, while passion fruit nectar and cream of coconut provide a taste of the tropics in the luscious Tropical Slush Punch.

Pink Tulip Punch

1 (12-ounce) package frozen unsweetened raspberries, thawed
2 medium-size ripe bananas, peeled and sliced
2 (12-ounce) cans frozen orange-pineapple-apple juice concentrate, thawed and undiluted
2 cups water
4 cups berry-flavored sparkling mineral water, chilled

Place raspberries in container of an electric blender; cover and process until smooth. Pour raspberry puree through a wire-mesh strainer into container, discarding pulp and seeds remaining in strainer. Add banana and 1 can juice concentrate; cover and process until smooth. Pour mixture into a large freezer-proof container. Stir in remaining concentrate and 2 cups water. Cover and freeze 4 hours or until slushy.

To serve, transfer juice mixture to a small punch bowl. Stir in mineral water, and serve immediately. Yield: 24 (½-cup) servings.

Per serving: Calories 61 (3% from fat)
Carbohydrate 14.7g Protein 0.9g Fat 0.2g (Sat. Fat 0.0g)
Cholesterol 0mg Sodium 9mg

Tropical Slush Punch

1½ cups passion fruit nectar
1 medium-size ripe banana, peeled and sliced
2 (12-ounce) cans frozen pineapple-orange-banana juice concentrate, thawed and undiluted
½ cup cream of coconut
2½ cups water
3½ cups lemon-lime carbonated beverage, chilled

Combine nectar, banana, 1 can juice concentrate, and cream of coconut in container of an electric blender; cover and process until smooth. Pour mixture into a large freezer-proof container. Stir in remaining concentrate and 2½ cups water. Cover and freeze 4 hours or until slushy.

To serve, transfer juice mixture to a small punch bowl. Stir in carbonated beverage, and serve immediately. Yield: 24 (½-cup) servings.

Per serving: Calories 94 (17% from fat)
Carbohydrate 19.7g Protein 0.6g Fat 1.8g (Sat. Fat 1.5g)
Cholesterol 0mg Sodium 2mg

From left: *Parmesan Breadsticks (page 54), Wheat-Lover's Bread (page 58), Velvet French Bread (page 57), Blueberry Oat Streusel Muffins (page 44)*

BREADS

You'll get tender, flaky biscuits when you prepare either of these recipes. For a down-home buttermilk biscuit, try the light version. Or bake Whipping Cream Biscuits and savor the melt-in-your-mouth buttery flavor.

BUTTERMILK BISCUITS

2 cups all-purpose flour
2 teaspoons baking powder
½ teaspoon baking soda
¼ teaspoon salt
1 tablespoon sugar
¼ cup reduced-calorie margarine
¾ cup plus 1 tablespoon nonfat buttermilk
1½ teaspoons all-purpose flour
Vegetable cooking spray

Combine first 5 ingredients in a medium bowl; cut in margarine with a pastry blender until mixture resembles coarse meal. Add buttermilk, stirring just until dry ingredients are moistened.

Sprinkle 1½ teaspoons flour evenly over work surface. Turn dough out onto floured surface, and knead 5 or 6 times. Roll dough to ½-inch thickness; cut into rounds with a 2½-inch biscuit cutter. Place rounds on a baking sheet coated with cooking spray. Bake at 425° for 10 to 12 minutes or until biscuits are golden. Yield: 8 biscuits.

Per biscuit: Calories 163 (23% from fat)
Carbohydrate 27.3g Protein 4.2g Fat 4.1g (Sat. Fat 0.6g)
Cholesterol 1mg Sodium 282mg

Whipping Cream Biscuits

2 cups all-purpose flour
1 tablespoon plus 1 teaspoon baking powder
¼ teaspoon salt
1 tablespoon sugar
¼ cup unsalted butter
1 cup plus 1 tablespoon whipping cream
1½ teaspoons all-purpose flour

Combine first 4 ingredients in a medium bowl; cut in butter with a pastry blender until mixture resembles coarse meal. Add whipping cream, stirring just until dry ingredients are moistened.

Sprinkle 1½ teaspoons flour evenly over work surface. Turn dough out onto floured surface, and knead 5 or 6 times. Roll dough to ½-inch thickness; cut into rounds with a 2½-inch biscuit cutter. Place rounds on a lightly greased baking sheet. Bake at 425° for 10 to 12 minutes or until biscuits are golden. Yield: 10 biscuits.

Per biscuit: Calories 230 (57% from fat)
Carbohydrate 21.7g Protein 3.2g Fat 14.6g (Sat. Fat 8.8g)
Cholesterol 47mg Sodium 236mg

Toasted almonds flavor both of these scone recipes. Fewer nuts and nonfat yogurt help keep the fat content low in the light Almond Yogurt Scones. Currants, butter, and sugar sprinkles combine to make a delectable treat in Toasted Almond Scones.

ALMOND YOGURT SCONES

1 cup all-purpose flour
1 cup sifted cake flour
2 teaspoons baking powder
½ teaspoon baking soda
¼ teaspoon salt
2 tablespoons brown sugar
2 tablespoons margarine
¼ cup chopped almonds, lightly toasted
1 (8-ounce) carton plain nonfat yogurt
1 tablespoon all-purpose flour
Vegetable cooking spray
1 egg white, lightly beaten

Combine first 6 ingredients in a medium bowl; cut in margarine with a pastry blender until mixture resembles coarse meal. Add almonds; toss well. Add yogurt to dry ingredients, stirring just until dry ingredients are moistened.

Sprinkle 1 tablespoon flour evenly over work surface. Turn dough out onto floured surface, and knead 3 or 4 times. Pat dough into an 8-inch round on a baking sheet coated with cooking spray. Cut round into 8 wedges, cutting to, but not through, bottom of dough. Brush wedges with egg white. Bake at 425° for 10 to 12 minutes or until golden. Yield: 8 scones.

Per scone: Calories 184 (25% from fat)
Carbohydrate 28.7g Protein 5.6g Fat 5.1g (Sat. Fat 0.8g)
Cholesterol 1mg Sodium 263mg

Toasted Almond Scones

¼ cup currants
¼ cup boiling water
2 cups all-purpose flour
1 tablespoon baking powder
¼ teaspoon salt
2 tablespoons brown sugar
¼ cup plus 2 tablespoons unsalted butter
¾ cup chopped almonds, lightly toasted
¾ cup buttermilk
1 tablespoon all-purpose flour
1 egg, lightly beaten
1 teaspoon water
1 tablespoon sugar

Combine currants and ¼ cup boiling water; let stand 10 minutes. Drain well, and set aside.

Combine 2 cups flour, baking powder, salt, and brown sugar in a medium bowl; cut in butter with a pastry blender until mixture resembles coarse meal. Add reserved currants and almonds; toss well. Add buttermilk to dry ingredients, stirring just until dry ingredients are moistened.

Sprinkle 1 tablespoon flour evenly over work surface. Turn dough out onto floured surface, and knead 3 or 4 times. Pat dough into an 8-inch round on a greased baking sheet. Cut round into 8 wedges, cutting to, but not through, bottom of dough. Combine beaten egg and 1 teaspoon water; mix well. Brush wedges with egg mixture, and sprinkle evenly with 1 tablespoon sugar. Bake at 425° for 10 to 12 minutes or until golden. Yield: 8 scones.

Per scone: Calories 311 (47% from fat)
Carbohydrate 34.7g Protein 7.4g Fat 16.3g (Sat. Fat 6.3g)
Cholesterol 52mg Sodium 223mg

Creamy Maple Topping, which contains nonfat frozen yogurt, adds just enough sweetness to the lighter spiced pancakes. The richer Maple Pecan Sauce is thick and full of nuts.

GINGER PANCAKES WITH CREAMY MAPLE TOPPING

2 cups all-purpose flour
1 tablespoon baking powder
1 teaspoon ground cinnamon
1 teaspoon ground ginger
½ teaspoon ground cloves
1 cup skim milk
⅓ cup molasses
2 tablespoons vegetable oil
1 egg, lightly beaten
2 egg whites
   Vegetable cooking spray
   Creamy Maple Topping
   Fresh strawberries (optional)

Combine first 5 ingredients in a large bowl; make a well in center of mixture. Combine milk, molasses, oil, egg, and egg whites; add to dry ingredients, stirring just until dry ingredients are moistened.

For each pancake, pour ¼ cup batter onto a hot griddle or skillet coated with cooking spray. Cook pancakes until tops are covered with bubbles and edges look cooked; turn and cook other side. Top each pancake with 2 tablespoons Creamy Maple Topping. Garnish with fresh strawberries, if desired. Yield: 12 (4-inch) pancakes.

Creamy Maple Topping

1½ cups vanilla nonfat frozen yogurt, softened
¼ cup plus 2 tablespoons reduced-calorie maple syrup
¼ teaspoon ground cinnamon

Combine all ingredients in a small bowl; stir well. Cover and chill. Yield: 1½ cups.

Per pancake with topping: Calories 159 (17% from fat)
Carbohydrate 28.5g Protein 4.8g Fat 3.0g (Sat. Fat 0.6g)
Cholesterol 19mg Sodium 121mg

Left: *Ginger Pancakes with Creamy Maple Topping*

Ginger Pancakes with Maple Pecan Sauce

3⅓ cups all-purpose flour
2¼ teaspoons baking powder
2¼ teaspoons baking soda
¾ teaspoon salt
1½ teaspoons ground cinnamon
1½ teaspoons ground ginger
¾ teaspoon ground cloves
1¼ cups buttermilk
1 cup water
2 eggs, lightly beaten
¼ cup plus 2 tablespoons margarine, melted
⅓ cup firmly packed brown sugar
   Maple Pecan Sauce

Combine first 7 ingredients in a large bowl; make a well in center of mixture. Combine buttermilk, water, eggs, margarine, and brown sugar; add to dry ingredients, stirring just until dry ingredients are moistened.

For each pancake, pour ¼ cup batter onto a hot, lightly greased griddle or skillet. Cook pancakes until tops are covered with bubbles and edges look cooked; turn and cook other side. Top pancakes evenly with Maple Pecan Sauce. Yield: 21 (4-inch) pancakes.

Maple Pecan Sauce

2 cups maple syrup
½ cup honey
¾ cup chopped pecans, toasted
½ teaspoon ground cinnamon

Combine syrup and honey in a medium saucepan; cook over medium heat 10 minutes or until very slightly thickened, stirring frequently. Remove from heat; stir in pecans and cinnamon. (Mixture will thicken as it cools.) Yield: 2¾ cups.

Per pancake with sauce: Calories 255 (23% from fat)
Carbohydrate 47.2g Protein 3.5g Fat 6.4g (Sat. Fat 1.1g)
Cholesterol 22mg Sodium 269mg

Start your day with Yogurt Waffles. Containing skim milk, nonfat yogurt, and very little oil, each waffle has only two grams of fat and one milligram of cholesterol. But for a special breakfast indulgence, enjoy the richness of whipping cream and butter in Rich Cream Waffles.

YOGURT WAFFLES

2 cups all-purpose flour
1 teaspoon baking soda
½ teaspoon baking powder
¼ teaspoon salt
1 tablespoon sugar
1½ cups skim milk
¾ cup plain nonfat yogurt
2 tablespoons vegetable oil
3 egg whites
⅛ teaspoon cream of tartar
   Vegetable cooking spray
   Reduced-calorie maple syrup (optional)

Combine first 5 ingredients in a large bowl; make a well in center of mixture. Combine milk, yogurt, and oil; stir with a wire whisk. Add to dry ingredients, stirring just until dry ingredients are moistened.

Beat egg whites and cream of tartar at high speed of an electric mixer until stiff peaks form; gently fold beaten egg white mixture into batter.

Coat an 8-inch square waffle iron with cooking spray; allow waffle iron to preheat. For each waffle, spoon 1¼ cups batter onto hot waffle iron, spreading batter to edges. Bake 4 to 5 minutes or until steaming stops. Repeat procedure with remaining batter. Cut each waffle into 4 squares. Top with maple syrup, if desired. Yield: 16 (4-inch) waffles.

Per waffle: Calories 93 (19% from fat)
Carbohydrate 14.8g Protein 3.6g Fat 2.0g (Sat. Fat 0.4g)
Cholesterol 1mg Sodium 129mg

Rich Cream Waffles

2 cups all-purpose flour
2 teaspoons baking powder
¼ teaspoon salt
2 tablespoons sugar
3 eggs, separated
1 cup whole milk
1 cup whipping cream
¼ cup butter, melted
⅛ teaspoon cream of tartar
   Vegetable cooking spray
   Maple syrup (optional)

Combine first 4 ingredients in a large bowl; make a well in center of mixture. Combine egg yolks, milk, cream, and butter; stir with a wire whisk. Add to dry ingredients, stirring just until dry ingredients are moistened.

Beat egg whites and cream of tartar at high speed of an electric mixer until stiff peaks form; gently fold beaten egg white mixture into batter.

Coat an 8-inch square waffle iron with cooking spray; allow waffle iron to preheat. For each waffle, spoon 1 cup batter onto hot waffle iron, spreading batter to edges. Bake 4 to 5 minutes or until steaming stops. Repeat procedure with remaining batter. Cut each waffle into 4 squares. Top with maple syrup, if desired. Yield: 20 (4-inch) waffles.

Per waffle: Calories 132 (55% from fat)
Carbohydrate 11.9g Protein 2.9g Fat 8.1g (Sat. Fat 4.7g)
Cholesterol 57mg Sodium 105mg

The light popovers have a characteristic crisp crust and moist interior but are lower in fat and calories than the luscious popovers because they contain skim milk and half the egg yolks. The light recipe saves even more calories by using cooking spray instead of oil to grease the pans.

LIGHT LEMON POPOVERS

Vegetable cooking spray
1 cup bread flour
1 cup skim milk
4 egg whites
1 egg yolk
1 tablespoon sugar
1 tablespoon fresh lemon juice
2 teaspoons grated lemon rind
¼ teaspoon salt

Heavily coat a popover pan with cooking spray, and set aside.

Combine flour and remaining ingredients in a large bowl; stir with a wire whisk until smooth. Pour batter evenly into prepared pan. Place in a cold oven. Turn oven on 450°, and bake 15 minutes. Reduce heat to 350°, and bake an additional 35 to 40 minutes or until popovers are crusty and brown. Serve immediately. Yield: 6 popovers.

Per popover: Calories 128 (11% from fat)
Carbohydrate 21.2g   Protein 6.9g   Fat 1.5g (Sat. Fat 0.4g)
Cholesterol 37mg   Sodium 156mg

Lemon Popovers

Vegetable oil
1 cup bread flour
1 cup whole milk
2 eggs
2 egg whites
2 tablespoons sugar
1 tablespoon fresh lemon juice
2 teaspoons grated lemon rind
¼ teaspoon salt

Heavily grease a popover pan with vegetable oil, and set aside.

Combine flour and remaining ingredients in a large bowl; stir with a wire whisk until smooth. Pour batter evenly into prepared pan. Place in a cold oven. Turn oven on 450°, and bake 15 minutes. Reduce heat to 350°, and bake an additional 35 to 40 minutes or until popovers are crusty and brown. Serve immediately. Yield: 6 popovers.

Per popover: Calories 175 (29% from fat)
Carbohydrate 23.2g   Protein 7.3g   Fat 5.7g (Sat. Fat 1.9g)
Cholesterol 79mg   Sodium 157mg

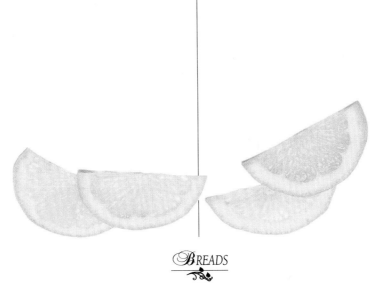

Blueberry muffins with crunchy, sweet toppings are sure to become breakfast favorites at your house. The light streusel mixture contains oats, reduced-calorie margarine instead of butter, and fewer almonds than the topping on Blueberry Almond Streusel Muffins.

BLUEBERRY OAT STREUSEL MUFFINS

⅓ cup regular oats, uncooked
3 tablespoons brown sugar
1 tablespoon all-purpose flour
1 tablespoon reduced-calorie margarine
2 tablespoons chopped almonds
2 cups all-purpose flour
2 teaspoons baking powder
¼ teaspoon baking soda
¼ teaspoon salt
½ cup sugar
2 teaspoons grated lemon rind
1½ cups fresh or frozen blueberries, thawed
¾ cup nonfat buttermilk
¼ cup vegetable oil
1 egg, lightly beaten
Vegetable cooking spray

Position knife blade in food processor bowl. Add first 3 ingredients; process 5 seconds or until mixture resembles fine meal. Add margarine, and pulse 5 times or until mixture resembles coarse meal. Transfer to a small bowl, and stir in chopped almonds. Set aside.

Combine 2 cups flour and next 5 ingredients in a large bowl. Add blueberries; toss gently to combine. Make a well in center of mixture. Combine buttermilk, oil, and egg; add to dry ingredients, stirring just until dry ingredients are moistened.

Spoon batter into muffin pans coated with cooking spray, filling two-thirds full. Sprinkle evenly with oat mixture. Bake at 400° for 15 to 20 minutes or until muffins are golden. Remove from pans immediately. Yield: 14 muffins.

Per muffin: Calories 177 (31% from fat)
Carbohydrate 27.9g Protein 3.5g Fat 6.0g (Sat. Fat 1.1g)
Cholesterol 16mg Sodium 128mg

Blueberry Almond Streusel Muffins

¼ cup all-purpose flour
¼ cup sugar
2 tablespoons unsalted butter, cut into pieces
¼ cup plus 2 tablespoons chopped almonds
2 cups all-purpose flour
1 tablespoon baking powder
½ teaspoon salt
⅔ cup sugar
2 teaspoons grated lemon rind
1½ cups fresh or frozen blueberries, thawed
½ cup whole milk
½ cup unsalted butter, melted and cooled
2 eggs, lightly beaten

Combine ¼ cup flour and ¼ cup sugar in a medium bowl. Cut in 2 tablespoons butter with a pastry blender until mixture is crumbly. Stir in chopped almonds. Set aside.

Combine 2 cups flour and next 4 ingredients in a large bowl. Add blueberries; toss gently to combine. Make a well in center of mixture. Combine milk, ½ cup butter, and eggs; add to dry ingredients, stirring just until dry ingredients are moistened.

Spoon batter into greased muffin pans, filling two-thirds full. Sprinkle evenly with almond mixture. Bake at 400° for 15 to 20 minutes or until muffins are golden. Remove from pans immediately. Yield: 16 muffins.

Per muffin: Calories 216 (43% from fat)
Carbohydrate 27.9g Protein 3.6g Fat 10.4g (Sat. Fat 5.1g)
Cholesterol 48mg Sodium 143mg

Right: *Blueberry Almond Streusel Muffins*

Substitutions go a long way in making a recipe lighter, and using less of a flavoring ingredient also makes a difference. The yogurt muffins contain nonfat yogurt instead of whole milk, vegetable oil rather than butter, and one-fourth the amount of coconut used in the luscious recipe.

BANANA YOGURT MUFFINS

    2   cups all-purpose flour
1½   teaspoons baking powder
  ½   teaspoon baking soda
  ½   teaspoon salt
  ⅓   cup sugar
    1   cup mashed ripe banana
  ¾   cup plain nonfat yogurt
  ¼   cup vegetable oil
    1   egg, lightly beaten
    1   teaspoon vanilla extract
  ¼   cup unsweetened shredded coconut,
         lightly toasted
         Vegetable cooking spray

Combine first 5 ingredients in a medium bowl; make a well in center of mixture. Combine banana, yogurt, oil, egg, and vanilla; stir well. Add coconut; stir just until blended. Add banana mixture to dry ingredients, stirring just until dry ingredients are moistened.

Spoon batter into muffin pans coated with cooking spray, filling two-thirds full. Bake at 400° for 20 minutes or until muffins are golden. Let cool on a wire rack 5 minutes, and remove from pans. Yield: 1 dozen muffins.

Per muffin: Calories 183 (31% from fat)
Carbohydrate 27.8g   Protein 3.8g   Fat 6.4g (Sat. Fat 1.9g)
Cholesterol 19mg   Sodium 187mg

Banana Coconut Muffins

    2   cups all-purpose flour
    1   tablespoon baking powder
  ½   teaspoon salt
  ⅓   cup sugar
    1   cup mashed ripe banana
  ⅔   cup whole milk
  ½   cup unsalted butter, melted and cooled
    1   egg, lightly beaten
    1   teaspoon vanilla extract
    1   cup flaked coconut, lightly toasted

Combine first 4 ingredients in a medium bowl; make a well in center of mixture. Combine banana, milk, butter, egg, and vanilla; stir well. Add coconut; stir just until blended. Add banana mixture to dry ingredients, stirring just until dry ingredients are moistened.

Spoon batter into greased muffin pans, filling two-thirds full. Bake at 400° for 20 minutes or until muffins are golden. Let cool on a wire rack 5 minutes, and remove from pans. Yield: 1 dozen muffins.

Per muffin: Calories 242 (45% from fat)
Carbohydrate 30.5g   Protein 3.6g   Fat 12.1g (Sat. Fat 7.7g)
Cholesterol 41mg   Sodium 205mg

Both of these spice loaf recipes yield a moist, flavorful bread. The Ginger Spice Loaf is lower in fat than the luscious loaf because it uses less margarine and omits the nuts. Its distinctive flavor comes from brewed coffee, while Pecan Spice Loaf is enhanced by pecans and orange juice.

GINGER SPICE LOAF

¼ cup margarine, softened
½ cup brown sugar
1 egg, lightly beaten
½ cup molasses
2 cups all-purpose flour
2 teaspoons baking powder
½ teaspoon baking soda
1 teaspoon ground ginger
1 teaspoon ground cinnamon
½ teaspoon ground nutmeg
¼ teaspoon ground cloves
¾ cup strong brewed coffee
   Vegetable cooking spray

Beat margarine in a large bowl at medium speed of an electric mixer until creamy; gradually add brown sugar, beating well. Add egg, and beat well. Stir in molasses.

Combine flour and next 6 ingredients; add flour mixture to creamed mixture alternately with coffee, beginning and ending with flour mixture. Mix after each addition.

Pour batter into a 9- x 5- x 3-inch loafpan coated with cooking spray. Bake at 350° for 55 minutes or until a wooden pick inserted in center comes out clean. Let cool in pan 5 minutes; remove from pan, and let cool completely on a wire rack. Yield: 18 (½-inch) slices.

Per slice: Calories 117 (23% from fat)
Carbohydrate 20.8g Protein 1.9g Fat 3.0g (Sat. Fat 0.6g)
Cholesterol 12mg Sodium 93mg

Pecan Spice Loaf

½ cup butter, softened
¾ cup brown sugar
1 egg, lightly beaten
½ cup molasses
1 tablespoon grated orange rind
2 cups all-purpose flour
2 teaspoons baking powder
½ teaspoon baking soda
1½ teaspoons ground ginger
½ teaspoon ground nutmeg
¼ teaspoon ground cloves
1 cup chopped pecans
¾ cup unsweetened orange juice

Beat butter in a large bowl at medium speed of an electric mixer until creamy; gradually add brown sugar, beating well. Add egg, and beat well. Stir in molasses and orange rind.

Combine flour and next 6 ingredients; add to creamed mixture alternately with orange juice, beginning and ending with flour mixture. Mix after each addition.

Pour batter into a greased and floured 9- x 5- x 3-inch loafpan. Bake at 350° for 55 minutes or until a wooden pick inserted in center comes out clean. Let cool in pan 5 minutes; remove from pan, and let cool completely on a wire rack. Yield: 18 (½-inch) slices.

Per slice: Calories 198 (46% from fat)
Carbohydrate 25.2g Protein 2.5g Fat 10.2g (Sat. Fat 3.7g)
Cholesterol 26mg Sodium 116mg

Packed full of walnuts and fresh banana, Banana Walnut Bread is a nut bread-lover's dream. Banana Yogurt Bread is full of banana flavor and has a light, cakelike texture, but it skips the nuts and reduces the number of egg yolks.

Banana Yogurt Bread

2	cups all-purpose flour
1½	teaspoons baking powder
½	teaspoon baking soda
½	teaspoon salt
1	(8-ounce) carton plain nonfat yogurt
1	cup mashed ripe banana
½	cup sugar
¼	cup margarine, melted
2	egg whites, lightly beaten
1	egg, lightly beaten
1	teaspoon vanilla extract
	Vegetable cooking spray
2	teaspoons all-purpose flour

Combine first 4 ingredients in a large bowl; make a well in center of mixture. Combine yogurt and next 6 ingredients; add to dry ingredients, stirring just until dry ingredients are moistened.

Coat a 9- x 5- x 3-inch loafpan with cooking spray; sprinkle with 2 teaspoons flour. Spoon batter into prepared pan. Bake at 350° for 1 hour or until a wooden pick inserted in center comes out clean. Let cool in pan 10 minutes; remove from pan, and let cool on a wire rack. Yield: 18 (½-inch) slices.

Per slice: Calories 123 (22% from fat)
Carbohydrate 20.9g Protein 3.1g Fat 3.1g (Sat. Fat 0.7g)
Cholesterol 13mg Sodium 162mg

Banana Walnut Bread

2	cups all-purpose flour
1	tablespoon baking powder
½	teaspoon salt
1	teaspoon ground cinnamon
½	teaspoon ground nutmeg
½	cup butter, softened
1	cup sugar
2	eggs
1	cup mashed ripe banana
¼	cup whole milk
1	cup chopped walnuts

Combine first 5 ingredients in a large bowl; stir well. Set aside.

Beat butter at medium speed of an electric mixer until creamy; gradually add sugar, beating well. Add eggs, one at a time, beating after each addition. Add banana and milk to creamed mixture; add to dry ingredients, stirring just until dry ingredients are moistened. Stir in walnuts.

Pour batter into a greased and floured 9- x 5- x 3-inch loafpan. Bake at 350° for 1 hour or until a wooden pick inserted in center comes out clean. Let cool in pan 10 minutes; remove from pan, and let cool on a wire rack. Yield: 18 (½-inch) slices.

Per slice: Calories 208 (44% from fat)
Carbohydrate 26.5g Protein 4.2g Fat 10.1g (Sat. Fat 3.8g)
Cholesterol 39mg Sodium 177mg

Right: *Banana Walnut Bread*

True cornbread fans will delight in both of these recipes. The light version is made with nonfat buttermilk, a small amount of vegetable oil, and egg substitute. The Yankee Cornbread Squares are more cakelike and are made with whole milk, margarine, and eggs.

LIGHT CORNBREAD SQUARES

1½ cups yellow cornmeal
½ cup all-purpose flour
1 teaspoon baking powder
1 teaspoon baking soda
¼ teaspoon salt
2 teaspoons sugar
1⅔ cups nonfat buttermilk
¼ cup frozen egg substitute, thawed
2 tablespoons vegetable oil
Vegetable cooking spray

Combine first 6 ingredients in a large bowl; make a well in center of mixture. Combine buttermilk, egg substitute, and oil; add to dry ingredients, stirring just until dry ingredients are moistened.

Pour batter into an 8-inch square pan coated with cooking spray. Bake at 400° for 22 to 25 minutes or until golden. Cut into squares. Yield: 9 servings.

Per serving: Calories 161 (21% from fat)
Carbohydrate 26.7g   Protein 5.0g   Fat 3.7g (Sat. Fat 0.7g)
Cholesterol 2mg   Sodium 250mg

Yankee Cornbread Squares

1¼ cups all-purpose flour
¾ cup yellow cornmeal
1 tablespoon baking powder
¼ teaspoon salt
½ cup sugar
1 cup whole milk
½ cup margarine, melted
2 eggs, lightly beaten

Combine first 5 ingredients in a large bowl; make a well in center of mixture. Combine milk, margarine, and eggs; add to dry ingredients, stirring just until dry ingredients are moistened.

Pour batter into a greased 8-inch square pan. Bake at 400° for 25 to 30 minutes or until golden. Cut into squares. Yield: 9 servings.

Per serving: Calories 275 (42% from fat)
Carbohydrate 35.0g   Protein 5.2g   Fat 12.7g (Sat. Fat 3.0g)
Cholesterol 53mg   Sodium 312mg

Add flavor as well as color to the light Chile-Jack Corn Loaf with corn, roasted red pepper, green chiles, and reduced-fat Monterey Jack cheese. Stir bacon and Cheddar cheese into the luscious batter to yield a savory corn loaf.

CHILE-JACK CORN LOAF

1 cup all-purpose flour
1 cup yellow cornmeal
2 teaspoons baking powder
½ teaspoon baking soda
½ teaspoon salt
1 cup canned no-salt-added cream-style corn
½ cup nonfat buttermilk
2 tablespoons margarine, melted
1 egg, lightly beaten
2 egg whites, lightly beaten
¼ cup chopped, drained, roasted red pepper in water
1 (4-ounce) can chopped green chiles, drained
½ cup (2 ounces) shredded reduced-fat Monterey Jack cheese
Vegetable cooking spray
2 teaspoons all-purpose flour

Combine first 5 ingredients in a medium bowl; make a well in center of mixture. Combine corn, buttermilk, margarine, egg, and egg whites; stir mixture well.

Press roasted red pepper and chiles between paper towels until barely moist. Add pepper and chiles to corn mixture, stirring well. Add corn mixture and cheese to dry ingredients, stirring just until dry ingredients are moistened.

Coat a 9- x 5- x 3-inch loafpan with cooking spray; sprinkle with 2 teaspoons flour. Spoon batter into prepared pan. Bake at 375° for 1 hour or until golden. Let cool in pan 10 minutes; remove loaf from pan, and let cool completely on a wire rack. Yield: 18 (½-inch) slices.

Per slice: Calories 95 (24% from fat)
Carbohydrate 14.8g Protein 3.6g Fat 2.5g (Sat. Fat 0.7g)
Cholesterol 15mg Sodium 178mg

Bacon Cheddar Corn Loaf

½ pound bacon
1½ cups all-purpose flour
½ cup yellow cornmeal
2 teaspoons baking powder
½ teaspoon salt
1½ cups (6 ounces) grated Cheddar cheese
½ cup sliced green onions
1 cup canned cream-style corn
¾ cup whole milk
¼ cup unsalted butter, melted and cooled
2 eggs, lightly beaten

Cook bacon in a large skillet until crisp; remove bacon, reserving 2 tablespoons drippings. Crumble bacon, and set aside.

Combine flour, cornmeal, baking powder, and salt in a large bowl; make a well in center of mixture. Combine bacon, reserved drippings, cheese, and remaining ingredients; add to dry ingredients, stirring just until dry ingredients are moistened.

Spoon batter into a greased and floured 9- x 5- x 3-inch loafpan. Bake at 350° for 1 hour and 5 minutes or until golden. Let cool in pan 10 minutes; remove loaf from pan, and let cool completely on a wire rack. Yield: 18 (½-inch) slices.

Per slice: Calories 179 (53% from fat)
Carbohydrate 14.6g Protein 6.3g Fat 10.6g (Sat. Fat 5.4g)
Cholesterol 48mg Sodium 294mg

Whole milk and butter give Super Dinner Rolls a rich flavor and tender texture. Lower the fat, but not the flavor, in the light buttermilk rolls by using nonfat buttermilk and fewer eggs.

BUTTERMILK DINNER ROLLS

2   packages active dry yeast
¼   cup warm water (105° to 115°)
1¾   cups nonfat buttermilk
¼   cup sugar
2   tablespoons margarine, softened
½   teaspoon salt
1   egg, lightly beaten
5   cups bread flour, divided
1   tablespoon bread flour
     Vegetable cooking spray

Combine yeast and warm water in a 1-cup liquid measuring cup; let stand 5 minutes. Combine yeast mixture, buttermilk, and next 4 ingredients in a large mixing bowl; beat at medium speed of an electric mixer until well blended. Add 2 cups flour, and beat 2 minutes at medium speed. Gradually stir in enough of the remaining 3 cups flour to make a soft dough.

Sprinkle 1 tablespoon flour evenly over work surface. Turn dough out onto floured surface, and knead until smooth and elastic (about 8 to 10 minutes). Place dough in a large bowl coated with cooking spray, turning to coat top. Cover and let rise in a warm place (85°), free from drafts, 45 minutes or until doubled in bulk.

Punch dough down; divide in half. Divide each half into 8 equal portions; shape each portion into a ball. Place at least 1 inch apart on large baking sheets coated with cooking spray.

Cover and let rise in a warm place, free from drafts, 30 minutes or until doubled in bulk. Bake at 325° for 18 to 20 minutes or until lightly browned. Remove rolls from baking sheets; let cool on wire racks. Yield: 16 rolls.

Per roll: Calories 199 (12% from fat)
Carbohydrate 36.3g Protein 6.9g Fat 2.6g (Sat. Fat 0.6g)
Cholesterol 15mg Sodium 123mg

Super Dinner Rolls

7¼   cups bread flour, divided
¾   cup sugar
1   teaspoon salt
2   packages active dry yeast
2   cups whole milk
½   cup unsalted butter
3   eggs, lightly beaten
1   tablespoon bread flour

Combine 2 cups flour, sugar, salt, and yeast in a large mixing bowl; stir well. Combine milk and butter in a saucepan; heat until butter melts, stirring occasionally. Cool to 120° to 130°. Gradually add liquid mixture to flour mixture, beating well at low speed of an electric mixer. Beat an additional 2 minutes at medium speed. Add eggs and ¾ cup flour, beating 2 minutes at medium speed. Gradually stir in enough of the remaining 4½ cups flour to make a soft dough.

Sprinkle 1 tablespoon flour evenly over work surface. Turn dough out onto floured surface, and knead until smooth and elastic (about 8 to 10 minutes). Place dough in a large well-greased bowl, turning to grease top. Cover and let rise in a warm place (85°), free from drafts, 45 minutes or until doubled in bulk.

Punch dough down; divide in half. Divide each half into 11 equal portions; shape each portion into a ball. Place at least 1 inch apart on large greased baking sheets.

Cover and let rise in a warm place, free from drafts, 30 minutes or until doubled in bulk. Bake at 325° for 18 to 20 minutes or until lightly browned. Remove rolls from baking sheets; let cool on wire racks. Yield: 22 rolls.

Per roll: Calories 257 (24% from fat)
Carbohydrate 41.2g Protein 7.3g Fat 6.8g (Sat. Fat 3.4g)
Cholesterol 45mg Sodium 128mg

Right: *Super Dinner Rolls*

The light breadsticks have no oil and are flavored with poppy seeds instead of kosher salt and cheese.

Poppy Seed Breadsticks

1 package active dry yeast
1⅓ cups warm water (105° to 115°)
1 tablespoon sugar
1 teaspoon salt
3 cups unbleached bread flour, divided
2 tablespoons unbleached bread flour
  Vegetable cooking spray
1 egg white, lightly beaten
2 teaspoons poppy seeds

Combine yeast and warm water in a 2-cup liquid measuring cup; let stand 5 minutes. Combine yeast mixture, sugar, and salt in a large mixing bowl; beat at medium speed of an electric mixer until well blended. Add 1 cup flour; beat 2 minutes at medium speed. Gradually stir in enough of the remaining 2 cups flour to make a soft dough.

Sprinkle 2 tablespoons flour evenly over work surface. Turn dough out onto floured surface, and knead until smooth and elastic (about 8 to 10 minutes). Place dough in a large bowl coated with cooking spray, turning to coat top. Cover and let rise in a warm place (85°), free from drafts, 1 hour or until doubled in bulk.

Punch dough down, and divide into 12 equal portions; roll each portion into a 10-inch rope. Place ropes 1 inch apart on a large baking sheet coated with cooking spray. Brush breadsticks with egg white, and sprinkle evenly with poppy seeds. Bake at 425° for 10 to 12 minutes or until golden. Remove from baking sheet, and let cool on a wire rack. Yield: 1 dozen breadsticks.

Per breadstick: Calories 139 (6% from fat)
Carbohydrate 27.3g Protein 4.9g Fat 0.9g (Sat. Fat 0.1g)
Cholesterol 0mg Sodium 201mg

Parmesan Breadsticks

1 package active dry yeast
1⅓ cups warm water (105° to 115°)
¼ cup extra-virgin olive oil
1 tablespoon honey
1 teaspoon salt
4¼ cups all-purpose flour, divided
½ cup freshly grated Parmesan cheese
2 teaspoons freshly ground pepper
2 tablespoons all-purpose flour
1 egg white, lightly beaten
2 teaspoons kosher salt

Combine yeast and warm water in a 2-cup liquid measuring cup; let stand 5 minutes. Combine yeast mixture, olive oil, honey, and 1 teaspoon salt in a large mixing bowl; beat at medium speed of an electric mixer until well blended. Add 2 cups flour; beat 2 minutes at medium speed. Stir in Parmesan cheese and pepper. Gradually stir in enough of the remaining 2¼ cups flour to make a soft dough.

Sprinkle 2 tablespoons flour evenly over work surface. Turn dough out onto floured surface, and knead until smooth and elastic (about 8 to 10 minutes). Place dough in a large, well-greased bowl, turning to grease top. Cover and let rise in a warm place (85°), free from drafts, 1 hour or until doubled in bulk.

Punch dough down, and divide into 12 equal portions; roll each portion into a 10-inch rope. Place ropes 1 inch apart on a large greased baking sheet. Brush breadsticks with egg white, and sprinkle evenly with kosher salt. Bake at 425° for 10 to 12 minutes or until golden. Remove from baking sheet, and let cool on a wire rack. Yield: 1 dozen breadsticks.

Per breadstick: Calories 235 (26% from fat)
Carbohydrate 35.9g Protein 6.8g Fat 6.8g (Sat. Fat 1.6g)
Cholesterol 3mg Sodium 667mg

Replace caramel with currants and decrease the nuts to lower calories in the light rolls.

CURRANT PECAN ROLLS

2 packages active dry yeast
2 cups warm water (105° to 115°)
¼ cup sugar
1 teaspoon salt
5 cups bread flour, divided
½ cup cooked potato, mashed
1 tablespoon vegetable oil
3 tablespoons bread flour
    Vegetable cooking spray
1 tablespoon margarine, melted
1¼ cups firmly packed brown sugar,
    divided
1 teaspoon ground cinnamon
⅓ cup currants
⅓ cup chopped pecans
⅓ cup evaporated skimmed milk

Combine yeast and warm water; let stand 5 minutes. Combine yeast mixture, ¼ cup sugar, and salt. Add 2 cups flour, potato, and oil; beat at medium speed of an electric mixer until well blended. Stir in enough of the remaining 3 cups flour to make a soft dough.

Sprinkle 3 tablespoons flour over work surface. Turn dough out; knead until smooth and elastic (about 8 minutes). Place in a bowl coated with cooking spray, turning to coat top. Cover and let rise in a warm place (85°), free from drafts, 1 hour or until doubled in bulk.

Punch dough down; roll to a 24- x 6-inch rectangle. Brush with margarine. Combine ½ cup brown sugar and cinnamon; sprinkle over dough. Roll up, starting at long side. Pinch seam to seal (do not seal ends). Cut into 16 (1½-inch) slices.

Spoon remaining ¾ cup brown sugar into a 13- x 9- x 2-inch baking dish coated with cooking spray. Sprinkle currants and pecans over sugar. Place slices over sugar. Pour milk around rolls. Cover and let rise in a warm place, free from drafts, 30 minutes or until doubled in bulk. Bake at 375° for 30 minutes or until done. Let cool 2 minutes. Yield: 16 rolls.

Per roll: Calories 294 (12% from fat)
Carbohydrate 58.3g Protein 6.6g Fat 4.0g (Sat. Fat 0.5g)
Cholesterol 0mg Sodium 169mg

Caramel Pecan Rolls

5 cups bread flour, divided
½ cup sugar
1 teaspoon salt
2 packages active dry yeast
2 cups whole milk
¼ cup unsalted butter
½ cup cooked potato, mashed
¼ cup bread flour
1 tablespoon unsalted butter, melted
2 cups firmly packed brown sugar,
    divided
1 teaspoon ground cinnamon
1½ cups chopped pecans
¾ cup whipping cream

Combine 2 cups flour, ½ cup sugar, salt, and yeast; stir well. Combine milk, ¼ cup butter, and potato in a saucepan; heat until butter melts, stirring occasionally. Cool to 120° to 130°. Add liquid mixture to flour mixture, beating at low speed of an electric mixer. Beat an additional 2 minutes at medium speed. Add ¾ cup flour, beating 2 minutes at medium speed. Stir in enough of the remaining 2¼ cups flour to make a soft dough.

Sprinkle ¼ cup flour over work surface. Turn dough out; knead until smooth and elastic (about 8 minutes). Place in a greased bowl, turning to grease top. Cover and let rise in a warm place (85°), free from drafts, 1 hour or until doubled in bulk.

Punch dough down; roll to a 24- x 6-inch rectangle. Brush with melted butter. Combine ½ cup brown sugar and cinnamon; sprinkle over dough. Roll up, starting at long side. Pinch seam to seal (do not seal ends). Cut into 16 (1½-inch) slices.

Spoon remaining 1½ cups brown sugar into a greased 13- x 9- x 2-inch baking dish. Sprinkle pecans over sugar. Place slices over sugar. Pour whipping cream around rolls. Cover and let rise in a warm place, free from drafts, 30 minutes or until doubled in bulk. Bake at 350° for 30 minutes or until done. Let cool 2 minutes. Yield: 16 rolls.

Per roll: Calories 472 (33% from fat)
Carbohydrate 72.8g Protein 8.1g Fat 17.3g (Sat. Fat 6.3g)
Cholesterol 29mg Sodium 177mg

French bread is typically low in calories and fat, but Velvet French Bread has butter in the dough and is brushed with additional butter for an extra-rich flavor.

LEAN FRENCH BREAD

2¾ cups bread flour, divided
1 teaspoon sugar
1 teaspoon salt
1 package active dry yeast
1 cup very warm water (120° to 130°)
2 tablespoons bread flour, divided
Vegetable cooking spray
1 egg white, lightly beaten

Combine 1½ cups flour, sugar, salt, and yeast; stir. Gradually add water to flour mixture, beating at low speed of an electric mixer. Beat an additional 2 minutes at medium speed. Stir in enough of the remaining 1¼ cups flour to make a soft dough.

Sprinkle 1 tablespoon flour over work surface. Turn dough out; knead until smooth and elastic (about 8 to 10 minutes). Place in a bowl coated with cooking spray, turning to coat top. Cover and let rise in a warm place (85°), free from drafts, 1 hour or until doubled in bulk.

Sprinkle remaining 1 tablespoon flour over work surface. Punch dough down; turn out onto floured surface, and knead 4 or 5 times. Divide dough in half. Roll 1 portion of dough into a 15- x 7-inch rectangle. Roll up dough, starting at long side, pressing firmly to eliminate air pockets; pinch seam and ends to seal. Repeat with remaining dough.

Place loaves, seam side down, in 2 French baguette pans coated with cooking spray. Cover and let rise in a warm place, free from drafts, 30 minutes or until doubled in bulk. Make ¼-inch-deep slits diagonally across loaves. Brush with egg white.

Place a shallow pan containing 1 inch of water on bottom rack of oven; place baguette pans on top rack. Bake at 400° for 20 minutes or until loaves are golden. Yield: 28 (1-inch) slices.

Per slice: Calories 52 (5% from fat)
Carbohydrate 10.4g Protein 1.9g Fat 0.3g (Sat. Fat 0g)
Cholesterol 0mg Sodium 86mg

Left: *Lean French Bread*

Velvet French Bread

2¾ cups bread flour, divided
1 tablespoon sugar
1 teaspoon salt
1 package active dry yeast
1 cup water
2 tablespoons butter
2 tablespoons bread flour, divided
3 tablespoons butter, melted and divided

Combine 1½ cups flour, sugar, salt, and yeast; stir. Combine water and 2 tablespoons butter in a saucepan; heat until butter melts, stirring occasionally. Cool to 120° to 130°. Gradually add water mixture to flour mixture, beating at low speed of an electric mixer. Beat an additional 2 minutes at medium speed. Stir in enough of the remaining 1¼ cups flour to make a soft dough.

Sprinkle 1 tablespoon flour over work surface. Turn dough out onto floured surface; knead until smooth and elastic (about 8 to 10 minutes). Place in a well-greased bowl, turning to grease top. Cover and let rise in a warm place (85°), free from drafts, 1 hour or until doubled in bulk.

Sprinkle remaining 1 tablespoon flour over work surface. Punch dough down; turn out onto surface; knead 4 or 5 times. Divide dough in half. Roll 1 portion of dough into a 15- x 7-inch rectangle. Roll up dough, starting at long side, pressing firmly to eliminate air pockets; pinch seam and ends to seal. Repeat with remaining dough.

Place loaves, seam side down, in 2 well-greased French baguette pans. Brush with 1 tablespoon melted butter. Cover and let rise in a warm place, free from drafts, 30 minutes or until doubled in bulk. Make ¼-inch-deep slits diagonally across loaves. Brush with 1 tablespoon melted butter.

Place a shallow pan containing 1 inch of water on bottom rack of oven; place baguette pans on top rack. Bake at 400° for 25 minutes or until loaves are golden. Remove from pans; brush with remaining butter. Yield: 32 (1-inch) slices.

Per slice: Calories 62 (29% from fat)
Carbohydrate 9.4g Protein 1.6g Fat 2.0g (Sat. Fat 1.2g)
Cholesterol 5mg Sodium 92mg

Use warm water instead of whole milk to activate the yeast in the light Wheat-Lover's Bread.

WHEAT-LOVER'S BREAD

2 cups stone-ground whole wheat flour
½ teaspoon salt
2 packages active dry yeast
2 cups very warm water (120° to 130°)
¼ cup molasses
2 tablespoons vegetable oil
½ cup toasted wheat germ
½ cup unprocessed wheat bran
1½ cups bread flour
3 tablespoons bread flour, divided
  Vegetable cooking spray

Combine first 3 ingredients; stir well. Add warm water to flour mixture, beating well at low speed of an electric mixer. Add molasses and oil; beat 2 minutes at medium speed. Gradually add wheat germ, wheat bran, and enough of the 1½ cups bread flour to make a soft dough.

Sprinkle 2 tablespoons bread flour over work surface. Turn dough out onto floured surface; knead until smooth and elastic (about 8 to 10 minutes). Place dough in a large bowl coated with cooking spray, turning to coat top. Cover and let rise in a warm place (85°), free from drafts, 35 minutes or until doubled in bulk.

Punch dough down; divide in half. Sprinkle 1½ teaspoons bread flour over work surface. Turn 1 portion of dough out onto surface; roll into a 14- x 7-inch rectangle. Roll up, starting at short side, pressing firmly to eliminate air pockets; pinch ends to seal. Place, seam side down, in an 8½- x 4½- x 3-inch loafpan coated with cooking spray. Repeat procedure with remaining bread flour and dough.

Cover and let rise in a warm place, free from drafts, 30 minutes or until doubled in bulk. Bake at 375° for 35 minutes or until loaves sound hollow when tapped. Remove from pans immediately; cool on wire racks. Yield: 34 (½-inch) slices.

Per slice: Calories 71 (16% from fat)
Carbohydrate 13.3g Protein 2.5g Fat 1.3g (Sat. Fat 0.2g)
Cholesterol 0mg Sodium 36mg

Country Wheat Bread

2 cups stone-ground whole wheat flour
1 teaspoon salt
2 packages active dry yeast
2 cups whole milk
½ cup unsalted butter
½ cup molasses
3 eggs
½ cup toasted wheat germ
½ cup unprocessed wheat bran
3¼ cups bread flour
2 tablespoons bread flour, divided
2 teaspoons vegetable oil, divided

Combine first 3 ingredients; stir well. Combine milk and butter in a saucepan; heat until butter melts, stirring occasionally. Cool to 120° to 130°.

Add liquid mixture to flour mixture, beating well at low speed of an electric mixer. Add molasses and eggs; beat 2 minutes at medium speed. Gradually add wheat germ, wheat bran, and enough of the 3¼ cups bread flour to make a soft dough.

Sprinkle 1 tablespoon bread flour over work surface. Turn dough out onto surface; knead until smooth and elastic (about 8 to 10 minutes). Place dough in a large well-greased bowl, turning to grease top. Cover and let rise in a warm place (85°), free from drafts, 45 minutes or until doubled in bulk.

Punch dough down; divide in half. Sprinkle 1½ teaspoons bread flour over work surface. Turn 1 portion of dough out onto surface; roll into a 14- x 7-inch rectangle. Roll up, starting at short side, pressing firmly to eliminate air pockets; pinch ends to seal. Place, seam side down, in a greased 8½- x 4½- x 3-inch loafpan. Brush with 1 teaspoon oil. Repeat procedure with remaining bread flour, dough, and oil.

Cover and let rise in a warm place, free from drafts, 25 minutes or until doubled in bulk. Bake at 375° for 35 minutes or until loaves sound hollow when tapped. (Cover with aluminum foil the last 15 minutes of baking to prevent over-browning, if necessary.) Remove from pans immediately; cool on wire racks. Yield: 34 (½-inch) slices.

Per slice: Calories 140 (32% from fat)
Carbohydrate 20.5g Protein 4.3g Fat 4.9g (Sat. Fat 2.3g)
Cholesterol 29mg Sodium 85mg

Process the parsley in Light Pesto Bread with two tablespoons oil instead of one-half cup butter.

LIGHT PESTO BREAD

5½ cups bread flour, divided
1 tablespoon sugar
2¼ teaspoons salt, divided
2 packages active dry yeast
2 cups very warm water (120° to 130°)
¼ cup extra-virgin olive oil, divided
¼ cup plus 2 tablespoons bread flour, divided
  Vegetable cooking spray
1 cup tightly packed fresh parsley
2 green onions, cut into 2-inch pieces
2 cloves garlic, halved
¼ teaspoon freshly ground pepper
½ cup grated Parmesan cheese, divided
1 egg white, lightly beaten

Combine 2 cups flour, sugar, 1¾ teaspoons salt, and yeast; stir. Add water and 2 tablespoons oil, beating at low speed of an electric mixer until blended. Beat 2 minutes at medium speed. Stir in enough of the remaining 3½ cups flour to make a soft dough.

Sprinkle ¼ cup flour over work surface. Turn dough out; knead until smooth and elastic (about 10 minutes). Place in a bowl coated with cooking spray, turning to coat top. Cover and let rise in a warm place (85°), free from drafts, 1 hour or until doubled.

Position knife blade in food processor bowl, and add parsley, onions, and garlic. Process 20 seconds. Add remaining ½ teaspoon salt, 2 tablespoons oil, and pepper; process 15 seconds.

Punch dough down; divide in half. Sprinkle 1 tablespoon flour over work surface. Roll 1 portion into a 16- x 10-inch rectangle. Spread half of parsley mixture over dough, leaving a 1-inch border; sprinkle with ¼ cup cheese. Roll up dough, starting at long side. Pinch seam and ends to seal. Repeat procedure.

Place loaves, seam side down, on a baking sheet coated with cooking spray. Make ¼-inch-deep slits in each loaf. Cover and let rise in a warm place, free from drafts, 35 minutes or until doubled. Brush with egg white. Bake at 375° for 30 minutes or until loaves sound hollow when tapped. Yield: 72 (½-inch) slices.

Per slice: Calories 52 (19% from fat)
Carbohydrate 8.5g Protein 1.7g Fat 1.1g (Sat. Fat 0.2g)
Cholesterol 0mg Sodium 85mg

Herb Butter Bread

6 cups bread flour, divided
2 tablespoons sugar
2½ teaspoons salt, divided
2 packages active dry yeast
2 cups whole milk
¾ cup butter, softened and divided
¼ cup plus 2 tablespoons bread flour, divided
1 cup tightly packed fresh parsley
2 green onions, cut into 2-inch pieces
2 cloves garlic, halved
¼ teaspoon freshly ground pepper
1 egg, lightly beaten
1 teaspoon water

Combine 2 cups flour, sugar, 2 teaspoons salt, and yeast; stir. Combine milk and ¼ cup butter in a saucepan; heat until butter melts, stirring occasionally. Cool to 120° to 130°. Add liquid mixture to flour mixture, beating at low speed of an electric mixer. Beat 2 minutes at medium speed. Stir in enough of the remaining 4 cups flour to make a soft dough.

Sprinkle ¼ cup flour over work surface. Turn dough out; knead until smooth and elastic (about 10 minutes). Place in a greased bowl, turning to grease top. Cover and let rise in a warm place (85°), free from drafts, 45 minutes or until doubled.

Position knife blade in food processor bowl, and add parsley, onions, and garlic. Process 20 seconds. Add remaining ½ cup butter, remaining ½ teaspoon salt, and pepper; process 15 seconds.

Punch dough down; divide in half. Sprinkle 1 tablespoon flour over work surface. Roll 1 portion into a 16- x 10-inch rectangle. Spread half of parsley mixture over dough, leaving a 1-inch border. Roll up dough, starting at long side. Pinch seam and ends to seal. Repeat procedure.

Place loaves, seam side down, on a greased baking sheet. Make ¼-inch-deep slits in each loaf. Cover and let rise in a warm place, free from drafts, 20 minutes or until doubled. Combine egg and water; brush over loaves. Bake at 375° for 30 minutes or until loaves sound hollow when tapped. Yield: 72 (½-inch) slices.

Per slice: Calories 69 (33% from fat)
Carbohydrate 9.6g Protein 1.9g Fat 2.5g (Sat. Fat 1.4g)
Cholesterol 9mg Sodium 106mg

Save fat by using only one cup cheese and replacing milk with broth in Parmesan Onion Twist.

Parmesan Onion Twist

¾ cup canned no-salt-added chicken broth,
    undiluted
1 tablespoon vegetable oil
2 cups finely chopped onion
1 teaspoon dried whole basil
1 teaspoon dried whole oregano
6 cups bread flour, divided
2 packages active dry yeast
2 cups very warm skim milk (120° to 130°)
1 cup freshly grated Parmesan cheese
1 tablespoon sugar
2 tablespoons bread flour
    Vegetable cooking spray
1 egg white, lightly beaten

Combine broth and oil in a nonstick skillet. Place over medium heat until hot. Add onion, basil, and oregano; sauté until onion is tender. Combine 2 cups flour and yeast; stir. Add milk to flour mixture, beating at low speed of an electric mixer. Beat 2 minutes at medium speed. Add onion mixture, cheese, and sugar. Stir in enough of the remaining 4 cups flour to make a soft dough.

Sprinkle 2 tablespoons flour over work surface. Turn dough out; knead until smooth and elastic. Place in a bowl coated with cooking spray, turning to coat top. Cover and let rise in a warm place (85°), free from drafts, 30 minutes or until doubled.

Punch dough down; divide in half. Divide each half into 3 equal portions. Roll each portion into a 16-inch rope. Braid 3 ropes together on a baking sheet coated with cooking spray, pinching ends to seal; tuck ends under. Repeat procedure with remaining ropes.

Cover and let rise in a warm place, free from drafts, 20 minutes or until doubled. Brush with egg white. Bake at 350° for 35 minutes or until loaves sound hollow when tapped. (Cover with aluminum foil the last 15 minutes of baking to prevent over-browning, if necessary.) Yield: 60 (½-inch) slices.

Per slice: Calories 65 (12% from fat)
Carbohydrate 11.3g Protein 2.7g Fat 0.9g (Sat. Fat 0.3g)
Cholesterol 1mg Sodium 28mg

Cheddar Onion Twist

2 cups finely chopped onion
1 teaspoon dried whole basil
1 teaspoon dried whole oregano
¼ cup unsalted butter, melted
6 cups bread flour, divided
2 packages active dry yeast
2 cups very warm whole milk (120° to 130°)
2 cups (8 ounces) shredded sharp
    Cheddar cheese
2 tablespoons sugar
2 teaspoons salt
2 tablespoons bread flour, divided
1 egg, lightly beaten
1 teaspoon water

Sauté onion, basil, and oregano in butter in a skillet over medium heat until onion is tender. Set aside. Combine 2 cups flour and yeast; stir. Add milk to flour mixture, beating at low speed of an electric mixer. Beat 2 minutes at medium speed. Add onion mixture, cheese, sugar, and salt. Stir in enough of the remaining 4 cups flour to make a soft dough.

Sprinkle 2 tablespoons flour over work surface. Turn dough out; knead until smooth and elastic. Place in a greased bowl, turning to grease top. Cover and let rise in a warm place (85°), free from drafts, 30 minutes or until doubled.

Punch dough down; divide in half. Divide each half into 3 equal portions. Roll each portion into a 16-inch rope. Braid 3 ropes together on a greased baking sheet, pinching ends to seal; tuck ends under. Repeat procedure with remaining ropes.

Cover and let rise in a warm place, free from drafts, 20 minutes or until doubled. Combine egg and water; brush over loaves. Bake at 350° for 35 minutes or until loaves sound hollow when tapped. (Cover with aluminum foil the last 15 minutes of baking to prevent over-browning, if necessary.) Yield: 60 (½-inch) slices.

Per slice: Calories 84 (29% from fat)
Carbohydrate 11.5g Protein 3.1g Fat 2.7g (Sat. Fat 1.5g)
Cholesterol 11mg Sodium 107mg

Left: *Parmesan Onion Twist*

Glazed Cornish Hens (page 106)

Entrées

The spinach lasagna is layered with all the noodles, sauce, and cheeses you expect in this classic Italian dish. Ground round and low-fat cheeses make it lower in fat than the pesto lasagna.

SPINACH BEEF LASAGNA

Vegetable cooking spray
1   pound ground round
½   cup chopped onion
1   (30¾-ounce) jar no-salt-added
    spaghetti sauce
1½ cups water
¼   teaspoon salt
2   (10-ounce) packages frozen chopped
    spinach, thawed
1   (15-ounce) carton nonfat ricotta cheese
1   cup (4 ounces) shredded part-skim
    mozzarella cheese, divided
½   cup frozen egg substitute, thawed
1   (2-ounce) jar diced pimiento, drained
9   lasagna noodles, uncooked

Coat a large nonstick skillet with cooking spray; place over medium-high heat until hot. Cook ground round and onion over medium heat until browned, stirring until meat crumbles. Drain and pat dry with paper towels. Wipe drippings from skillet with a paper towel.

Return meat mixture to skillet. Add spaghetti sauce, water, and salt; bring to a boil. Reduce heat and simmer, uncovered, 10 minutes; set aside.

Drain spinach; press between paper towels. Combine ricotta cheese, ½ cup mozzarella cheese, egg substitute, and pimiento; stir in spinach.

Coat a 13- x 9- x 2-inch baking dish with cooking spray. Spoon 1 cup meat mixture into dish. Place 3 uncooked lasagna noodles over meat mixture. Spoon one-third of remaining meat mixture over noodles; top with half of spinach mixture. Place 3 lasagna noodles over spinach mixture; spoon half of remaining beef mixture over noodles. Top with remaining spinach mixture. Top with remaining 3 noodles and remaining meat mixture.

Cover and bake at 350° for 55 minutes. Uncover; sprinkle with remaining ½ cup mozzarella cheese. Bake, uncovered, 5 minutes or until cheese melts. Let stand 10 minutes; serve. Yield: 10 servings.

Per serving: Calories 306 (22% from fat)
Carbohydrate 36.6g Protein 26.3g Fat 7.5g (Sat. Fat 2.5g)
Cholesterol 39mg Sodium 241mg

Pesto Beef Lasagna

9   lasagna noodles, uncooked
2   cups ricotta cheese
2   eggs, lightly beaten
¼   teaspoon coarsely ground pepper
1   (8-ounce) jar sun-dried tomatoes in oil,
    undrained
1   cup chopped fresh basil
½   cup pine nuts
½   cup grated Parmesan cheese
1   clove garlic
1½ pounds ground beef
1   (30-ounce) jar spaghetti sauce
3   cups (12 ounces) shredded mozzarella
    cheese, divided

Cook lasagna noodles according to package directions. Combine ricotta cheese, eggs, and pepper; stir well with a wire whisk, and set aside.

Drain tomatoes, reserving ⅓ cup oil and ½ cup tomatoes. Reserve remaining tomatoes for another use. Position knife blade in food processor bowl, and add ½ cup tomatoes, basil, and next 3 ingredients; process until smooth. With processor running, pour reserved ⅓ cup oil through food chute in a slow, steady stream; process until blended. Fold basil mixture (pesto) into ricotta mixture.

Cook ground beef in a large skillet over medium heat until browned, stirring until meat crumbles; drain. Stir in spaghetti sauce. Spoon one-third of meat mixture into a greased 13- x 9- x 2-inch baking dish. Arrange 3 cooked lasagna noodles over meat mixture. Spread half of pesto over noodles, and sprinkle with ½ cup mozzarella cheese. Repeat layers once. Top with remaining 3 noodles and remaining meat mixture.

Cover and bake at 350° for 25 minutes. Uncover and sprinkle with remaining 2 cups mozzarella cheese. Bake, uncovered, an additional 5 minutes or until cheese melts. Let stand 10 minutes; serve. Yield: 10 servings.

Per serving: Calories 617 (59% from fat)
Carbohydrate 33.8g Protein 32.7g Fat 40.4g (Sat. Fat 14.8g)
Cholesterol 134mg Sodium 955mg

Give meat loaf a flavor make-over in the luscious Reuben recipe with sauerkraut, bacon, and Swiss cheese. Top the light gingersnap version with a creamy sauce of nonfat sour cream and skim milk.

GINGERSNAP MEAT LOAF

Vegetable cooking spray
½ cup finely chopped onion
½ cup finely chopped celery
2 pounds ground round
½ cup soft breadcrumbs
½ cup finely chopped gingersnaps
½ cup frozen egg substitute, thawed
3 tablespoons cider vinegar
1½ teaspoons prepared mustard
¼ cup canned no-salt-added beef broth, undiluted
2 tablespoons all-purpose flour
¼ teaspoon salt
¼ teaspoon ground ginger
¾ cup skim milk
¼ cup nonfat sour cream alternative

Coat a large nonstick skillet with cooking spray; place over medium-high heat until hot. Add onion and celery; sauté until tender.

Combine sautéed vegetables, ground round, and next 5 ingredients in a large bowl; stir well. Shape mixture into a 9- x 5-inch loaf; place on a rack in a roasting pan coated with cooking spray. Bake at 350° for 1 hour and 15 minutes.

Combine beef broth, flour, salt, and ginger in a small saucepan; stir until smooth. Gradually add milk, stirring constantly. Cook over medium heat, stirring constantly, until thickened. Remove from heat, and add sour cream, stirring just until blended. Spoon evenly over meat loaf. Yield: 10 servings.

Per serving: Calories 186 (24% from fat)
Carbohydrate 9.7g Protein 23.9g Fat 4.9g (Sat. Fat 1.6g)
Cholesterol 54mg Sodium 181mg

Reuben Meat Loaf

2 pounds ground beef
2 cups soft rye breadcrumbs
1 (10-ounce) can shredded sauerkraut, drained
½ cup chopped onion
¼ cup whole milk
¼ cup commercial Thousand Island salad dressing
1 teaspoon caraway seeds
1 teaspoon dry mustard
2 eggs, beaten
5 slices bacon
½ cup (2 ounces) shredded Swiss cheese

Combine first 9 ingredients in a medium bowl; stir well. Shape mixture into a 9- x 5-inch loaf; place on a rack in a lightly greased roasting pan. Arrange bacon slices over loaf. Bake at 350° for 1 hour and 30 minutes. Sprinkle cheese over meat loaf, and bake an additional 5 minutes. Let stand 10 minutes before serving. Yield: 10 servings.

Per serving: Calories 420 (69% from fat)
Carbohydrate 9.2g Protein 21.8g Fat 32.3g (Sat. Fat 12.4g)
Cholesterol 127mg Sodium 445mg

Fresh zucchini puts a new twist on spaghetti. This light entrée contains ultra-lean ground beef and has no added fat. Whipping cream thickens the sauce in the pepperoni version, and sun-dried tomatoes and pepperoni make it chunky and spicy.

ZUCCHINI BEEF SPAGHETTI

Vegetable cooking spray
1 pound ultra-lean ground beef
2 cups sliced fresh mushrooms
2 cups thinly sliced zucchini
1 cup chopped onion
½ teaspoon salt
¼ teaspoon crushed red pepper
4 cloves garlic, minced
1 (14½-ounce) can no-salt-added whole tomatoes, undrained and chopped
1 cup water
1 (6-ounce) can no-salt-added tomato paste
1 teaspoon dried whole oregano
6 cups cooked spaghetti (cooked without salt or fat)
½ cup finely shredded zucchini
2 tablespoons grated Parmesan cheese
  Fresh oregano sprigs (optional)

Coat a large nonstick skillet with cooking spray; place over medium heat until hot. Cook ground beef over medium heat until browned, stirring until it crumbles. Drain and pat dry with paper towels. Wipe drippings from skillet with a paper towel.

Coat skillet with cooking spray; place over medium-high heat until hot. Add mushrooms and next 5 ingredients; sauté 5 minutes, stirring frequently. Stir in beef, tomato, water, tomato paste, and dried oregano. Bring to a boil; cover, reduce heat, and simmer 10 to 15 minutes or to desired consistency. Serve over cooked spaghetti; top with shredded zucchini and cheese. Garnish with fresh oregano sprigs, if desired. Yield: 6 servings.

Per serving: Calories 365 (16% from fat)
Carbohydrate 54.3g Protein 24.3g Fat 6.6g (Sat. Fat 2.4g)
Cholesterol 49mg Sodium 412mg

Left: *Zucchini Beef Spaghetti*

Pepperoni Beef Spaghetti

½ ounce dried porcini mushrooms
1 pound ground beef
¼ cup chopped onion
¼ cup finely chopped carrot
¼ cup finely chopped celery
2 cloves garlic, minced
2 tablespoons olive oil
1 (28-ounce) can whole tomatoes, undrained and pureed
½ cup oil-packed sun-dried tomatoes, thinly sliced
1 (3-ounce) package whole pepperoni, sliced
½ cup whipping cream
2 tablespoons minced fresh basil
1 teaspoon coarsely ground pepper
½ cup plus 2 tablespoons grated fresh Parmesan cheese, divided
6 cups cooked spaghetti

Pour boiling water to cover over mushrooms; let stand 15 minutes. Drain mushrooms, reserving ⅓ cup liquid; coarsely chop mushrooms. Set mushrooms and liquid aside.

Cook ground beef in a large skillet over medium heat until browned, stirring until it crumbles. Drain and set aside.

Sauté onion, carrot, celery, and garlic in hot olive oil in a large skillet over medium-high heat until tender. Stir in reserved mushrooms, mushroom liquid, ground beef, pureed tomato, sun-dried tomato, and pepperoni; bring to a boil. Reduce heat, and simmer, uncovered, 35 minutes. Stir in whipping cream, basil, and pepper. Simmer, uncovered, 5 minutes or until slightly thickened. Stir in ½ cup Parmesan cheese. Serve over cooked spaghetti. Sprinkle with remaining 2 tablespoons Parmesan cheese. Yield: 6 servings.

Per serving: Calories 631 (47% from fat)
Carbohydrate 52.8g Protein 31.6g Fat 33.1g (Sat. Fat 13.4g)
Cholesterol 93mg Sodium 961mg

The beef ribbons use an oil-free marinade with fragrant lemon grass and fiery serrano pepper. The kabobs marinate in a peanut oil-soy sauce mixture and are served with a gingered peanut sauce.

VIETNAMESE BEEF RIBBONS

1 pound lean boneless beef sirloin
   steak
1 tablespoon chopped fresh lemon grass
1 teaspoon minced serrano pepper
   with seeds
2 tablespoons lime juice
2 tablespoons low-sodium soy sauce
1 clove garlic, minced
1 medium onion, thinly sliced and
   separated into rings
3 tablespoons sugar
3 tablespoons white wine vinegar
¼ teaspoon pepper
4 cups shredded carrot
⅓ cup chopped fresh mint
   Vegetable cooking spray
1 tablespoon chopped unsalted
   dry-roasted peanuts

Partially freeze steak; trim fat from steak. Slice steak diagonally across grain into ¼-inch-wide strips, and set aside.

Combine lemon grass and next 4 ingredients in a large heavy-duty, zip-top plastic bag; seal bag, and shake well. Add steak to bag; seal bag, and shake until steak is well coated. Marinate in refrigerator 8 hours, turning bag occasionally.

Combine onion, sugar, vinegar, and ¼ teaspoon pepper in a bowl; cover and chill at least 30 minutes. Stir in carrot and mint.

Remove steak from marinade; discard marinade. Thread steak onto 4 (12-inch) metal skewers.

Coat grill rack with cooking spray; place on grill over medium-hot coals (350° to 400°). Place kabobs on rack; grill, covered, 5 minutes or to desired degree of doneness, turning skewers once. Transfer carrot mixture to a serving platter using a slotted spoon; top with steak, and sprinkle evenly with peanuts. Yield: 4 servings.

Per serving: Calories 302 (27% from fat)
Carbohydrate 25.2g Protein 29.3g Fat 9.1g (Sat. Fat 3.3g)
Cholesterol 79mg Sodium 286mg

Indonesian Beef Kabobs

1 pound lean boneless beef sirloin
   steak
3 tablespoons minced fresh cilantro
⅓ cup peanut oil
2 tablespoons soy sauce
1 tablespoon rice wine vinegar
1 tablespoon honey
½ cup chunky peanut butter
½ cup canned coconut milk
2 tablespoons peeled, minced
   gingerroot
2 tablespoons soy sauce
1½ tablespoons lime juice
¼ teaspoon crushed red pepper
4 cups cooked long-grain rice
¼ cup chopped green onions

Partially freeze steak; trim fat from steak. Slice steak diagonally across grain into ¼-inch-wide strips, and set aside.

Combine cilantro and next 4 ingredients in a large heavy-duty, zip-top plastic bag; seal bag, and shake well. Add steak to bag; seal bag, and shake until steak is well coated. Marinate in refrigerator 8 hours, turning bag occasionally.

Combine peanut butter, coconut milk, minced gingerroot, soy sauce, lime juice, and red pepper in a small bowl; stir well. Cover and chill at least 1 hour.

Remove steak from marinade; discard marinade. Thread steak onto 4 (12-inch) metal skewers.

Place greased grill rack on grill over medium-hot coals (350° to 400°). Place kabobs on rack; grill, covered, 5 minutes or to desired degree of doneness, turning skewers once.

Combine rice and green onions; toss well. Transfer rice mixture to a serving platter, and top with steak. Serve with peanut butter mixture. Yield: 4 servings.

Per serving: Calories 867 (53% from fat)
Carbohydrate 62.1g Protein 41.9g Fat 51.0g (Sat. Fat 13.0g)
Cholesterol 81mg Sodium 1633mg

Both stroganoffs are rich and creamy, but the light recipe is lower in fat because it uses nonfat sour cream and has more mushrooms and less steak than the luscious version.

LIGHT BEEF STROGANOFF

1 pound lean boneless beef sirloin steak
  Vegetable cooking spray
3 cups sliced fresh mushrooms
¾ cup chopped onion
2 cloves garlic, crushed
¾ cup hot water
1 teaspoon beef-flavored bouillon
  granules
½ cup Burgundy or other dry red wine
2 tablespoons all-purpose flour
1 tablespoon margarine
2 teaspoons low-sodium Worcestershire
  sauce
1 teaspoon dry mustard
½ teaspoon dried whole thyme
¼ teaspoon pepper
1 (8-ounce) carton nonfat sour cream
  alternative
3 cups cooked medium egg noodles
  (cooked without salt or fat)
2 tablespoons sliced green onions

Partially freeze steak; trim fat from steak. Slice steak diagonally across grain into 2- x ¼-inch strips.

Coat a large nonstick skillet with cooking spray; place over medium-high heat until hot. Add steak, mushrooms, chopped onion, and garlic; cook 15 minutes or until steak and vegetables are tender. Drain and wipe drippings from skillet with a paper towel. Set steak mixture aside, and keep warm.

Combine water and bouillon granules in skillet. Combine wine and flour; stir well, and add to broth. Stir in margarine and next 4 ingredients. Cook over medium heat, stirring constantly with a wire whisk, until thickened and bubbly. Add reserved steak mixture. Cook over medium heat until thoroughly heated. Remove from heat, and stir in sour cream. To serve, spoon steak mixture over noodles, and sprinkle with green onions. Yield: 6 servings.

Per serving: Calories 312 (26% from fat)
Carbohydrate 28.9g Protein 26.6g Fat 9.0g (Sat. Fat 2.9g)
Cholesterol 81mg Sodium 263mg

Brandied Beef Stroganoff

1½ pounds lean boneless beef sirloin steak
2 tablespoons vegetable oil
2 ounces fresh shiitake mushrooms,
  sliced
½ cup sweet red pepper strips
½ cup sweet yellow pepper strips
¼ cup minced shallots
¼ cup margarine, melted
3 tablespoons brandy
2 cups sour cream
½ cup canned ready-to-serve beef broth
1 tablespoon paprika
½ teaspoon salt
3 cups cooked medium egg noodles

Partially freeze steak; trim fat from steak. Slice steak diagonally across grain into 2- x ¼-inch strips.

Cook steak in 2 tablespoons hot oil in a large skillet over medium heat until browned. Remove steak from skillet; set aside, and keep warm.

Sauté mushrooms, peppers, and shallots in margarine in skillet over medium-high heat until tender. Remove from heat. Add brandy, and immediately ignite with a long match. Let flames die down.

Combine sour cream and next 3 ingredients; add to vegetable mixture. Cook over medium-low heat 8 minutes, stirring frequently. Stir in steak, and cook until thoroughly heated. To serve, spoon steak mixture over noodles. Yield: 6 servings.

Per serving: Calories 587 (57% from fat)
Carbohydrate 27.2g Protein 35.1g Fat 37.5g (Sat. Fat 15.8g)
Cholesterol 144mg Sodium 623mg

Adding an acidic ingredient to the marinade is essential for tenderizing lean cuts of meat. Papaya nectar contributes fruit-flavored acidity in Tropical Flank Steak. Fresh papaya slices enhance this light recipe, while creamy papaya butter accompanies the luscious version.

TROPICAL FLANK STEAK

1   (1-pound) lean flank steak
1   cup canned papaya nectar
2   teaspoons ground ginger
1   teaspoon coconut extract
1   teaspoon cracked black pepper
1   teaspoon crushed white peppercorns
1   teaspoon crushed green peppercorns
    Vegetable cooking spray
1   fresh papaya, peeled, sliced, and cut
       into decorative shapes
    Edible flowers (optional)

Trim fat from steak. Combine papaya nectar, ginger, and coconut extract in a large heavy-duty, zip-top plastic bag; seal bag, and shake well. Add steak to bag; seal bag, and shake until steak is well coated. Marinate steak in refrigerator 8 hours, turning bag occasionally.

Remove steak from marinade; reserve marinade. Combine pepper and peppercorns, and press onto both sides of steak. Coat grill rack with cooking spray; place on grill over medium-hot coals (350° to 400°). Place steak on rack; grill, covered, 6 minutes on each side or to desired degree of doneness, brushing steak frequently with reserved marinade. Remove steak from grill, and let stand 10 minutes; cut diagonally across grain into thin slices. Weave meat slices into a criss-cross pattern, if desired. Serve with papaya slices. Garnish with edible flowers, if desired. Yield: 4 servings.

Per serving: Calories 294 (42% from fat)
Carbohydrate 19.0g Protein 23.2g Fat 13.6g (Sat. Fat 5.7g)
Cholesterol 62mg Sodium 77mg

Flank Steak with Papaya Butter

1   (1-pound) lean flank steak
2   tablespoons soy sauce
2   tablespoons vegetable oil
2   tablespoons peeled, minced gingerroot
⅛   teaspoons hot sauce
1   clove garlic, minced
¼   cup butter, softened
¼   cup flaked coconut
3   tablespoons finely chopped ripe
       papaya
2   teaspoons finely minced fresh parsley
1   teaspoon curry powder

Trim fat from steak. Combine soy sauce and next 4 ingredients in a large heavy-duty, zip-top plastic bag; seal bag, and shake well. Add steak to bag; seal bag, and shake until steak is well coated. Marinate steak in refrigerator 8 hours, turning bag occasionally.

Remove steak from marinade; discard marinade. Place greased grill rack on grill over medium-hot coals (350° to 400°). Place steak on rack; grill, covered, 6 minutes on each side or to desired degree of doneness. Remove steak from grill, and let stand 10 minutes; cut diagonally across grain into thin slices.

Combine butter and remaining ingredients in a small mixing bowl; beat at medium speed of an electric mixer until fluffy. Serve butter mixture with steak. Yield: 4 servings.

Per serving: Calories 411 (70% from fat)
Carbohydrate 7.3g Protein 23.6g Fat 43.5g (Sat. Fat 23.0g)
Cholesterol 93mg Sodium 488mg

Left: *Tropical Flank Steak*

Top the light fajitas with fresh salsa instead of the traditional sour cream and cheese.

BEEF AND SALSA FAJITAS

¼ cup lime juice
¼ cup light beer
2 tablespoons minced fresh cilantro
1 teaspoon dried whole oregano
¼ teaspoon ground red pepper
2 cloves garlic, minced
1 small green pepper
1 small sweet red pepper
1 small sweet yellow pepper
1 (1-pound) lean boneless top round steak
1 small purple onion, cut into 8 wedges
1 cup diced tomato
2 tablespoons chopped green onions
2 tablespoons minced fresh cilantro
2 tablespoons red wine vinegar
1 tablespoon chopped ripe olives
1 tablespoon seeded and minced jalapeño pepper
   Vegetable cooking spray
8 (8-inch) flour tortillas

Combine first 6 ingredients in a heavy-duty, zip-top plastic bag; seal bag, and shake well. Seed green and sweet peppers; cut each into 8 wedges. Place pepper wedges, steak, and onion in bag; seal bag, and shake. Marinate in refrigerator 8 hours. Combine tomato and next 5 ingredients. Cover and chill.

Remove steak and vegetables from marinade, reserving marinade. Thread vegetables onto 4 (10-inch) metal skewers. Coat grill rack with cooking spray; place on grill over medium-hot coals (350° to 400°). Place steak and skewers on rack. Grill vegetables, covered, 12 minutes or until tender, turning and basting occasionally. Grill steak 5 to 6 minutes on each side or to desired doneness, basting occasionally. Wrap tortillas in aluminum foil. Grill, covered, 2 minutes.

Cut steak diagonally across grain into ¼-inch-wide slices. Divide steak and vegetables among tortillas. Top each with 3 tablespoons tomato salsa mixture; roll up tortillas. Yield: 8 fajitas.

Per fajita: Calories 234 (23% from fat)
Carbohydrate 26.6g Protein 18.2g Fat 5.9g (Sat. Fat 1.4g)
Cholesterol 37mg Sodium 212mg

Beef and Cheese Fajitas

1   (1-pound) lean flank steak
½   cup tequila
¼   cup lime juice
¼   cup vegetable oil
¼   cup chopped fresh cilantro
1   tablespoon coarsely ground pepper
1½   teaspoons ground cumin
4   cloves garlic, minced
1   cup frozen whole kernel corn
8   (8-inch) flour tortillas
2   tablespoons vegetable oil, divided
1   large sweet red pepper, cut into julienne strips
¾   cup sliced green onions
2   jalapeño peppers, seeded and minced
1   cup diced tomato
1   cup (4 ounces) shredded Monterey Jack cheese
½   cup sour cream

Partially freeze steak; trim fat from steak. Slice steak diagonally across grain into ¼-inch-wide strips. Combine tequila and next 6 ingredients in a heavy-duty, zip-top plastic bag; seal bag, and shake well. Add steak; seal bag, and shake. Marinate in refrigerator 8 hours. Remove steak from marinade; discard marinade. Cook corn according to package directions, and set aside. Wrap tortillas in aluminum foil, and bake at 325° for 15 minutes.

Pour 2 teaspoons oil around top of preheated wok, coating sides; heat at medium-high (375°) for 2 minutes. Add red pepper strips and green onions; stir-fry 2 minutes. Remove from wok. Add 2 teaspoons oil to wok. Add steak; stir-fry 5 minutes. Remove steak from wok. Add remaining 2 teaspoons oil to wok. Return vegetables and steak to wok. Stir in corn and jalapeño pepper; stir-fry 1 minute. Divide steak mixture among tortillas. Top each with tomato, cheese, and sour cream; roll up tortillas. Yield: 8 fajitas.

Per fajita: Calories 386 (47% from fat)
Carbohydrate 34.5g Protein 19.4g Fat 20.0g (Sat. Fat 8.4g)
Cholesterol 46mg Sodium 131mg

Both recipes start with lean flank steak, but the Jamaican stir-fry uses only a minimal amount of oil.

JAMAICAN BEEF STIR-FRY

1 (1-pound) lean flank steak
¼ cup rum
2 teaspoons Dijon mustard
1 teaspoon cornstarch
1 teaspoon dried whole thyme
¾ teaspoon ground red pepper
¼ teaspoon ground allspice
   Dash of ground cinnamon
   Dash of ground nutmeg
   Vegetable cooking spray
1 teaspoon vegetable oil
1 medium-size green pepper, cut into
      julienne strips
½ cup sliced green onions
1 cup diced fresh mango
2 carambolas (starfruit), sliced
4 cups shredded romaine lettuce

Partially freeze steak; trim fat from steak. Slice steak diagonally across grain into ¼-inch-wide strips.

Combine rum and next 7 ingredients in a small bowl; stir well, and set aside.

Coat a wok with cooking spray; drizzle oil around top of wok, coating sides. Heat at medium-high (375°) for 2 minutes or until hot. Add steak, and stir-fry 5 minutes or until browned. Remove from wok; drain well on paper towels, and set aside. Wipe wok dry with a paper towel.

Coat wok with cooking spray. Add green pepper and green onions; stir-fry 3 minutes. Add steak, rum mixture, mango, and carambola; stir-fry 1 to 2 minutes or until mixture is slightly thickened.

Arrange 1 cup lettuce on each of 4 individual serving plates. Spoon 1 cup steak mixture in center of each serving. Yield: 4 servings.

Per serving: Calories 312 (45% from fat)
Carbohydrate 19.3g Protein 24.4g Fat 15.6g (Sat. Fat 6.0g)
Cholesterol 62mg Sodium 159mg

Szechuan Shredded Beef

1 (1-pound) lean flank steak
¼ cup soy sauce, divided
1 tablespoon plus 1 teaspoon cornstarch,
      divided
1½ tablespoons dry sherry
¼ cup plus 2 tablespoons vegetable oil,
      divided
2 teaspoons sugar
2 teaspoons rice wine vinegar
2 teaspoons dark sesame oil
2 ounces cellophane noodles, uncooked
1 clove garlic, crushed
4 dried red chile pepper pods
1 cup shredded carrot
1 cup shredded celery
¼ cup sliced green onions

Partially freeze steak. Slice with the grain into 2-inch-wide strips. Cut strips diagonally across the grain into ⅛-inch-wide slices; stack slices, and cut meat into thin shreds. Combine 1 tablespoon soy sauce, 1 tablespoon cornstarch, sherry, and 1 tablespoon vegetable oil. Add steak, and stir. Cover and marinate in refrigerator 1 hour. Combine sugar, vinegar, sesame oil, and remaining soy sauce and cornstarch.

Pour ¼ cup vegetable oil around top of preheated wok, coating sides; heat at medium-high (375°) for 2 minutes or until hot. Add noodles, a small amount at a time, and stir-fry 2 to 3 seconds or until noodles expand and turn white. Remove and drain on paper towels. Transfer to a serving platter.

Remove steak from marinade. Discard marinade. Add steak and garlic to wok; stir-fry 5 minutes. Remove steak. Pour remaining 1 tablespoon oil around top of wok, coating sides. Add pepper pods; stir-fry 1 minute. Add carrot and celery; stir-fry 1 minute. Add vinegar mixture; cook, stirring constantly, 1 minute or until slightly thickened. Add steak; cook until thoroughly heated. Spoon over noodles; sprinkle with green onions. Yield: 4 servings.

Per serving: Calories 461 (66% from fat)
Carbohydrate 15.3g Protein 24.3g Fat 33.6g (Sat. Fat 8.6g)
Cholesterol 57mg Sodium 953mg

ENTRÉES

73

Our eye-of-round roast is leaner than the rib roast, and its marinade has wine and vinegar instead of oil.

EYE-OF-ROUND ROAST WITH ONION SAUCE

1   (3-pound) beef eye-of-round roast
½   cup Chablis or other dry white wine
¼   cup white wine vinegar
1   tablespoon minced fresh parsley
1   teaspoon dried whole thyme
1   teaspoon dried whole rosemary, crushed
¼   teaspoon ground red pepper
1   clove garlic, minced
    Vegetable cooking spray
2   cups water
2   large onions, thinly sliced and separated into rings
1   cup skim milk
1   tablespoon cornstarch
2   tablespoons Dijon mustard

Trim fat from roast. Place roast in a shallow dish. Combine wine and next 6 ingredients, stirring well. Pour mixture over roast. Cover and marinate in refrigerator 8 to 10 hours, turning occasionally.

Remove roast from marinade, reserving marinade. Place roast on rack of a broiler pan coated with cooking spray. Insert meat thermometer into thickest part of roast, if desired. Pour water into broiler pan. Cover with aluminum foil, and bake at 450° for 20 minutes. Uncover and bake an additional 55 minutes or until meat thermometer registers 150° (medium-rare), basting roast frequently with marinade.

Let roast stand 15 minutes; cut diagonally across grain into thin slices. Transfer sliced meat to a serving platter, and keep warm.

Coat a Dutch oven with cooking spray; place over medium-high heat until hot. Add onion; cook 15 minutes or until tender, stirring frequently. Combine milk, cornstarch, and mustard, stirring until smooth. Gradually add milk mixture to onion, stirring constantly until thickened and bubbly. (Mixture will first appear curdled but will smooth out as it cooks.) Serve with roast. Yield: 12 servings.

Per serving: Calories 184 (28% from fat)
Carbohydrate 6.0g Protein 25.3g Fat 5.8g (Sat. Fat 2.1g)
Cholesterol 57mg Sodium 139mg

Rib Roast with Mustard Sauce

1   (3-pound) boneless rib roast
1   cup vegetable oil
⅔   cup dry sherry
1   teaspoon dried whole thyme
1   teaspoon dried whole rosemary, crushed
1   teaspoon coarsely ground pepper
½   teaspoon onion salt
¼   cup whipping cream, whipped
¼   cup sour cream
2   tablespoons prepared mustard
    Dash of hot sauce

Trim fat from roast. Place roast in a shallow dish. Combine oil and next 5 ingredients, stirring well. Pour mixture over roast. Cover and marinate in refrigerator 8 to 10 hours, turning occasionally.

Remove roast from marinade, reserving marinade. Place roast on a rack in a roasting pan. Insert meat thermometer into thickest part of roast, if desired. Bake at 350° for 1 hour and 45 minutes or until meat thermometer registers 150° (medium-rare), basting roast frequently with marinade.

Let roast stand 15 minutes; cut diagonally across grain into thin slices. Transfer sliced meat to a serving platter, and keep warm.

Combine whipped cream, sour cream, mustard, and hot sauce in a small bowl, stirring gently. Serve mustard mixture with roast. Yield: 12 servings.

Per serving: Calories 360 (69% from fat)
Carbohydrate 1.2g Protein 26.3g Fat 27.4g (Sat. Fat 8.6g)
Cholesterol 83mg Sodium 189mg

Right: *Rib Roast with Mustard Sauce*

Whether you prefer Southwestern or traditional barbecue flavor, you'll savor both of these fork-tender roasts. Picante Pot Roast uses lean bottom round roast, and the barbecued version uses chuck roast, which contains more marbling and exterior fat.

PICANTE POT ROAST

2 medium onions, cut into ¼-inch-thick slices
1 tablespoon chili powder
1¼ teaspoons ground cumin
1 teaspoon sugar
½ teaspoon dried whole oregano
¼ teaspoon ground red pepper
1 (4-pound) lean bottom round roast
    Vegetable cooking spray
1 (8-ounce) can no-salt-added tomato sauce
2 cups commercial picante sauce
½ cup water

Combine first 6 ingredients in a medium bowl; toss well. Set aside.

Trim fat from roast. Coat a Dutch oven with cooking spray; place over medium-high heat until hot. Add roast; cook until browned on all sides. Combine tomato sauce, picante sauce, and water; pour over roast. Add onion mixture, and bring to a boil. Cover, reduce heat, and simmer 4½ to 5 hours or until roast is tender.

Transfer roast to a serving platter; serve with picante sauce mixture. Yield: 16 servings.

Per serving: Calories 154 (24% from fat)
Carbohydrate 5.1g   Protein 22.9g   Fat 4.1g (Sat. Fat 1.5g)
Cholesterol 56mg   Sodium 392mg

Barbecued Pot Roast

1 (4-pound) boneless chuck roast
2 teaspoons salt
¼ teaspoon pepper
3 tablespoons vegetable oil
2 (8-ounce) cans tomato sauce
¾ cup beer
⅓ cup catsup
⅓ cup white vinegar
⅓ cup lemon juice
3 tablespoons brown sugar
2 tablespoons Worcestershire sauce
¾ teaspoon dry mustard
½ teaspoon paprika
2 cloves garlic, minced
3 medium onions, cut into ¼-inch-thick slices
⅓ cup all-purpose flour
⅓ cup water

Sprinkle roast with salt and pepper. Cook roast in hot oil in a Dutch oven over medium-high heat until browned on all sides. Combine tomato sauce and next 9 ingredients; pour over roast. Add onion, and bring to a boil. Cover, reduce heat, and simmer 3½ to 4 hours or until roast is tender.

Transfer roast to a serving platter, reserving liquid in pan. Combine flour and water, stirring until smooth; stir into liquid in pan. Cook over medium heat, stirring constantly, until thickened and bubbly. Spoon 1 cup sauce over roast, and serve remaining sauce with roast. Yield: 16 servings.

Per serving: Calories 365 (62% from fat)
Carbohydrate 12.0g   Protein 22.0g   Fat 25.2g (Sat. Fat 10.1g)
Cholesterol 78mg   Sodium 612mg

Fresh pears and a small amount of blue cheese provide a sweet and tangy stuffing for the light tenderloin. Stilton cheese, toasted walnuts, and fresh mushrooms make the luscious beef tenderloin a regal entrée.

PEAR AND CHEESE STUFFED TENDERLOIN

1¾ cups finely chopped fresh pear
½ cup minced green onions
3 tablespoons crumbled blue cheese
1 tablespoon lemon juice
1 teaspoon cracked pepper
1 (4½-pound) beef tenderloin
Vegetable cooking spray
¼ cup port wine

Combine first 5 ingredients in a small bowl, and set aside.

Trim fat from tenderloin. Slice tenderloin lengthwise, cutting to, but not through, the center, leaving one long edge intact. Spoon pear mixture into opening of tenderloin. Bring sides of meat back together, enclosing pear mixture, and secure at 2-inch intervals with heavy string. Place tenderloin, seam side down, on a rack in a roasting pan coated with cooking spray. Insert meat thermometer into thickest part of tenderloin, if desired.

Brush wine over tenderloin. Heat oven to 500°; place tenderloin in oven. Reduce heat to 350°, and bake, uncovered, for 1 hour or until meat thermometer registers 140° (rare) to 160° (medium). Remove from oven, and let stand 10 minutes. Remove string, and cut tenderloin diagonally across grain into ¼-inch-thick slices; arrange on a serving platter. Yield: 18 servings.

Per serving: Calories 192 (39% from fat)
Carbohydrate 3.2g Protein 24.6g Fat 8.4g (Sat. Fat 3.3g)
Cholesterol 73mg Sodium 71mg

Stilton and Walnut Stuffed Tenderloin

1 (8-ounce) package presliced fresh mushrooms
½ cup chopped fresh parsley
¼ cup minced green onions
1 tablespoon vegetable oil
1 cup finely chopped walnuts, toasted
½ cup crumbled Stilton cheese
1 egg, beaten
2 tablespoons port wine
1 teaspoon dried whole thyme
½ teaspoon salt
1 (4½-pound) beef tenderloin
½ cup port wine

Sauté mushrooms, parsley, and green onions in hot oil in a large skillet over medium-high heat until tender. Remove from heat. Combine walnuts and next 5 ingredients, stirring with a wire whisk until blended. Stir walnut mixture into mushroom mixture. Set aside.

Trim fat from tenderloin. Slice tenderloin lengthwise, cutting to, but not through, the center, leaving one long edge intact. Spoon mushroom mixture into opening of tenderloin. Bring sides of meat back together, enclosing mushroom mixture, and secure at 2-inch intervals with heavy string. Place tenderloin, seam side down, on a rack in a lightly greased roasting pan. Insert meat thermometer into thickest portion of tenderloin, if desired.

Brush ½ cup wine over tenderloin. Heat oven to 500°; place tenderloin in oven. Reduce heat to 350°, and bake, uncovered, for 1 hour or until meat thermometer registers 140° (rare) to 160° (medium). Remove from oven, and let stand 10 minutes. Remove string, and cut tenderloin diagonally across grain into ¼-inch-thick slices; arrange on a serving platter. Yield: 18 servings.

Per serving: Calories 242 (51% from fat)
Carbohydrate 1.8g Protein 27.1g Fat 13.8g (Sat. Fat 4.2g)
Cholesterol 87mg Sodium 169mg

Artichokes and colorful peppers heighten the delicate flavor of veal without adding fat. Top the luscious veal chops with a cream-based sauce containing leeks and shiitake mushrooms.

ARTICHOKE VEAL CHOPS

4 (6-ounce) lean veal loin chops (¾ inch thick)
½ teaspoon cracked pepper
½ teaspoon green peppercorns, crushed
   Vegetable cooking spray
⅓ cup sliced green pepper
¼ cup sliced sweet orange pepper
¼ cup sliced sweet red pepper
¼ cup sliced sweet yellow pepper
¼ cup dry vermouth
2 tablespoons canned no-salt-added chicken broth, undiluted
¼ teaspoon dried whole thyme
2 cloves garlic, minced
1 (14-ounce) can artichoke hearts, drained and quartered
2 tablespoons chopped fresh parsley

Trim fat from veal chops. Combine cracked pepper and crushed peppercorns in a small bowl; rub mixture over chops.

Coat a large nonstick skillet with cooking spray; place over medium-high heat until hot. Add chops, and cook 3 to 4 minutes on each side or until browned. Remove chops from skillet. Drain chops, and pat dry with paper towels. Wipe drippings from skillet with a paper towel. Place chops in an 11- x 7- x 1½-inch baking dish coated with cooking spray; set aside.

Place green pepper and next 7 ingredients in skillet. Bring to a boil; reduce heat, and simmer 5 minutes. Stir in artichoke hearts. Spoon artichoke mixture over veal chops. Cover and bake at 350° for 25 minutes or until veal is tender. Transfer veal and vegetable mixture to a serving platter; sprinkle with chopped fresh parsley. Yield: 4 servings.

Per serving: Calories 176 (23% from fat)
Carbohydrate 9.4g Protein 24.7g Fat 4.4g (Sat. Fat 1.3g)
Cholesterol 91mg Sodium 293mg

Veal Chops with Creamed Leeks

4 (6-ounce) lean veal loin chops (¾ inch thick)
2 tablespoons margarine
1½ cups sliced leeks
3 ounces fresh shiitake mushrooms, sliced
1 tablespoon margarine, melted
¾ cup Chablis or other dry white wine
¾ cup whipping cream
1 tablespoon prepared horseradish
1½ teaspoons green peppercorns, crushed
1 tablespoon chopped fresh parsley

Trim fat from veal chops. Place 2 tablespoons margarine in a large nonstick skillet. Place over medium-high heat until margarine melts. Add chops, and cook 3 to 4 minutes on each side or until browned. Transfer veal to a serving platter, and keep warm. Reserve drippings in skillet.

Sauté leeks and mushrooms in 1 tablespoon margarine in skillet over medium-high heat until tender. Stir in wine, whipping cream, horseradish, and crushed peppercorns. Cook, uncovered, over medium-low heat, stirring frequently, 8 to 10 minutes or until slightly thickened. Spoon sauce evenly over veal, and sprinkle with parsley. Yield: 4 servings.

Per serving: Calories 399 (66% from fat)
Carbohydrate 9.8g Protein 25.2g Fat 29.1g (Sat. Fat 13.1g)
Cholesterol 152mg Sodium 237mg

Left: *Artichoke Veal Chops*

The lighter veal Parmesan has a crisp cereal coating and a piquant salsa topping.
Classic Veal Parmigiana is rich with spicy tomato sauce and lots of
Parmesan and mozzarella cheeses.

VEAL PARMESAN WITH TOMATO SALSA

2 cups peeled, seeded, and chopped
　　plum tomato
1 cup thinly sliced arugula
½ cup sliced green onions
2 tablespoons minced fresh basil
2 tablespoons red wine vinegar
1 tablespoon olive oil
¼ teaspoon garlic powder
¼ teaspoon pepper
8 (6-ounce) lean veal loin chops (¾ inch
　　thick)
1 cup crushed toasted whole grain wheat
　　flake cereal
¼ cup grated Parmesan cheese
2 egg whites, lightly beaten
　　Vegetable cooking spray
½ cup (2 ounces) shredded part-skim
　　mozzarella cheese

Combine first 8 ingredients in a small bowl. Cover and set aside.

Trim fat from veal chops. Combine cereal and Parmesan cheese in a shallow bowl. Dip chops in egg whites, and dredge in cereal mixture. Place chops in a 13- x 9- x 2-inch baking dish coated with cooking spray. Cover and chill 1 hour.

Bake chops, uncovered, at 375° for 30 to 35 minutes or until tender. Sprinkle with mozzarella cheese; bake an additional 5 minutes or until cheese melts. Transfer to a serving platter, and spoon tomato mixture evenly over chops. Yield: 8 servings.

Per serving: Calories 251 (28% from fat)
Carbohydrate 16.8g Protein 28.5g Fat 7.8g (Sat. Fat 2.6g)
Cholesterol 97mg   Sodium 310mg

Classic Veal Parmigiana

2 pounds veal cutlets
1⅔ cups plus 2 tablespoons grated
　　Parmesan cheese, divided
⅔ cup all-purpose flour
¼ cup butter, melted
2 eggs, beaten
2 (15-ounce) cans tomato sauce
¼ cup Burgundy or other dry red wine
1 teaspoon dried Italian seasoning
½ teaspoon pepper
½ cup olive oil
3 cups (12 ounces) shredded mozzarella
　　cheese

Trim fat from cutlets. Place cutlets between 2 sheets of heavy-duty plastic wrap, and flatten to ¼-inch thickness, using a meat mallet or rolling pin. Cut veal into serving-size pieces.

Combine 1⅔ cups Parmesan cheese and flour in a shallow bowl. Dip cutlets in melted butter; dredge in cheese mixture. Cover and chill 30 minutes. Dip cutlets in egg; dredge again in remaining cheese mixture. Cover and chill 1 hour.

Combine tomato sauce and next 3 ingredients in a saucepan; cook, uncovered, over medium heat 5 minutes, stirring occasionally. Set aside.

Cook veal in hot oil in a large skillet 2 to 3 minutes on each side or until browned. Transfer veal to a lightly greased 13- x 9- x 2-inch baking dish. Pour tomato sauce mixture over veal. Sprinkle with remaining 2 tablespoons Parmesan cheese. Cover and bake at 350° for 30 minutes. Uncover and top with mozzarella cheese; bake an additional 5 minutes or until cheese melts. Yield: 8 servings.

Per serving: Calories 514 (56% from fat)
Carbohydrate 13.9g Protein 41.8g Fat 32.1g (Sat. Fat 14.9g)
Cholesterol 211mg   Sodium 986mg

The distinctive flavor of Tangy Lamb Chops Véronique comes from hot-sweet mustard and a spicy breadcrumb coating. In the luscious recipe, the secret lies in the sauce. It contains brandy, whipping cream, and blue cheese.

TANGY LAMB CHOPS VÉRONIQUE

½ cup fine, dry breadcrumbs
2 teaspoons dried whole dillweed
½ teaspoon garlic powder
¼ teaspoon pepper
8 (3-ounce) lean lamb loin chops
   (¾ inch thick)
3 tablespoons hot-sweet mustard
3 tablespoons cider vinegar
   Vegetable cooking spray
½ cup seedless green grapes, quartered
½ cup seedless red grapes, quartered

Combine first 4 ingredients in a shallow bowl; stir well.

Trim fat from lamb chops. Combine mustard and vinegar; brush mustard mixture evenly over chops. Dredge chops in breadcrumb mixture.

Coat a large nonstick skillet with cooking spray; place over medium heat until hot. Add chops; cover and cook 4 minutes on each side or until browned. Uncover and cook 5 minutes on each side or to desired degree of doneness. Transfer chops to a serving platter, and sprinkle evenly with grapes. Yield: 4 servings.

Per serving: Calories 254 (30% from fat)
Carbohydrate 17.5g Protein 26.4g Fat 8.4g (Sat. Fat 2.7g)
Cholesterol 75mg Sodium 280mg

Lamb Chops with Blue Cheese Sauce

4 (5-ounce) lean lamb loin chops
   (1 inch thick)
1 tablespoon olive oil
¼ cup brandy
½ cup whipping cream
1 egg yolk, beaten
½ cup sliced seedless green grapes
¼ cup crumbled blue cheese

Trim fat from chops. Cook lamb chops in hot oil in a large skillet over medium-high heat 8 to 10 minutes on each side or until browned. Cover, reduce heat, and cook 20 minutes or to desired degree of doneness, turning once. Transfer chops to a serving platter, and keep warm.

Pour brandy into skillet. Combine whipping cream and egg yolk; add to brandy in skillet, stirring well. Cook over low heat, stirring constantly, until thickened. Stir in grapes and cheese. Spoon sauce evenly over chops, and serve immediately. Yield: 4 servings.

Per serving: Calories 350 (63% from fat)
Carbohydrate 4.8g Protein 26.7g Fat 24.6g (Sat. Fat 11.5g)
Cholesterol 175mg Sodium 191mg

The luscious leg of lamb is baked with bacon and marmalade and served with hazelnut-accented honey butter. The light parslied lamb's flavor comes from the fresh herbs and orange coating.

Parslied Leg of Lamb

1 cup chopped fresh parsley
½ cup chopped green onions
2 teaspoons grated orange rind
¼ cup plus 2 tablespoons unsweetened orange juice
1 tablespoon chopped hazelnuts
½ teaspoon pepper
1 (3½-pound) lean boneless leg of lamb
   Vegetable cooking spray
   Fresh orange slices (optional)
   Fresh parsley sprigs (optional)

Combine first 6 ingredients in container of an electric blender or food processor; cover and process until mixture forms a paste.

Trim fat from lamb, and place lamb in a shallow dish. Rub parsley mixture over lamb. Cover and marinate in refrigerator 8 hours.

Place lamb on a rack in a roasting pan coated with cooking spray. Insert meat thermometer into thickest part of roast, if desired. Bake, uncovered, at 325° for 1 hour and 45 minutes or until meat thermometer registers 140° (rare) to 160° (medium). Transfer lamb to a serving platter. Let stand 15 minutes. If desired, garnish with orange slices and parsley sprigs. Yield: 14 servings.

Per serving: Calories 155 (38% from fat)
Carbohydrate 1.4g Protein 21.5g Fat 6.5g (Sat. Fat 2.1g)
Cholesterol 67mg Sodium 53mg

Leg of Lamb with Honey Butter

1 (3½-pound) lean boneless leg of lamb
3 cloves garlic, thinly sliced
4 slices bacon
½ cup orange marmalade
½ cup commercial French dressing
3 tablespoons lemon juice
½ cup butter, softened
½ cup honey
½ cup chopped hazelnuts, toasted
1 tablespoon bourbon
   Chive blossoms (optional)
   Fresh mint (optional)
   Fresh oregano (optional)
   Fresh thyme (optional)
   Assorted cooked vegetables (optional)

Trim fat from lamb. Make lengthwise slits halfway through lamb. Insert a garlic slice into each slit. Arrange bacon slices in a crisscross pattern over lamb.

Combine orange marmalade, French dressing, and lemon juice in a small saucepan. Bring to a boil over medium heat, stirring occasionally. Remove from heat, and set aside.

Place lamb on a rack in a roasting pan. Insert meat thermometer into thickest part of roast, if desired. Brush lamb with marmalade mixture. Bake, uncovered, at 325° for 1 hour and 45 minutes or until meat thermometer registers 140° (rare) to 160° (medium), basting occasionally with marmalade mixture. Transfer lamb to a serving platter. Let stand 15 minutes.

Beat butter and honey at medium speed of an electric mixer until smooth. Stir in hazelnuts and bourbon. Serve butter mixture with lamb. If desired, garnish with chive blossoms, mint, oregano, thyme, and vegetables. Yield: 14 servings.

Per serving: Calories 386 (56% from fat)
Carbohydrate 20.9g Protein 22.2g Fat 24.0g (Sat. Fat 7.5g)
Cholesterol 91mg Sodium 274mg

Right: *Leg of Lamb with Honey Butter*

Spicy chimichangas are frequently in demand. Try our baked version filled with lean pork and reduced-fat cheese, or the crispy fried ones brimming with ground beef, chorizo, and cheese.

BAKED CHIMICHANGAS

2 pounds lean boneless pork
2 cups water
2 tablespoons chili powder
2 tablespoons white vinegar
½ teaspoon dried whole oregano
½ teaspoon ground cumin
2 cloves garlic, minced
1 (8-ounce) can no-salt-added tomato
    sauce
1 (4-ounce) can chopped green chiles
1 cup (4 ounces) shredded reduced-fat
    Monterey Jack cheese
½ cup sliced green onions
12 (10-inch) flour tortillas
    Vegetable cooking spray
12 cups shredded iceberg lettuce
¾ cup nonfat sour cream alternative
¼ teaspoon hot sauce
¾ cup commercial no-salt-added salsa

Trim fat from pork; cut pork into 2-inch pieces. Combine pork, water, and next 5 ingredients in a saucepan; bring to a boil. Cover, reduce heat, and simmer 30 minutes. Uncover; cook over medium-low heat 1 hour or until liquid evaporates. Remove from heat; shred meat with 2 forks. Stir in tomato sauce, chiles, cheese, and green onions.

Wrap tortillas in aluminum foil; heat at 350° for 15 minutes. Working with 1 tortilla at a time, coat both sides of tortilla with cooking spray. Spoon about ⅓ cup meat mixture just below center of tortilla. Fold over left and right sides of tortilla to partially enclose filling. Fold remaining edges to form a rectangle, and secure with a wooden pick. Repeat procedure with remaining tortillas and meat mixture. Place filled tortillas on an ungreased baking sheet. Bake at 425° for 20 minutes or until crisp. Remove wooden picks. Place 1 cup lettuce on each of 12 plates; top with chimichangas. Combine sour cream and hot sauce. Top each chimichanga with sour cream mixture and salsa. Yield: 12 servings.

Per serving: Calories 391 (29% from fat)
Carbohydrate 47.4g Protein 25.4g Fat 12.5g (Sat. Fat 4.2g)
Cholesterol 52mg Sodium 180mg

Crispy Chimichangas

1 pound chorizo, casings removed
1 pound ground beef
½ cup chopped onion
½ cup chopped green pepper
1 (15-ounce) can refried beans
½ cup wheat germ
1 teaspoon dried whole oregano
½ teaspoon ground cumin
12 (10-inch) flour tortillas
    Vegetable oil
1 cup (4 ounces) shredded Monterey Jack
    cheese
1 cup (4 ounces) shredded Cheddar
    cheese
1 (6-ounce) carton frozen guacamole,
    thawed
1 (8-ounce) carton sour cream
1 cup chopped tomato
1 (2.2-ounce) can sliced ripe olives,
    drained

Cook chorizo, ground beef, onion, and green pepper in a large skillet over medium heat until browned, stirring until meat crumbles; drain. Stir in beans and next 3 ingredients.

Wrap tortillas in aluminum foil; heat at 350° for 15 minutes. Working with 1 tortilla at a time, spoon about ⅓ cup meat mixture just below center of tortilla. Fold over left and right sides of tortilla to partially enclose filling. Fold remaining edges to form a rectangle, and secure with a wooden pick. Repeat procedure with remaining tortillas and meat mixture.

Pour vegetable oil to depth of 2 to 3 inches into a Dutch oven; heat to 375°. Fry filled tortillas in hot oil 1 to 2 minutes or until golden. Drain. Remove wooden picks. Place chimichangas on an ungreased baking sheet. Sprinkle with cheeses. Broil 5½ inches from heat (with electric oven door partially opened) 1 minute or until cheese melts. Top with guacamole, sour cream, tomato, and olives. Yield: 12 servings.

Per serving: Calories 773 (61% from fat)
Carbohydrate 54.4g Protein 25.9g Fat 52.3g (Sat. Fat 17.6g)
Cholesterol 77mg Sodium 690mg

Reduce fat in Curried Pork Medaillons by using reduced-calorie margarine and omitting the coconut milk and peanuts. Add a finishing flair to Pork Curry with green onions and peanuts.

CURRIED PORK MEDAILLONS

2   teaspoons reduced-calorie margarine
2   medium-size firm bananas, peeled and
      cut into ½-inch-thick slices
½   teaspoon ground cinnamon
2   (¾-pound) pork tenderloins
      Vegetable cooking spray
1¼ cups unsweetened orange juice, divided
¾   cup thinly sliced green onions
1   medium-size sweet red pepper, cut into
      thin strips
1½ teaspoons cornstarch
¼   cup plus 2 tablespoons raisins
1   teaspoon curry powder
½   teaspoon ground cumin

Melt margarine in a large nonstick skillet over medium-high heat. Add banana and cinnamon; sauté 5 minutes or until golden, tossing gently. Transfer to a bowl, and keep warm.

Partially freeze tenderloins; trim fat from tenderloins. Cut tenderloins diagonally across grain into ¼-inch-thick slices. Coat skillet with cooking spray. Place over medium-high heat until hot. Add half of pork, and cook 3 minutes on each side or until pork is lightly browned. Remove pork from skillet. Drain; set aside, and keep warm. Repeat procedure with remaining pork slices. Wipe drippings from skillet with a paper towel.

Combine 2 tablespoons orange juice, green onions, and red pepper in skillet; stir well. Cook over medium-high heat, stirring constantly, 2 minutes or until vegetables are tender.

Combine cornstarch and remaining 1 cup plus 2 tablespoons orange juice, stirring until smooth. Add cornstarch mixture to vegetable mixture in skillet; stir well. Add raisins, curry powder, and cumin. Bring to a boil; reduce heat, and simmer, stirring constantly, 1 minute. Return pork to skillet, and simmer an additional 3 to 4 minutes or until pork is tender, stirring frequently. Serve with banana slices. Yield: 6 servings.

Per serving: Calories 258 (20% from fat)
Carbohydrate 25.2g Protein 27.4g Fat 5.7g (Sat. Fat 1.7g)
Cholesterol 83mg Sodium 78mg

Pork Curry

2   (¾-pound) pork tenderloins
3   tablespoons margarine, melted and
      divided
¾   cup sliced celery
1   clove garlic, crushed
1½ cups chopped cooking apple
1   tablespoon curry powder
¼   teaspoon ground ginger
1½ tablespoons all-purpose flour
¼   teaspoon ground red pepper
1½ cups canned ready-to-serve chicken
      broth
⅓   cup cream of coconut
⅓   cup tomato sauce
4   cups cooked long-grain rice
¼   cup sliced green onions
¼   cup chopped dry-roasted peanuts

Partially freeze tenderloins; trim fat from tenderloins. Cut tenderloins diagonally across grain into ¼-inch-thick slices; cut slices into 1-inch pieces. Cook half of pork in 1 tablespoon margarine in a large skillet over medium-high heat 3 minutes on each side or until lightly browned. Remove pork from skillet. Drain; set aside, and keep warm. Repeat procedure with remaining pork and 1 tablespoon oil.

Sauté celery and garlic in remaining 1 tablespoon margarine in skillet over medium-high heat until tender. Add apple, curry powder, and ginger; sauté over medium heat 6 minutes or until apple is crisp-tender. Stir in flour and red pepper. Gradually add chicken broth, cream of coconut, and tomato sauce. Return pork to skillet. Bring to a boil; reduce heat, and simmer, uncovered, 10 minutes or until pork is tender, stirring frequently. Spoon pork mixture over rice, and sprinkle with green onions and peanuts. Yield: 6 servings.

Per serving: Calories 483 (37% from fat)
Carbohydrate 44.6g Protein 31.8g Fat 19.8g (Sat. Fat 7.1g)
Cholesterol 74mg Sodium 902mg

These sweet-and-sour combinations offer similar flavors. The light one contains no added fat and relies on low-sodium ingredients, while the luscious nuggets are breaded and fried.

LIGHT SWEET AND SOUR PORK STRIPS

1 pound lean boneless pork loin
Vegetable cooking spray
1 (8-ounce) can no-salt-added tomato sauce
¼ cup rice wine vinegar
2 tablespoons brown sugar
2 teaspoons low-sodium soy sauce
¼ teaspoon minced garlic
⅛ teaspoon ground red pepper
1 (20-ounce) can pineapple chunks in juice
1 medium-size green pepper, seeded and cut into 1-inch pieces
¼ cup chopped green onions
2 tablespoons cornstarch
2 cups cooked long-grain rice (cooked without salt or fat)
Pepper triangles (optional)

Partially freeze pork; trim fat from pork. Slice pork diagonally across grain into thin slices; slice into 1-inch-wide strips. Coat a nonstick skillet with cooking spray; place over medium-high heat until hot. Add pork; cook 8 minutes or until browned, stirring frequently. Remove from skillet. Drain and pat dry. Wipe drippings from skillet with a paper towel.

Combine pork, tomato sauce, and next 5 ingredients in skillet; bring to a boil. Cover, reduce heat, and simmer 15 minutes or until pork is tender. Drain pineapple, reserving juice. Add enough water to juice to make 1 cup liquid. Set aside. Add pineapple, green pepper pieces, and green onions to skillet; cover and simmer 5 to 7 minutes or until vegetables are crisp-tender. Combine cornstarch and reserved pineapple juice mixture; stir into pork mixture. Cook, stirring constantly, until thickened. Spoon pork mixture over rice. Garnish with pepper triangles, if desired. Yield: 4 servings.

Per serving: Calories 445 (24% from fat)
Carbohydrate 57.9g Protein 25.3g Fat 11.8g (Sat. Fat 3.9g)
Cholesterol 73mg Sodium 140mg

Sweet and Sour Pork Nuggets

¼ cup plus 2 tablespoons all-purpose flour
2 eggs, beaten
1 tablespoon ground ginger
1 tablespoon whole milk
2 teaspoons sesame oil
1 pound lean boneless pork, cut into ¾-inch cubes
Vegetable oil
1 (8-ounce) can pineapple chunks in juice
1½ tablespoons cornstarch
¼ cup plus 1 tablespoon sugar
¼ cup white vinegar
3 tablespoons soy sauce
3 tablespoons catsup
2 tablespoons dry sherry
¼ teaspoon garlic salt
1 (11-ounce) can mandarin oranges in light syrup, drained
½ cup thinly sliced green onions
2 cups cooked long-grain rice

Combine first 5 ingredients in a bowl, stirring well. Dip pork cubes in batter, a few at a time, coating well. Pour vegetable oil to depth of 1 inch into a large heavy skillet. Fry pork in hot oil over medium-high heat 5 to 6 minutes. Drain on paper towels.

Drain pineapple, reserving 3 tablespoons juice. Combine cornstarch and reserved pineapple juice in a Dutch oven, stirring well. Add sugar and next 5 ingredients; stir well. Cook over medium heat, stirring constantly, until thickened. Stir in pork, pineapple, oranges, and green onions; cook just until thoroughly heated. Spoon pork mixture over rice. Yield: 4 servings.

Per serving: Calories 636 (34% from fat)
Carbohydrate 72.3g Protein 31.2g Fat 24.2g (Sat. Fat 6.1g)
Cholesterol 179mg Sodium 1146mg

Left: *Light Sweet and Sour Pork Strips*

Make the light cherry sauce by skimming the fat from the pork roast drippings and simmering the drippings with the fruit and sugar. Or cook a thick chutney made of whole-berry cranberry sauce and brown sugar to serve with the other pork roast recipe.

PORK ROAST WITH CHERRY SAUCE

1	(2½-pound) lean boneless double pork loin roast, tied
½	teaspoon ground ginger
½	teaspoon dry mustard
½	teaspoon pepper
	Vegetable cooking spray
2	tablespoons honey
2	tablespoons fine, dry breadcrumbs
1	cup Chablis or other dry white wine
1	tablespoon balsamic vinegar
½	cup unsweetened pitted dried cherries
¼	cup firmly packed brown sugar
2	teaspoons cornstarch
1	tablespoon water

Untie roast; trim fat from roast. Retie roast. Combine ginger, dry mustard, and pepper; rub mixture over surface of roast. Place roast on a rack in a roasting pan coated with cooking spray. Insert meat thermometer into thickest part of roast, if desired. Place roast in a 450° oven. Reduce heat to 350°, and bake 1 hour and 15 minutes.

Brush roast with honey, and sprinkle with breadcrumbs. Combine wine and vinegar; pour over roast. Bake, uncovered, an additional 30 minutes or until meat thermometer registers 160°.

Remove roast from pan, reserving drippings. Let roast stand 10 minutes. Skim fat from drippings, and place drippings in a small saucepan. Bring to a boil; add cherries, and simmer 10 minutes. Combine brown sugar, cornstarch, and water; stir well. Add to cherry mixture. Cook, stirring constantly, until thickened.

Remove string from roast; cut diagonally across grain into ¼-inch-thick slices. Serve with cherry sauce. Yield: 10 servings.

Per serving: Calories 235 (31% from fat)
Carbohydrate 18.4g Protein 21.8g Fat 8.2g (Sat. Fat 2.8g)
Cholesterol 61mg Sodium 80mg

Pork Roast with Cranberry Chutney

3	tablespoons butter, divided
1	(2½-pound) lean boneless double pork loin roast, tied
1	tablespoon all-purpose flour
1	tablespoon cracked pepper
1	tablespoon Dijon mustard
2	teaspoons ground ginger
2	teaspoons brown sugar
1	(16-ounce) can whole-berry cranberry sauce
½	cup firmly packed brown sugar
¼	cup cider vinegar
1	teaspoon ground cinnamon
¼	teaspoon ground cloves
2	teaspoons cornstarch
1½	tablespoons water

Melt 1 tablespoon butter in a large heavy skillet. Add roast; cook 4 minutes on each side or until browned. Remove roast from skillet, and let cool 10 minutes. Transfer roast to a rack in a lightly greased roasting pan.

Combine remaining 2 tablespoons butter, flour, and next 4 ingredients. Spread mustard mixture evenly over top and sides of roast. Insert meat thermometer into thickest part of roast, if desired. Place roast in a 450° oven. Reduce heat to 350°, and bake 1 hour and 20 minutes or until meat thermometer registers 160°.

Combine cranberry sauce and next 4 ingredients. Bring to a boil over medium heat, stirring frequently. Dissolve cornstarch in water; stir into cranberry mixture. Cook, stirring constantly, until mixture thickens.

Remove roast from pan, and let stand 10 minutes. Remove string from roast; cut diagonally across grain into ¼-inch-thick slices. Serve with cranberry mixture. Yield: 10 servings.

Per serving: Calories 351 (38% from fat)
Carbohydrate 31.3g Protein 22.3g Fat 15.0g (Sat. Fat 6.1g)
Cholesterol 83mg Sodium 154mg

A broth-based mustard sauce dresses up the light pork tenderloins, while a brandied cream sauce accompanies the richer version. Different preparation methods also affect the fat content in these recipes—the light one is baked, and the other is pan-fried in oil.

LIGHT PORK TENDERLOINS WITH MUSTARD SAUCE

2 (¾-pound) pork tenderloins
12 (2-inch) fresh thyme sprigs
2 tablespoons brandy, divided
2 teaspoons olive oil, divided
¼ teaspoon salt
¼ teaspoon pepper
½ cup sliced onion
1 tablespoon brown sugar
1 cup halved seedless red grapes
1 cup canned no-salt-added chicken broth, undiluted
1½ tablespoons coarse-grained mustard
1 teaspoon cornstarch
1 tablespoon water

Trim fat from tenderloins. Fold a piece of aluminum foil in half, crosswise; place tenderloins on aluminum foil lengthwise. Place thyme sprigs evenly on tenderloins.

Combine 1 tablespoon brandy, 1 teaspoon olive oil, salt, and pepper in a small bowl; stir well. Pour over tenderloins, and wrap securely. Place on an ungreased baking sheet. Insert meat thermometer into thickest part of tenderloin, if desired. Bake at 400° for 30 to 35 minutes or until meat thermometer registers 160°. Remove tenderloins from foil; remove and discard thyme sprigs. Transfer tenderloins to a serving platter, and keep warm.

Heat remaining 1 teaspoon olive oil in a skillet over medium-high heat until hot; add onion. Sauté until tender. Add remaining 1 tablespoon brandy, brown sugar, and next 3 ingredients; stir well. Combine cornstarch and water; add to onion mixture, and stir. Bring to a boil; cook over medium-high heat until thickened, stirring occasionally.

To serve, slice tenderloins diagonally across grain into thin slices, and serve with mustard sauce. Yield: 6 servings.

Per serving: Calories 202 (28% from fat)
Carbohydrate 8.7g Protein 26.5g Fat 6.2g (Sat. Fat 1.8g)
Cholesterol 83mg Sodium 212mg

Pork Tenderloins with Brandied Cream Sauce

2 (¾-pound) pork tenderloins
1 tablespoon all-purpose flour
1 teaspoon pepper
¼ cup vegetable oil
¼ cup butter, divided
1 cup fresh mushrooms, sliced
½ cup brandy
½ cup canned ready-to-serve chicken broth
1 cup whipping cream
3 tablespoons hot-sweet mustard
1 teaspoon dried whole sage

Trim fat from tenderloins. Combine flour and pepper in a shallow bowl; dredge tenderloins in flour mixture. Cook tenderloins, uncovered, in hot oil in a large skillet over medium heat 10 minutes, turning occasionally. Insert meat thermometer into thickest part of tenderloin, if desired. Cover and cook an additional 20 minutes or until meat thermometer registers 160°. Transfer tenderloins to a serving platter, and keep warm.

Melt 2 tablespoons butter in a large saucepan; add mushrooms, and cook 5 minutes. Add brandy and chicken broth. Bring to a boil, and cook over medium-high heat until mixture is reduced by half, stirring occasionally. Stir in whipping cream, and cook over medium-high heat 10 to 15 minutes or until mixture thickens. Remove from heat; add remaining 2 tablespoons butter, mustard, and sage, and stir with a wire whisk.

To serve, cut tenderloins diagonally across grain into thin slices, and serve with cream sauce. Yield: 6 servings.

Per serving: Calories 458 (72% from fat)
Carbohydrate 4.4g Protein 28.1g Fat 36.4g (Sat. Fat 17.1g)
Cholesterol 158mg Sodium 323mg

A peachy mixture with mango chutney and green onions provides a light, flavorful accompaniment to pork. Mandarin oranges and toasted pecans distinguish the flavor of the chutney sauce in the luscious recipe.

PEACHY PORK MEDAILLONS

2   (¾-pound) pork tenderloins
    Vegetable cooking spray
½   cup peach nectar
¼   cup Chablis or other dry white wine
1   teaspoon peeled, minced gingerroot
¼   teaspoon pepper
1   teaspoon cornstarch
1   tablespoon water
⅓   cup mango chutney
2   cups peeled, sliced fresh peaches
½   cup sliced green onions
    Green onion curls (optional)

Partially freeze tenderloins; trim fat from tenderloins. Cut tenderloins diagonally across grain into ¼-inch-thick slices.

Coat a large nonstick skillet with cooking spray. Place over medium-high heat until hot. Add half of pork, and cook 3 minutes on each side or until pork is lightly browned. Remove pork from skillet. Drain; set aside, and keep warm. Repeat procedure with remaining pork slices. Wipe drippings from skillet with a paper towel.

Combine peach nectar and next 3 ingredients in skillet. Return pork to skillet. Bring to a boil; cover, reduce heat, and simmer 4 to 5 minutes or until pork is tender.

Transfer pork to a serving platter, using a slotted spoon. Set aside, and keep warm. Combine cornstarch and water; stir until smooth. Add cornstarch mixture and chutney to peach nectar mixture; stir well. Add peaches and sliced green onions. Bring to a boil; reduce heat, and simmer, stirring constantly, until thickened. Spoon peach mixture over pork. Garnish with green onion curls, if desired. Yield: 6 servings.

Per serving: Calories 231 (18% from fat)
Carbohydrate 20.7g   Protein 26.7g   Fat 4.6g (Sat. Fat 1.5g)
Cholesterol 83mg   Sodium 94mg

Left: *Peachy Pork Medaillons*

Pork Medaillons with Chutney Sauce

2   (¾-pound) pork tenderloins
2   tablespoons olive oil, divided
2   (11-ounce) cans mandarin oranges in light syrup
½   teaspoon grated orange rind
½   teaspoon peeled, minced gingerroot
½   teaspoon pepper
¼   cup dark rum
½   cup mango chutney
¼   cup sliced green onions
1   teaspoon cornstarch
1   tablespoon water
⅓   cup chopped pecans, toasted

Partially freeze tenderloins; trim fat from tenderloins. Cut tenderloins diagonally across grain into ¼-inch-thick slices.

Cook half of pork in 1 tablespoon hot olive oil in a large skillet over medium-high heat 3 minutes on each side or until pork is lightly browned. Remove pork from skillet, and keep warm. Repeat procedure with remaining pork slices and remaining 1 tablespoon olive oil.

Drain oranges, reserving ½ cup liquid. Add reserved liquid, orange rind, and next 3 ingredients to skillet. Return pork to skillet. Bring to a boil; cover, reduce heat, and simmer 4 to 5 minutes or until pork is tender.

Transfer pork to a serving platter, using a slotted spoon. Set aside, and keep warm. Add chutney and green onions to pan drippings. Combine cornstarch and water, stirring until smooth. Add cornstarch mixture to chutney mixture. Bring to a boil; reduce heat, and simmer, uncovered, until chutney mixture is thickened and bubbly. Stir in oranges and pecans. Cook over medium-low heat until thoroughly heated. Spoon sauce evenly over pork. Yield: 6 servings.

Per serving: Calories 331 (32% from fat)
Carbohydrate 31.4g   Protein 24.8g   Fat 11.8g (Sat. Fat 1.9g)
Cholesterol 74mg   Sodium 106mg

Splurge with double-crust pastry for Home-Style Pot Pie, or top the lighter pies with a biscuit crust.

CHICKEN POT PIES

Vegetable cooking spray
1 cup diced carrot
1 cup sliced fresh mushrooms
½ cup chopped celery
½ cup frozen English peas, thawed
¼ cup minced onion
1½ (10¾-ounce) cans 99% fat-free,
   one-third-less-salt cream of chicken
   soup, undiluted
1½ cups water
½ teaspoon pepper
¼ teaspoon dried whole thyme
3 cups diced cooked chicken breast
   (skinned before cooking and cooked
   without salt)
1 cup self-rising flour
1½ tablespoons margarine
¼ cup skim milk

Coat a large nonstick skillet with cooking spray; place over medium-high heat until hot. Add carrot, mushrooms, celery, peas, and onion. Sauté 5 minutes or until vegetables are tender.

Combine soup, water, pepper, and thyme in a medium bowl; stir well. Add vegetables and cooked chicken, stirring well.

Spoon chicken mixture evenly into 6 (8-ounce) round baking dishes coated with cooking spray.

Place flour in a small bowl; cut in margarine with a pastry blender until mixture is crumbly. Sprinkle milk (1 tablespoon at a time) evenly over surface, stirring with a fork until dry ingredients are moistened. Drop dough evenly by spoonfuls onto chicken mixture. Bake at 425° for 15 to 18 minutes or until crusts are golden. Yield: 6 servings.

Per serving: Calories 281 (22% from fat)
Carbohydrate 28.5g Protein 24.7g Fat 6.8g (Sat. Fat 1.5g)
Cholesterol 61mg Sodium 716mg

Home-Style Pot Pie

3 cups all-purpose flour
1 teaspoon salt
1 cup vegetable shortening
2 eggs, lightly beaten and divided
¼ cup plus 2 tablespoons cold water
1 tablespoon white vinegar
½ cup chopped onion
2 tablespoons margarine, melted
3 cups diced cooked chicken breast
1¼ cups canned ready-to-serve chicken
   broth
1 cup chopped celery
1 cup sliced fresh mushrooms
¾ cup diced carrot
¾ cup frozen English peas, thawed
¾ cup frozen diced potatoes, thawed
2 tablespoons cornstarch
2 tablespoons water
1 (10¾-ounce) can cream of chicken soup
½ cup sour cream
¾ cup (3 ounces) shredded Cheddar cheese
1 tablespoon whole milk

Combine flour and salt; cut in shortening. Combine 1 egg, cold water, and vinegar; sprinkle over surface, stirring until dry ingredients are moistened. Shape into a ball; chill. Sauté onion in margarine in a skillet 5 minutes. Stir in chicken and next 6 ingredients. Bring to a boil; cover, reduce heat, and simmer 20 minutes. Combine cornstarch and 2 tablespoons water; add to chicken mixture. Cook, stirring constantly, until mixture boils. Remove from heat; stir in soup, sour cream, and cheese.

Roll half of pastry to ⅛-inch thickness. Fit into a deep 2-quart casserole. Spoon chicken mixture into casserole. Roll remaining pastry; place over chicken mixture. Trim, seal, and flute edges. Cut slits in pastry. Combine 1 egg and milk; brush over pastry. Bake at 400° for 30 minutes. Yield: 6 servings.

Per serving: Calories 848 (53% from fat)
Carbohydrate 63.4g Protein 35.4g Fat 49.7g (Sat. Fat 8.7g)
Cholesterol 152mg Sodium 1209mg

Right: *Home-Style Pot Pie*

Top the light enchiladas with a spicy tomato mixture instead of a cream-based red sauce.

LIGHT ENCHILADAS

Vegetable cooking spray
4 (4-ounce) skinned, boned chicken breast halves, cut into bite-size pieces
¾ cup chopped onion
1 sweet red pepper, seeded and chopped
1 large green pepper, seeded and chopped
1½ tablespoons chopped fresh cilantro
2 (16-ounce) cans pinto beans, drained and mashed
1 (14½-ounce) can no-salt-added tomatoes, undrained and chopped
1 (8-ounce) can no-salt-added tomato sauce
1 (4-ounce) can green chiles, drained
¼ teaspoon pepper
10 (8-inch) flour tortillas
¾ cup (3 ounces) shredded reduced-fat Monterey Jack cheese

Coat a nonstick skillet with cooking spray; place over medium-high heat until hot. Add chicken; sauté 2 minutes or until lightly browned. Add onion and next 3 ingredients; sauté 3 minutes or until chicken is done. Remove from heat. Add beans; stir. Combine tomato and next 3 ingredients in a bowl; stir. Spoon ⅓ cup tomato mixture into a 13- x 9- x 2-inch baking dish coated with cooking spray. Set remaining tomato mixture aside.

Place a damp paper towel in center of a sheet of aluminum foil. Stack tortillas on paper towel. Cover stack with another damp paper towel; seal foil. Bake at 250° for 10 minutes. Spoon chicken mixture evenly down centers of tortillas. Roll tortillas; place, seam side down, in prepared dish. Pour remaining tomato mixture over tortillas. Cover and bake at 350° for 30 minutes or until thoroughly heated. Uncover and sprinkle with cheese. Bake 5 minutes or until cheese melts. Yield: 10 enchiladas.

Per enchilada: Calories 265 (21% from fat)
Carbohydrate 33.3g Protein 18.9g Fat 6.1g (Sat. Fat 2.2g)
Cholesterol 33mg Sodium 455mg

Enchiladas Olé

1½ cups coarsely chopped onion, divided
1 jalapeño pepper, seeded and chopped
2 cloves garlic
1 (16-ounce) can crushed tomatoes
¼ cup chili powder
1 teaspoon dried whole oregano
3¾ cups vegetable oil, divided
2 tablespoons cornstarch
2 cups canned chicken broth, divided
1 cup whipping cream
¼ teaspoon salt
⅛ teaspoon freshly ground pepper
2 cloves garlic, minced
4 cups shredded, cooked chicken breast
12 (6-inch) corn tortillas
1½ cups (6 ounces) shredded Monterey Jack cheese
1 (8-ounce) carton sour cream
½ cup chopped green onions

Position blade in food processor, and add ½ cup onion and next 3 ingredients; process. Sauté chili powder and oregano in 2 tablespoons oil in a skillet 3 minutes. Add tomato mixture; simmer 5 minutes. Combine cornstarch and 2 tablespoons broth. Add remaining broth and cream to tomato mixture; cook 2 minutes. Add cornstarch mixture; cook until thickened. Stir in salt and pepper.

Sauté remaining 1 cup onion and minced garlic in 2 tablespoons hot oil in a skillet over medium-high heat until tender. Add chicken; cook until lightly browned. Stir in 1 cup tomato mixture.

Pour 3½ cups oil into a skillet. Fry tortillas, one at a time, over medium-high heat 8 seconds on each side. Drain on paper towels. Brush one side with tomato mixture. Spoon about ¼ cup chicken mixture down center. Roll tortilla; place, seam side down, in a greased 13- x 9- x 2-inch baking dish. Repeat with remaining tortillas. Pour remaining tomato mixture over tortillas; sprinkle with cheese. Bake, uncovered, at 375° for 15 minutes. Top with sour cream and green onions. Yield: 12 enchiladas.

Per enchilada: Calories 445 (67% from fat)
Carbohydrate 19.8g Protein 18.4g Fat 33.3g (Sat. Fat 13.2g)
Cholesterol 79mg Sodium 419mg

Light Creole Chicken and Rice offers everything you love in traditional jambalaya except the sausage.

CREOLE CHICKEN AND RICE

Vegetable cooking spray
1 tablespoon reduced-calorie margarine
1½ cups chopped onion
1½ cups chopped celery
1½ cups chopped green pepper, divided
1 teaspoon minced garlic
1 teaspoon dry mustard
1 teaspoon dried whole oregano
½ teaspoon salt
½ teaspoon dried whole thyme
¼ teaspoon ground white pepper
¼ teaspoon freshly ground black pepper
¼ teaspoon ground red pepper
¼ teaspoon hot sauce
3 cups canned no-salt-added stewed tomato
3 cups canned no-salt-added chicken broth, undiluted
5 (4-ounce) skinned, boned chicken breast halves, cut into ½-inch pieces
2 cups converted rice, uncooked
¼ cup sliced green onions

Coat a large Dutch oven with cooking spray; add margarine. Place over medium-high heat until margarine melts. Add onion, celery, ¾ cup green pepper, and garlic; sauté until tender.

Stir in dry mustard and next 7 ingredients; cook 2 minutes, stirring occasionally. Stir in tomato; cook over medium heat 10 minutes, stirring occasionally. Add broth; bring to a boil. Add remaining ¾ cup green pepper, chicken, rice, and green onions; stir well. Bring to a boil; cover, reduce heat, and simmer 20 minutes or until rice is tender. Yield: 8 (1½-cup) servings.

Per serving: Calories 203 (9% from fat)
Carbohydrate 25.3g Protein 19.5g Fat 2.2g (Sat. Fat 0.4g)
Cholesterol 41mg Sodium 251mg

Chicken Jambalaya

¾ pound andouille or other smoked sausage
1½ cups chopped onion
1½ cups chopped celery
1½ cups chopped green pepper, divided
1 teaspoon minced garlic
2 tablespoons butter, melted
½ teaspoon salt
1 teaspoon dry mustard
1 teaspoon dried whole oregano
½ teaspoon dried whole thyme
¼ teaspoon ground white pepper
¼ teaspoon freshly ground black pepper
¼ teaspoon ground red pepper
3 cups canned crushed tomato
3 cups canned ready-to-serve chicken broth
6 (4-ounce) skinned, boned chicken breast halves, cut into ½-inch pieces
2 cups converted rice, uncooked
¼ cup sliced green onions

Cook sausage in a large Dutch oven until browned; remove from pan with a slotted spoon, and set aside.

Add onion, celery, ¾ cup green pepper, garlic, and butter to pan; sauté over medium-high heat until tender. Add salt and next 6 ingredients, stirring well; cook 2 minutes, stirring occasionally. Stir in tomato; cook over medium heat 10 minutes, stirring occasionally. Add broth; bring to a boil. Add remaining ¾ cup green pepper, sausage, chicken, rice, and green onions; stir well. Bring to a boil; cover, reduce heat, and simmer 20 minutes or until rice is tender. Yield: 8 (1½-cup) servings.

Per serving: Calories 403 (41% from fat)
Carbohydrate 24.2g Protein 33.9g Fat 18.5g (Sat. Fat 7.1g)
Cholesterol 86mg Sodium 1308mg

Chicken Linguine is so creamy, you'll never guess it uses nonfat sour cream in place of half-and-half.

CHICKEN LINGUINE

1 pound sliced fresh mushrooms
½ cup dry sherry
2 tablespoons reduced-calorie margarine, melted and divided
4 (4-ounce) skinned, boned chicken breast halves
 Vegetable cooking spray
½ cup chopped onion
¼ cup plus 2 tablespoons all-purpose flour
3 cups canned no-salt-added chicken broth, undiluted and divided
1 (8-ounce) carton nonfat sour cream alternative
1 (16-ounce) package linguine, uncooked
½ cup (2 ounces) shredded reduced-fat Monterey Jack cheese
¼ cup plus 2 tablespoons freshly grated Parmesan cheese, divided
⅛ teaspoon freshly ground black pepper
¼ cup fine, dry breadcrumbs

Sauté mushrooms in sherry and 1 tablespoon margarine in a nonstick skillet over high heat 5 minutes.

Place chicken in a saucepan; add water to cover. Bring to a boil; cover, reduce heat, and simmer 20 minutes. Drain; let cool, and shred. Coat a saucepan with cooking spray; place over medium heat until hot. Add onion, and sauté until tender. Combine flour and ½ cup broth. Add 2½ cups broth and flour mixture to onion. Cook over medium heat until thickened. Remove from heat; stir in sour cream. Cook linguine according to package directions, omitting salt and fat; drain. Combine mushroom mixture, chicken, sour cream mixture, Monterey Jack cheese, ¼ cup Parmesan cheese, and pepper. Stir in linguine. Spoon into a 13- x 9- x 2-inch baking dish coated with cooking spray.

Combine breadcrumbs and remaining Parmesan cheese and margarine; sprinkle over chicken. Bake, uncovered, at 350° for 30 minutes. Yield: 12 servings.

Per serving: Calories 289 (19% from fat)
Carbohydrate 37.7g Protein 18.7g Fat 6.1g (Sat. Fat 2.0g)
Cholesterol 31mg Sodium 167mg

Left: *Chicken Linguine*

Chicken Tetrazzini

1 pound sliced fresh mushrooms
½ cup plus 1 tablespoon margarine, melted and divided
½ cup dry sherry
1½ teaspoons salt, divided
½ teaspoon ground white pepper, divided
6 (4-ounce) skinned, boned chicken breast halves
½ cup chopped onion
½ teaspoon minced garlic
¼ cup plus 2 tablespoons all-purpose flour
2½ cups half-and-half
1½ cups canned ready-to-serve chicken broth
1 cup shredded fontina cheese
¾ cup freshly grated Parmesan cheese, divided
1 (16-ounce) package linguine, uncooked
¼ cup fine, dry breadcrumbs

Sauté mushrooms in 2 tablespoons margarine in a skillet 5 minutes. Add sherry; cook 2 minutes or until reduced to ¼ cup. Add ½ teaspoon salt and ⅛ teaspoon pepper.

Place chicken in a saucepan; add water to cover. Bring to a boil; cover, reduce heat, and simmer 20 minutes. Drain; let cool, and shred. Cook onion in ¼ cup plus 2 tablespoons margarine in a saucepan over low heat 15 minutes. Add garlic; cook 1 minute. Add flour, stirring until smooth. Cook 1 minute, stirring constantly. Add half-and-half and chicken broth; cook over medium heat, stirring constantly, until thickened. Remove from heat; add fontina cheese, ½ cup Parmesan cheese, ½ teaspoon salt, and ⅛ teaspoon pepper. Stir until cheeses melt. Cook linguine according to package directions; drain. Combine mushroom mixture, chicken, cheese mixture, ½ teaspoon salt, and ¼ teaspoon pepper. Stir in linguine. Spoon into a greased 13- x 9- x 2-inch dish.

Combine breadcrumbs and remaining ¼ cup Parmesan cheese and 1 tablespoon margarine; sprinkle over chicken. Bake, uncovered, at 350° for 20 minutes. Yield: 12 servings.

Per serving: Calories 465 (45% from fat)
Carbohydrate 38.4g Protein 24.5g Fat 23.4g (Sat. Fat 9.3g)
Cholesterol 68mg Sodium 709mg

Gruyère cheese provides distinctive flavor to both chicken recipes, but Chicken Broccoli Casserole stays trimmer than Gruyère Chicken Divan because it uses a minimum amount of reduced-fat cheese.

CHICKEN BROCCOLI CASSEROLE

2 tablespoons chopped shallots
½ teaspoon minced garlic
2 tablespoons reduced-calorie margarine, melted and divided
¼ cup plus 2 tablespoons all-purpose flour
1½ cups canned no-salt-added chicken broth, undiluted and divided
1 cup nonfat sour cream alternative
¼ cup (1 ounce) shredded reduced-fat Gruyère cheese
¼ cup grated Parmesan cheese
¼ teaspoon salt
⅛ teaspoon ground white pepper
   Vegetable cooking spray
6 cups chopped cooked broccoli
3 cups chopped cooked chicken breast (skinned before cooking and cooked without salt)
¼ cup fine, dry breadcrumbs
2 tablespoons grated Parmesan cheese
2 tablespoons minced fresh parsley

Sauté shallots and garlic in 1 tablespoon margarine in a saucepan over medium-high heat until tender. Combine flour and ½ cup chicken broth; stir well. Add flour mixture and remaining 1 cup chicken broth to saucepan. Cook over medium heat, stirring constantly, until mixture is thickened. Remove from heat; add sour cream and next 4 ingredients.

Spread ½ cup sour cream mixture in an 11- x 7- x 1½-inch baking dish coated with cooking spray. Add broccoli and 1¼ cups sour cream mixture. Top with chicken and remaining sour cream mixture.

Combine breadcrumbs, 2 tablespoons Parmesan cheese, parsley, and remaining 1 tablespoon margarine; stir well. Sprinkle evenly over top of casserole. Bake, uncovered, at 350° for 30 minutes or until thoroughly heated. Yield: 8 servings.

Per serving: Calories 208 (25% from fat)
Carbohydrate 14.2g Protein 23.6g Fat 5.8g (Sat. Fat 2.0g)
Cholesterol 47mg Sodium 288mg

Gruyère Chicken Divan

2 tablespoons chopped shallots
½ teaspoon minced garlic
½ cup margarine, melted and divided
¼ cup plus 2 tablespoons all-purpose flour
1½ cups half-and-half
1 cup canned ready-to-serve chicken broth
1½ cups (6 ounces) shredded Gruyère cheese
¼ teaspoon salt
⅛ teaspoon ground white pepper
4 cups chopped cooked broccoli
4 cups chopped cooked chicken breast (skinned before cooking and cooked without salt)
⅓ cup grated Parmesan cheese
⅓ cup fine, dry breadcrumbs
2 teaspoons paprika

Sauté shallots and garlic in ¼ cup plus 2 tablespoons margarine in a saucepan over medium-high heat until tender. Add flour, stirring until smooth. Cook 1 minute over medium heat, stirring constantly. Gradually add half-and-half and chicken broth; cook over medium heat, stirring constantly, until mixture is thickened and bubbly. Remove from heat; add Gruyère cheese, salt, and pepper, stirring until cheese melts.

Spread ½ cup cheese sauce in a greased 11- x 7- x 1½-inch baking dish. Add broccoli and 1½ cups cheese sauce. Top with chicken and remaining cheese sauce.

Combine Parmesan cheese, breadcrumbs, paprika, and remaining 2 tablespoons margarine; stir well. Sprinkle evenly over top of casserole. Bake, uncovered, at 350° for 30 minutes or until thoroughly heated. Yield: 8 servings.

Per serving: Calories 438 (58% from fat)
Carbohydrate 13.4g Protein 32.8g Fat 28.1g (Sat. Fat 11.2g)
Cholesterol 98mg Sodium 572mg

Stuff the chicken medaillons with light ricotta, light cream cheese, and herbs, but fill the luscious chicken breast rolls with rich mascarpone cheese and prosciutto.

CHICKEN MEDAILLONS WITH PEPPER SAUCE

2 cups chopped sweet red pepper
1⅓ cups peeled, diced round red potato
⅔ cup Chablis or other dry white wine
⅔ cup canned no-salt-added chicken broth, undiluted
⅛ teaspoon salt
8 (4-ounce) skinned, boned chicken breast halves
¾ cup light ricotta cheese
¼ cup light process cream cheese product
2 tablespoons minced fresh basil
2 tablespoons minced fresh oregano
2 tablespoons minced fresh parsley
1 teaspoon minced garlic
½ teaspoon pepper
¼ teaspoon salt
½ teaspoon salt-free lemon-pepper seasoning
Vegetable cooking spray

Combine first 5 ingredients in a medium saucepan; stir well. Bring to a boil; cover, reduce heat, and simmer 20 minutes or until pepper and potato are tender. Transfer mixture to container of an electric blender; cover and process until smooth. Pour mixture through a wire-mesh strainer into a bowl.

Place chicken between 2 sheets of heavy-duty plastic wrap, and flatten to ¼-inch thickness.

Combine ricotta cheese and next 7 ingredients in a bowl; stir well. Spread cheese mixture evenly over chicken. Roll up jellyroll fashion, starting with short end, tucking ends under. Secure chicken rolls with wooden picks; sprinkle with lemon-pepper seasoning. Place chicken rolls on a baking sheet coated with cooking spray. Bake at 375° for 35 minutes or until lightly browned. Remove wooden picks, and cut chicken rolls into ½-inch slices. Spoon pepper sauce evenly onto individual serving plates. Arrange chicken, cut side down, on sauce. Yield: 8 servings.

Per serving: Calories 194 (17% from fat)
Carbohydrate 9.3g Protein 30.4g Fat 3.7g (Sat. Fat 1.6g)
Cholesterol 73mg Sodium 245mg

Prosciutto Chicken Rolls

8 (4-ounce) skinned, boned chicken breast halves
¼ teaspoon pepper
1 cup mascarpone cheese
¼ cup minced fresh parsley
1 teaspoon minced garlic
¼ teaspoon salt
8 thin slices prosciutto
⅔ cup Italian-seasoned breadcrumbs
½ cup grated Parmesan cheese
¼ cup whole milk
⅓ cup margarine, melted
2 tablespoons lemon juice
⅛ teaspoon paprika

Place chicken between 2 sheets of heavy-duty plastic wrap, and flatten to ¼-inch thickness. Sprinkle chicken with pepper.

Combine mascarpone cheese and next 3 ingredients in a medium bowl; beat at medium speed of an electric mixer. Place 1 slice prosciutto on each chicken breast half; spread cheese mixture evenly over prosciutto. Roll up chicken, jellyroll fashion, starting at short end.

Combine breadcrumbs and Parmesan cheese; stir well. Dip each chicken roll in milk; dredge in breadcrumb mixture. Place in a lightly greased 13- x 9- x 2-inch baking dish. Combine melted margarine and lemon juice; drizzle over chicken rolls. Sprinkle evenly with paprika. Bake, uncovered, at 350° for 30 to 35 minutes or until lightly browned. Yield: 8 servings.

Per serving: Calories 385 (52% from fat)
Carbohydrate 9.8g Protein 35.2g Fat 22.3g (Sat. Fat 9.7g)
Cholesterol 109mg Sodium 905mg

A chicken breast becomes an elegant entrée when drizzled with a creamy Madeira sauce. In the orange sauce for the lighter recipe, evaporated skimmed milk replaces whipping cream to cut fat calories, and no-salt-added chicken broth reduces the sodium content.

BREAST OF CHICKEN WITH ORANGE SAUCE

Breast of Chicken Madeira

6	(4-ounce) skinned, boned chicken breast halves
¼	teaspoon freshly ground pepper
1	tablespoon reduced-calorie margarine, melted
	Vegetable cooking spray
1	tablespoon reduced-calorie margarine
1	tablespoon minced shallots
1	cup unsweetened orange juice
¼	cup Madeira
½	teaspoon minced garlic
1½	cups canned no-salt-added chicken broth, undiluted
¼	cup evaporated skimmed milk
⅛	teaspoon salt
⅛	teaspoon freshly ground pepper

Sprinkle chicken with ¼ teaspoon pepper, and brush with 1 tablespoon melted margarine. Place chicken on rack of a broiler pan coated with cooking spray. Bake at 375° for 16 to 18 minutes or until chicken is done. Transfer chicken to a serving platter, and keep warm.

Coat a small nonstick skillet with cooking spray; add 1 tablespoon margarine. Place over medium-high heat until margarine melts. Add shallots, and sauté 1 minute or until tender. Add orange juice, Madeira, and garlic; cook over high heat 14 minutes or until mixture is reduced to about ¼ cup. Add broth, and cook 15 minutes or until mixture is reduced to about ¾ cup. Add evaporated skimmed milk, and cook 10 minutes or until mixture turns caramel colored and is reduced to about ¼ cup. Stir in salt and ⅛ teaspoon pepper. Drizzle sauce evenly over chicken breast halves. Yield: 6 servings.

Per serving: Calories 198 (25% from fat)
Carbohydrate 7.1g Protein 27.7g Fat 5.6g (Sat. Fat 1.2g)
Cholesterol 73mg Sodium 164mg

6	(4-ounce) skinned, boned chicken breast halves
½	teaspoon salt
¼	teaspoon freshly ground pepper
¼	cup all-purpose flour
2	tablespoons margarine
2	tablespoons vegetable oil
1	cup Madeira
¼	cup unsweetened orange juice
1½	cups canned ready-to-serve chicken broth
½	cup whipping cream
⅛	teaspoon salt
⅛	teaspoon freshly ground pepper

Sprinkle chicken with ½ teaspoon salt and ¼ teaspoon pepper. Dredge chicken in flour. Combine margarine and oil in a large skillet. Place over medium-high heat until margarine melts. Add chicken, and cook 4 to 5 minutes on each side or until done. Transfer chicken to a serving platter, and keep warm.

Discard pan drippings; add Madeira and orange juice to skillet. Cook over medium-high heat 6 minutes or until mixture is reduced to about ½ cup, deglazing pan by scraping particles that cling to pan. Add broth, and cook 10 minutes or until mixture is reduced to about ¾ cup. Add cream, and cook 5 minutes or until mixture turns caramel colored and is reduced to about ¼ cup. Stir in ⅛ teaspoon salt and ⅛ teaspoon pepper. Drizzle sauce evenly over chicken breast halves. Yield: 6 servings.

Per serving: Calories 309 (51% from fat)
Carbohydrate 7.6g Protein 28.5g Fat 17.5g (Sat. Fat 6.6g)
Cholesterol 93mg Sodium 568mg

Right: *Breast of Chicken Madeira*

Instead of lightening the dumplings, we replaced them with mushrooms and onions in Chicken Fricassee.

CHICKEN FRICASSEE

1 (3-pound) broiler-fryer, cut up and skinned
½ teaspoon freshly ground black pepper
¼ teaspoon salt
1 teaspoon dried whole thyme
    Vegetable cooking spray
1 teaspoon vegetable oil
12 small boiling onions
3 cups canned no-salt-added chicken broth, undiluted and divided
1 cup Chablis or other dry white wine
1 pound small fresh mushrooms, sliced
2 teaspoons minced garlic
¼ cup all-purpose flour
1 cup nonfat sour cream alternative
¼ teaspoon ground white pepper
⅛ teaspoon salt
1 tablespoon minced parsley

Sprinkle chicken with ½ teaspoon pepper, ¼ teaspoon salt, and thyme. Coat a Dutch oven with cooking spray; add oil. Place over medium heat until hot. Add chicken and onions; cook until chicken is browned on all sides. Remove chicken, and set aside.

Add 2¾ cups chicken broth and wine to pan; bring to a boil. Cover, reduce heat and simmer 15 minutes. Return chicken to pan; cover and simmer 10 minutes.

Coat a large nonstick skillet with cooking spray; place over medium-high heat until hot. Add mushrooms, and sauté until tender. Add garlic, and sauté 1 minute.

Combine remaining ¼ cup broth and flour, stirring with a wire whisk until smooth. Gradually add to chicken mixture, stirring well. Stir in mushroom mixture, sour cream, white pepper, and ⅛ teaspoon salt. Cook over low heat 5 minutes or until thoroughly heated, stirring frequently. Sprinkle with parsley. Yield: 6 servings.

Per serving: Calories 232 (18% from fat)
Carbohydrate 16.0g Protein 28.8g Fat 4.6g (Sat. Fat 1.1g)
Cholesterol 76mg Sodium 268mg

Chicken and Dumplings

1 (3-pound) broiler-fryer, cut up
1 teaspoon dried whole thyme
1 teaspoon salt, divided
¾ teaspoon freshly ground pepper, divided
3 tablespoons vegetable oil, divided
3 cups canned ready-to-serve chicken broth
1 cup Chablis or other dry white wine
12 small boiling onions
2 teaspoons minced garlic
¼ cup margarine
¼ cup all-purpose flour
1 cup whipping cream
1⅓ cups all-purpose flour
2 teaspoons baking powder
¼ cup shortening
⅔ cup whole milk

Sprinkle chicken with thyme, ½ teaspoon salt, and ½ teaspoon pepper. Cook in 2 tablespoons hot oil in a Dutch oven over medium-high heat 8 minutes, turning to brown all sides. Stir in broth and wine; bring to a boil. Cover, reduce heat, and simmer 15 minutes. Drain chicken, reserving broth mixture. Wipe drippings from pan with a paper towel. Sauté onions in 1 tablespoon hot oil in a skillet over medium-high heat 5 minutes. Add garlic; sauté 1 minute.

Melt margarine in Dutch oven over low heat; add ¼ cup flour, stirring until smooth. Cook 1 minute, stirring constantly. Add reserved broth mixture; cook over medium heat, stirring constantly, until mixture is slightly thickened and bubbly. Stir in whipping cream. Add chicken and onion mixture to broth mixture; bring to a boil.

Combine 1⅓ cups flour, baking powder, and remaining ½ teaspoon salt and ¼ teaspoon pepper; cut in shortening with a pastry blender until mixture is crumbly. Add milk; stir with a fork until dry ingredients are moistened. Drop batter by large spoonfuls into boiling broth mixture; cover, reduce heat to medium-low, and simmer 20 minutes or until dumplings are done. Yield: 6 servings.

Per serving: Calories 837 (66% from fat)
Carbohydrate 33.7g Protein 36.9g Fat 61.3g (Sat. Fat 20.9g)
Cholesterol 174mg Sodium 1112mg

Chicken with a crisp oven-fried coating and low-fat gravy offers a satisfying alternative to fried chicken.

OVEN-FRIED CHICKEN

¼ cup fine, dry breadcrumbs
1 teaspoon paprika
½ teaspoon dried whole thyme
¼ teaspoon freshly ground pepper
1 (3-pound) broiler-fryer, skinned and
   cut up
   Vegetable cooking spray
1½ tablespoons reduced-calorie
   margarine
1 cup evaporated skimmed milk
½ cup canned no-salt-added chicken
   broth, undiluted
2 tablespoons all-purpose flour
¼ teaspoon salt
⅛ teaspoon ground white pepper

Combine first 4 ingredients in a shallow dish; stir well. Dredge chicken pieces in crumb mixture, coating each piece well. Place on a baking sheet coated with cooking spray. Bake at 375° for 45 minutes or until chicken is done.

Melt margarine in a small saucepan over medium heat. Combine milk, broth, and flour; stir until smooth. Gradually add to margarine, stirring constantly. Cook over medium heat, stirring constantly, until mixture is thickened and bubbly. Stir in salt and white pepper. Serve with chicken. Yield: 6 servings.

Per serving: Calories 208 (24% from fat)
Carbohydrate 10.4g Protein 27.4g Fat 5.6g (Sat. Fat 1.2g)
Cholesterol 78mg Sodium 289mg

Southern Fried Chicken

½ cup all-purpose flour
1 teaspoon paprika
½ teaspoon salt
½ teaspoon dried whole thyme
¼ teaspoon freshly ground pepper
1 (3-pound) broiler-fryer, cut up
   Vegetable oil
¼ cup all-purpose flour
1½ cups canned ready-to-serve chicken
   broth
⅔ cup whipping cream
¼ teaspoon salt
¼ teaspoon ground white pepper

Combine first 5 ingredients in a shallow dish; stir well. Dredge chicken pieces in flour mixture, coating each piece well.

Pour oil to depth of 1 inch into a large heavy skillet; heat to 350°. Fry chicken over medium heat 20 to 25 minutes or until golden, turning to brown all sides. Drain well on paper towels.

Pour off all but ¼ cup drippings from skillet; place skillet over medium heat. Add ¼ cup flour, and cook over medium-high heat, stirring constantly, 6 minutes or until browned. Gradually add broth and cream; cook, stirring constantly, until thickened and bubbly. Stir in ¼ teaspoon salt and white pepper. Serve with chicken. Yield: 6 servings.

Per serving: Calories 652 (72% from fat)
Carbohydrate 13.3g Protein 32.1g Fat 51.8g (Sat. Fat 16.2g)
Cholesterol 152mg Sodium 605mg

In Honey Barbecued Chicken Breasts, using skinned breasts in place of chicken pieces saves fat calories. And barbecuing with a mixture of reduced-calorie catsup and low-sodium Worcestershire sauce doesn't sacrifice flavor but greatly reduces sodium content.

HONEY BARBECUED CHICKEN BREASTS

1 cup reduced-calorie catsup
3 tablespoons lemon juice
2 tablespoons low-sodium
   Worcestershire sauce
2 tablespoons honey
1 tablespoon peeled, minced gingerroot
1 teaspoon minced garlic
   Vegetable cooking spray
6 (6-ounce) skinned chicken breast
   halves

Combine first 6 ingredients in a saucepan. Bring to a boil, stirring frequently; reduce heat, and simmer 2 minutes. Remove from heat, and set aside.

Coat grill rack with cooking spray; place on grill over medium-hot coals (350° to 400°). Place chicken on rack; grill, covered, 5 minutes, turning frequently. Brush chicken with catsup mixture. Grill an additional 12 minutes or until done, turning and basting frequently with remaining catsup mixture. Transfer to a large serving platter. Yield: 6 servings.

Per serving: Calories 190 (15% from fat)
Carbohydrate 11.2g Protein 26.5g Fat 3.1g (Sat. Fat 0.9g)
Cholesterol 72mg Sodium 92mg

Honey Barbecued Chicken

1 cup catsup
3 tablespoons lemon juice
3 tablespoons butter
2 tablespoons Worcestershire
   sauce
2 tablespoons honey
1 tablespoon peeled, minced gingerroot
1 teaspoon minced garlic
   Vegetable cooking spray
1 (3-pound) broiler-fryer, cut up

Combine first 7 ingredients in a saucepan. Bring to a boil, stirring frequently; reduce heat, and simmer 2 minutes. Remove from heat, and set aside.

Coat grill rack with cooking spray; place on grill over medium-hot coals (350° to 400°). Place chicken on rack; grill, covered, 10 minutes, turning frequently. Brush chicken with catsup mixture. Grill an additional 10 minutes or until done, turning and basting frequently with remaining catsup mixture. Transfer to a large serving platter. Yield: 6 servings.

Per serving: Calories 369 (48% from fat)
Carbohydrate 19.4g Protein 28.4g Fat 19.7g (Sat. Fat 7.4g)
Cholesterol 104mg Sodium 665mg

Left: *Honey Barbecued Chicken Breast and Nutty Pineapple Slaw (page 143)*

In the lighter recipe, Cornish hens are skinned and basted with a tangy honey-lemon mixture. Glazed Cornish Hens glisten with a red currant jelly sauce.

Honey Lemon Cornish Hens

3 (1-pound) Cornish hens, skinned
¼ teaspoon freshly ground pepper
  Vegetable cooking spray
½ cup honey
⅓ cup lemon juice
¼ cup low-sodium soy sauce
1 tablespoon margarine
  Wild rice (optional)
  Fresh herbs (optional)

Remove giblets from hens; reserve for another use. Rinse hens under cold running water, and pat dry. Split each hen in half lengthwise, using an electric knife. Sprinkle evenly with pepper. Place hens, cut side down, on rack of a broiler pan coated with cooking spray.

Combine honey and next 3 ingredients in a small saucepan. Bring to a boil; reduce heat, and simmer 5 minutes.

Brush hens with half of honey mixture. Bake at 350° for 20 minutes. Brush with additional honey mixture, and bake an additional 30 to 35 minutes or until hens are done, basting frequently with remaining honey mixture. Transfer hens to a serving platter. If desired, serve with wild rice and garnish with fresh herbs. Yield: 6 servings.

Per serving: Calories 267 (27% from fat)
Carbohydrate 24.5g Protein 23.8g Fat 8.1g (Sat. Fat 2.0g)
Cholesterol 73mg Sodium 353mg

Glazed Cornish Hens

3 (1-pound) Cornish hens
  Vegetable cooking spray
¼ cup plus 2 tablespoons red currant jelly
2½ tablespoons Madeira
¼ teaspoon grated orange rind
1 tablespoon unsweetened orange juice
2 teaspoons lemon juice
1½ teaspoons water
1 teaspoon cornstarch
½ teaspoon dry mustard
½ teaspoon salt
  Dash of ground red pepper
½ teaspoon salt
¼ teaspoon freshly ground black pepper
2 tablespoons margarine, melted
  Wild rice (optional)
  Fresh herbs (optional)

Remove giblets from hens; reserve for another use. Rinse hens under cold running water, and pat dry. Split each hen in half lengthwise, using an electric knife. Place hens, cut side down, on rack of a broiler pan coated with cooking spray.

Combine jelly and next 9 ingredients in a small saucepan; stir well. Bring to a boil, stirring constantly. Cook, stirring constantly, 1 minute. Remove from heat, and set aside.

Sprinkle hens with ½ teaspoon salt and black pepper. Brush with melted margarine. Bake, uncovered, at 350° for 20 minutes. Brush hens with half of jelly mixture. Bake an additional 45 to 50 minutes or until done, basting frequently with remaining jelly mixture. Transfer hens to a serving platter. If desired, serve with wild rice and garnish with fresh herbs. Yield: 6 servings.

Per serving: Calories 331 (48% from fat)
Carbohydrate 14.5g Protein 27.4g Fat 17.6g (Sat. Fat 4.5g)
Cholesterol 88mg Sodium 525mg

Top the light turkey cutlets with a reduced amount of part-skim mozzarella cheese and a zesty tomato sauce. Add a mellow flavor to Turkey Prosciutto Scallopini with fontina cheese.

TURKEY CUTLETS ITALIANO

Vegetable cooking spray
2 teaspoons reduced-calorie margarine
1 pound turkey breast cutlets
1/4 cup canned no-salt-added chicken broth, undiluted
1/2 cup chopped onion
1/3 cup chopped green pepper
1/4 cup sliced celery
1 (8-ounce) can no-salt-added tomato sauce
1/4 cup no-salt-added tomato paste
1/8 teaspoon salt
1/8 teaspoon pepper
1/8 teaspoon dried whole oregano
1/8 teaspoon dried whole basil
3 ounces part-skim mozzarella cheese, thinly sliced

Coat a large nonstick skillet with cooking spray; add margarine, and place over medium-high heat until margarine melts. Add cutlets, and cook 2 to 3 minutes on each side or until lightly browned. Remove from skillet, and place in an 11- x 7- x 1½-inch baking dish coated with cooking spray. Wipe drippings from skillet with a paper towel.

Add chicken broth, onion, green pepper, and celery to skillet. Cover, reduce heat, and simmer 10 minutes or until vegetables are tender. Stir in tomato sauce and next 5 ingredients; bring to a boil. Reduce heat, and simmer, uncovered, 10 minutes.

Spoon sauce over cutlets; cover and bake at 325° for 30 to 40 minutes or until cutlets are tender. Arrange cheese slices on cutlets, and bake an additional 5 minutes or until cheese melts. Yield: 4 servings.

Per serving: Calories 242 (28% from fat)
Carbohydrate 10.3g Protein 31.9g Fat 7.6g (Sat. Fat 3.2g)
Cholesterol 71mg Sodium 268mg

Turkey Prosciutto Scallopini

4 (4-ounce) boneless turkey breast slices
1/4 teaspoon salt
1/8 teaspoon freshly ground pepper
1/8 teaspoon dried whole thyme
1/4 cup all-purpose flour
1½ tablespoons margarine, melted
1 tablespoon vegetable oil
4 thin slices prosciutto
1 cup (4 ounces) grated fontina cheese
1 tablespoon grated Parmesan cheese
1/4 cup canned ready-to-serve chicken broth

Place turkey between 2 sheets of heavy-duty plastic wrap, and flatten to 1/4-inch thickness, using a meat mallet or rolling pin. Sprinkle turkey with salt, pepper, and thyme. Dredge in flour.

Cook turkey breast slices in margarine and hot oil in a large skillet over medium heat 2 to 3 minutes on each side or until tender. Transfer turkey to a greased 13- x 9- x 2-inch baking dish. Place 1 slice of prosciutto on each turkey slice. Sprinkle evenly with cheeses. Pour broth into dish. Bake, uncovered, at 350° for 15 minutes or until bubbly. Serve immediately. Yield: 4 servings.

Per serving: Calories 376 (52% from fat)
Carbohydrate 6.6g Protein 36.6g Fat 21.7g (Sat. Fat 8.6g)
Cholesterol 99mg Sodium 567mg

Bake both turkeys with the skin on to keep them moist, but serve the light slices without skin.

LIGHT TURKEY WITH LEEK ONION STUFFING

Vegetable cooking spray
1 tablespoon reduced-calorie margarine
4 cups coarsely chopped leeks
1 cup chopped onion
1 teaspoon dried whole thyme
1¾ cups canned no-salt-added chicken broth, undiluted and divided
2 (6-ounce) packages plain croutons
⅓ cup chopped fresh parsley
1 tablespoon grated orange rind
½ teaspoon freshly ground pepper
1 (10-pound) turkey
1 tablespoon reduced-calorie margarine, melted

Coat a nonstick skillet with cooking spray; add 1 tablespoon margarine. Place over medium heat until margarine melts. Add leeks, onion, thyme, and ½ cup broth. Bring to a boil. Cover, reduce heat, and simmer until vegetables are tender. Uncover and cook over high heat until liquid evaporates. Transfer leek mixture to a bowl; add croutons and next 3 ingredients. Add 1¼ cups broth; cover and chill.

Remove giblets and neck from turkey. Rinse turkey under cold water; pat dry. Pack about 7 cups leek mixture into cavity of turkey. Tuck legs under flap of skin around tail, or close cavity with skewers, and truss. Tie ends of legs to tail with cord. Lift wingtips up and over back; tuck under turkey.

Coat turkey with cooking spray; place, breast side up, on a rack in a roasting pan coated with cooking spray. Insert meat thermometer in meaty part of thigh. Cover with heavy-duty aluminum foil; bake at 325° for 2 hours. Uncover and baste with melted margarine. Bake 2 hours or until meat thermometer registers 180°.

Spoon remaining leek mixture into a 1-quart casserole coated with cooking spray. Bake at 325° for 25 minutes. Serve with skinned turkey slices. Yield: 20 servings.

Per serving: Calories 282 (26% from fat)
Carbohydrate 14.8g Protein 34.3g Fat 8.2g (Sat. Fat 2.2g)
Cholesterol 92mg Sodium 273mg

Turkey with Leek Nut Stuffing

4 cups coarsely chopped leeks
1 cup chopped onion
1 teaspoon dried whole thyme
¾ cup unsalted butter, melted and divided
½ cup chopped hazelnuts, toasted
2 (6-ounce) packages plain croutons
⅓ cup chopped fresh parsley
1 tablespoon grated orange rind
1 teaspoon salt
½ teaspoon freshly ground pepper
1⅓ cups canned ready-to-serve chicken broth
1 (10-pound) turkey
Vegetable cooking spray
Fresh fruit (optional)
Fresh thyme (optional)

Sauté leeks, onion, and thyme in ½ cup butter in a large skillet until tender. Transfer leek mixture to a bowl; add hazelnuts and next 6 ingredients. Cover and chill.

Remove giblets and neck from turkey. Rinse turkey under cold water; pat dry. Pack about 7 cups leek mixture into cavity of turkey. Tuck legs under flap of skin around tail, or close cavity with skewers, and truss. Tie ends of legs to tail with cord. Lift wing tips up and over back; tuck under turkey.

Brush turkey with 2 tablespoons butter, and place, breast side up, on a rack in a roasting pan. Insert meat thermometer in meaty part of thigh. Cover with heavy-duty aluminum foil, and bake at 325° for 2 hours. Uncover and baste with remaining 2 tablespoons butter. Bake 2 hours or until meat thermometer registers 180°.

Spoon remaining leek mixture into a 1-quart casserole coated with cooking spray. Bake at 325° for 25 minutes. Serve with turkey. If desired, garnish with fresh fruit and thyme. Yield: 20 servings.

Per serving: Calories 447 (49% from fat)
Carbohydrate 15.1g Protein 39.2g Fat 24.3g (Sat. Fat 8.8g)
Cholesterol 249mg Sodium 448mg

Right: *Turkey with Leek Nut Stuffing*

Top the poached amberjack fillets in the light recipe with an oil-free tomato-fennel sauce. Serve the luscious fried fillets with a hearty Provençal sauce.

AMBERJACK WITH TOMATO-FENNEL SAUCE

Vegetable cooking spray
1 cup canned no-salt-added chicken broth, undiluted
½ cup chopped onion
½ cup chopped fennel bulb
1 teaspoon minced garlic
¼ teaspoon crushed dried fennel seeds
1 (14½-ounce) can no-salt-added stewed tomatoes
1 (8-ounce) can no-salt-added tomato sauce
¼ cup chopped fresh parsley, divided
½ teaspoon sugar
½ teaspoon freshly ground pepper, divided
¼ teaspoon salt
6 (4-ounce) amberjack fillets
4 cups water

Coat a large nonstick skillet with cooking spray; add chicken broth. Place over medium-high heat until hot. Add onion and next 3 ingredients; cook until vegetables are tender and liquid evaporates. Stir in stewed tomatoes and tomato sauce. Cook, uncovered, over low heat 30 minutes or until thickened. Stir in 2 tablespoons parsley, sugar, ¼ teaspoon pepper, and salt.

Rinse fillets and pat dry; sprinkle with remaining ¼ teaspoon pepper. Bring water to a boil in a large nonstick skillet over medium heat. Reduce heat, and add fillets; cover and simmer 8 minutes or until fish flakes easily when tested with a fork. Remove fish from liquid, and place on a serving platter; discard liquid. Spoon tomato mixture evenly over fillets; sprinkle with remaining 2 tablespoons parsley. Yield: 6 servings.

Per serving: Calories 169 (13% from fat)
Carbohydrate 10.2g Protein 25.8g Fat 2.5g (Sat. Fat 0.5g)
Cholesterol 49mg Sodium 163mg

Amberjack with Provençal Sauce

1 cup chopped onion
1 teaspoon minced garlic
½ teaspoon dried whole thyme
½ bay leaf
2 tablespoons margarine, melted
1 (16-ounce) can crushed tomatoes, undrained
1 (8-ounce) can tomato sauce
¼ cup chopped fresh parsley, divided
¾ teaspoon salt, divided
½ teaspoon sugar
½ teaspoon freshly ground pepper, divided
6 (4-ounce) amberjack fillets
3 tablespoons all-purpose flour
2 tablespoons vegetable oil
Fresh thyme sprigs (optional)
Fresh green beans (optional)

Sauté first 4 ingredients in margarine in a skillet over medium-high heat until tender. Stir in crushed tomatoes and tomato sauce. Cook, uncovered, over low heat 30 minutes or until thickened. Remove and discard bay leaf. Stir in 2 tablespoons parsley, ¼ teaspoon salt, sugar, and ¼ teaspoon pepper.

Rinse fillets and pat dry; sprinkle with remaining ½ teaspoon salt and ¼ teaspoon pepper. Dredge fillets in flour. Cook fillets in hot oil in a large nonstick skillet over medium-high heat 2 to 3 minutes on each side or until fish flakes easily when tested with a fork. Transfer to a serving platter. Spoon sauce evenly over fillets; sprinkle with remaining 2 tablespoons parsley. If desired, garnish with fresh thyme and serve with green beans. Yield: 6 servings.

Per serving: Calories 249 (37% from fat)
Carbohydrate 11.7g Protein 26.1g Fat 11.0g (Sat. Fat 2.1g)
Cholesterol 49mg Sodium 708mg

Right: *Amberjack with Provençal Sauce*

The light champagne sauce depends on skim milk instead of butter, whipping cream, and eggs.

FLOUNDER WITH LIGHT CHAMPAGNE SAUCE

1 tablespoon reduced-calorie margarine
2 tablespoons minced shallots
1 teaspoon minced garlic
1 pound fresh mushrooms, sliced
1½ pounds flounder fillets
   Vegetable cooking spray
½ teaspoon salt, divided
½ teaspoon ground white pepper, divided
1½ cups champagne
1 tablespoon lemon juice
¼ cup plus 2 tablespoons all-purpose flour
1 cup skim milk, divided
½ cup (2 ounces) shredded reduced-fat Swiss cheese
¼ cup freshly grated Parmesan cheese

Heat margarine in a nonstick skillet over medium-high heat until margarine melts. Add shallots and garlic; sauté until tender. Add mushrooms; sauté until liquid evaporates. Arrange fillets in an 11- x 7- x 1½-inch baking dish coated with cooking spray. Sprinkle with ¼ teaspoon salt and ¼ teaspoon pepper. Pour champagne and lemon juice over fillets. Cover and bake at 400° for 10 minutes. Drain, reserving liquid. Strain liquid through cheesecloth. Cook strained liquid in a saucepan over high heat until liquid is reduced to 1 cup.

Combine flour and ½ cup milk in a bowl, stirring with a wire whisk until smooth. Add remaining ½ cup milk to reduced liquid, stirring constantly; bring to a boil. Add flour mixture, stirring constantly with a wire whisk. Bring to a boil, stirring constantly. Stir in remaining ¼ teaspoon salt and ¼ teaspoon pepper.

Spoon mushroom mixture over fillets; top with sauce, and sprinkle with cheeses. Bake, uncovered, at 375° for 15 minutes or until thoroughly heated. Broil 5½ inches from heat (with electric oven door partially opened) 2 minutes or until lightly browned. Serve immediately. Yield: 6 servings.

Per serving: Calories 229 (24% from fat)
Carbohydrate 13.3g Protein 30.2g Fat 6.0g (Sat. Fat 2.3g)
Cholesterol 64mg Sodium 425mg

Flounder with Champagne Sauce

2 tablespoons minced shallots
1 teaspoon minced garlic
2 tablespoons butter, melted
1 pound fresh mushrooms, sliced
1 teaspoon salt, divided
¼ teaspoon freshly ground black pepper
1½ pounds flounder fillets
½ teaspoon ground white pepper, divided
1½ cups champagne
2 tablespoons lemon juice
¼ cup butter
¼ cup all-purpose flour
1 cup whipping cream
2 egg yolks, lightly beaten
1 cup (4 ounces) shredded Gruyère cheese

Sauté shallots and garlic in butter in a skillet over medium-high heat until tender. Add mushrooms; sauté until liquid evaporates. Stir in ¼ teaspoon salt and black pepper. Arrange fillets in a greased 11- x 7- x 1½-inch baking dish. Sprinkle with ½ teaspoon salt and ¼ teaspoon white pepper. Pour champagne and lemon juice over fillets. Cover and bake at 400° for 10 minutes. Drain, reserving liquid. Strain liquid through cheesecloth. Cook strained liquid in a saucepan over high heat until liquid is reduced to 1 cup.

Melt ¼ cup butter in a heavy saucepan over low heat; add flour, stirring until smooth. Cook 1 minute, stirring constantly. Add whipping cream; cook over medium heat, stirring constantly, until mixture is thickened and bubbly. Stir in remaining ¼ teaspoon salt and ¼ teaspoon white pepper. Stir about one-fourth hot mixture into egg yolks; add to remaining hot mixture, stirring constantly.

Spoon mushroom mixture over fillets; top with sauce, and sprinkle with cheese. Bake, uncovered, at 375° for 15 minutes or until thoroughly heated. Broil 5½ inches from heat (with electric oven door partially opened) 2 minutes or until lightly browned. Serve immediately. Yield: 6 servings.

Per serving: Calories 493 (67% from fat)
Carbohydrate 10.6g Protein 31.2g Fat 36.7g (Sat. Fat 21.4g)
Cholesterol 236mg Sodium 699mg

The light fillets are poached and served with a lemon sauce; the luscious ones are pan-fried in butter.

POACHED LEMON GROUPER

3   (8-ounce) grouper fillets, halved
1   teaspoon dried whole tarragon, crumbled
¼   teaspoon freshly ground pepper
⅛   teaspoon salt
4   cups water
1   teaspoon extra-virgin olive oil
½   teaspoon minced garlic
¼   cup Madeira
2   tablespoons fresh lemon juice
¼   cup capers
2   tablespoons minced fresh parsley

Sprinkle fillets with tarragon, pepper, and salt. Bring 4 cups water to a boil in a large nonstick skillet over medium heat. Reduce heat, and add fillets; cover, and simmer 8 to 10 minutes or until fish flakes easily when tested with a fork. Remove fish from liquid, and place on a serving platter; discard liquid. Set fish aside, and keep warm.

Heat olive oil in a nonstick skillet over medium-high heat until hot. Add garlic; sauté 1 minute or until tender. Add Madeira; cook 1 minute or until reduced to 2 tablespoons. Stir in lemon juice and capers; cook until thoroughly heated. Pour sauce over fish, and sprinkle with parsley. Yield: 6 servings.

Per serving: Calories 118 (14% from fat)
Carbohydrate 1.5g Protein 22.4g Fat 1.9g (Sat. Fat 0.4g)
Cholesterol 42mg Sodium 544mg

Pan-Fried Grouper Meunière

3   (8-ounce) grouper fillets, halved
1   teaspoon dried whole tarragon, crumbled
½   teaspoon salt
¼   teaspoon freshly ground pepper
¼   cup all-purpose flour
3   tablespoons butter, melted
2   tablespoons vegetable oil
¼   cup Madeira
3   tablespoons lemon juice
¼   cup capers
2   tablespoons minced fresh parsley

Sprinkle fillets with tarragon, salt, and pepper; dredge lightly in flour.

Cook fish in butter and hot oil in a large skillet over medium heat 7 to 8 minutes on each side or until fish flakes easily when tested with a fork. Remove fish from skillet, and place on a serving platter. Set aside, and keep warm.

Drain drippings from skillet, reserving 2 tablespoons in skillet. Add Madeira; cook over medium heat 4 minutes or until reduced to 2 tablespoons, deglazing skillet by scraping particles that cling to pan. Stir in lemon juice and capers; cook until thoroughly heated. Pour sauce over fish, and sprinkle with parsley. Yield: 6 servings.

Per serving: Calories 163 (30% from fat)
Carbohydrate 4.7g Protein 22.8g Fat 5.4g (Sat. Fat 1.9g)
Cholesterol 47mg Sodium 724mg

A fat-free tomato and chive sauce accentuates the succulent flavor of salmon fillets in the light recipe. In the luscious version, a tangy tomato cream sauce adds richness to the buttery fillets.

FILLETS OF SALMON WITH TOMATO AND CHIVES

6 (4-ounce) salmon fillets
¼ teaspoon salt
¼ teaspoon freshly ground pepper
4 cups water
    Olive oil-flavored vegetable cooking spray
1 tablespoon minced shallots
½ teaspoon minced garlic
¼ cup Chablis or other dry white wine
1 cup seeded, diced tomato
2 tablespoons chopped fresh chives
2 tablespoons fresh lemon juice
¼ teaspoon salt
⅛ teaspoon ground white pepper
    Fresh chives (optional)

Sprinkle fillets with ¼ teaspoon salt and ¼ teaspoon pepper. Bring 4 cups of water just to a boil in a large nonstick skillet over medium heat. Reduce heat, and add fillets; cover and simmer 4 to 5 minutes or until fish flakes easily when tested with a fork. Remove fillets from skillet, using a slotted spatula, and place on a serving platter. Set aside; keep warm.

Coat a small nonstick skillet with cooking spray; place over medium-high heat until hot. Add shallots and garlic; sauté 1 minute. Add wine, and cook until reduced by half. Stir in tomato, 2 tablespoons chives, lemon juice, ¼ teaspoon salt, and white pepper. Spoon sauce evenly over salmon fillets, and serve immediately. Garnish with fresh chives, if desired. Yield: 6 servings.

Per serving: Calories 177 (36% from fat)
Carbohydrate 2.4g Protein 24.9g Fat 7.0g (Sat. Fat 1.3g)
Cholesterol 44mg Sodium 251mg

Fillets of Salmon with Tomato Cream

6 (4-ounce) salmon fillets
½ teaspoon salt
¼ teaspoon freshly ground pepper
3 tablespoons all-purpose flour
¼ cup plus 2 tablespoons butter, divided
2 tablespoons vegetable oil
¼ cup Chablis or other dry white wine
½ cup whipping cream
1 tablespoon tomato paste
½ cup seeded, diced tomato
2 tablespoons chopped fresh chives
¼ teaspoon salt
⅛ teaspoon ground white pepper
    Fresh chives (optional)

Sprinkle fillets with ½ teaspoon salt and ¼ teaspoon pepper; dredge fillets in flour.

Cook fillets in 3 tablespoons butter and hot oil in a large skillet over medium-high heat 2 to 3 minutes on each side or until fish flakes easily when tested with a fork. Remove fillets from skillet, and place on a serving platter. Set aside; keep warm.

Drain fat from skillet. Add wine; bring to a boil. Reduce heat, and simmer until reduced by half. Add whipping cream and tomato paste; cook, stirring constantly, until slightly thickened. Reduce heat, and add remaining 3 tablespoons butter, stirring until butter melts.

Add tomato and next 3 ingredients; stir well. Spoon sauce evenly over salmon fillets, and serve immediately. Garnish with fresh chives, if desired. Yield: 6 servings.

Per serving: Calories 351 (64% from fat)
Carbohydrate 5.0g Protein 25.7g Fat 25.1g (Sat. Fat 11.6g)
Cholesterol 95mg Sodium 445mg

Left: *Fillet of Salmon with Tomato and Chives*

Doubling up on vegetables, the lighter gratin substitutes evaporated skimmed milk for cream.

SNAPPER-VEGETABLE GRATIN

1 pound red snapper fillets
½ teaspoon freshly ground black pepper, divided
  Vegetable cooking spray
½ cup Chablis or other dry white wine
½ cup water
1½ tablespoons lemon juice, divided
6 cups sliced fresh mushrooms
2 small zucchini, thinly sliced
1 large sweet red pepper, chopped
¼ teaspoon salt
½ cup minced celery
2 tablespoons minced green onions
¼ teaspoon crushed red pepper
1 cup evaporated skimmed milk, divided
¼ cup all-purpose flour
½ cup minced fresh parsley
½ cup (2 ounces) shredded Cheddar cheese

Rinse fillets, and pat dry; sprinkle with ¼ teaspoon black pepper. Place in a 13- x 9- x 2-inch baking dish coated with cooking spray. Combine wine and water; pour over fillets. Bake, uncovered, at 400° for 12 minutes. Drain, pouring liquid into a glass measure; let solids settle. Reserve ¾ cup clear liquid.

Coat a nonstick skillet with cooking spray; add ¼ cup of the reserved liquid and 1 tablespoon lemon juice. Place over medium-high heat until hot. Add mushrooms; sauté 3 minutes. Add zucchini and sweet red pepper; sauté 3 minutes. Stir in salt and remaining ¼ teaspoon black pepper. Spoon over fillets.

Combine ¼ cup reserved liquid, celery, green onions, and crushed red pepper in a saucepan. Bring to a boil; reduce heat, and simmer until vegetables are tender. Combine ¼ cup milk and flour, stirring until smooth. Stir in remaining ¾ cup milk and ¼ cup reserved liquid; stir into celery mixture. Cook, stirring constantly, 2 minutes or until slightly thickened. Remove from heat; stir in parsley and remaining ½ tablespoon lemon juice. Spoon over vegetables and fillets; sprinkle with cheese. Bake at 400° for 15 minutes. Yield: 4 servings.

Per serving: Calories 298 (17% from fat)
Carbohydrate 26.1g Protein 37.1g Fat 5.5g (Sat. Fat 2.1g)
Cholesterol 54mg Sodium 425mg

Snapper Gratin Supreme

1 pound red snapper fillets
1 teaspoon salt, divided
¼ teaspoon freshly ground pepper
½ cup Chablis or other dry white wine
½ cup water
6 cups sliced fresh mushrooms
½ cup margarine, melted and divided
1½ tablespoons fresh lemon juice, divided
⅛ teaspoon freshly ground pepper
½ cup minced celery
2 tablespoons minced green onions
¼ teaspoon crushed red pepper
¼ cup all-purpose flour
¾ cup whipping cream
½ cup minced fresh parsley
⅛ teaspoon ground white pepper
¼ cup freshly grated Parmesan cheese
½ cup (2 ounces) shredded Cheddar cheese
½ cup soft breadcrumbs

Rinse fillets, and pat dry; sprinkle with ½ teaspoon salt and ¼ teaspoon pepper. Place in a greased 13- x 9- x 2-inch baking dish. Combine wine and water; pour over fillets. Bake, uncovered, at 400° for 12 minutes. Drain, pouring liquid into a glass measure; let solids settle. Reserve ½ cup clear liquid.

Sauté mushrooms in 2 tablespoons margarine and 1 tablespoon lemon juice 3 minutes or until tender. Stir in ¼ teaspoon salt and ⅛ teaspoon pepper. Spoon over fillets.

Sauté celery, green onions, and crushed red pepper in ¼ cup margarine in a saucepan over medium-high heat until tender. Add flour, stirring until smooth. Cook 1 minute, stirring constantly. Add whipping cream and ½ cup reserved liquid; cook over medium heat, stirring constantly, 1 minute or until thickened. Remove from heat; stir in parsley, white pepper, ½ tablespoon lemon juice, and ¼ teaspoon salt. Spoon over vegetables and fillets; sprinkle with cheeses. Combine 2 tablespoons margarine and breadcrumbs; sprinkle over casserole. Bake at 400° for 15 minutes. Yield: 4 servings.

Per serving: Calories 647 (67% from fat)
Carbohydrate 15.9g Protein 34.1g Fat 48.4g (Sat. Fat 19.4g)
Cholesterol 123mg Sodium 1181mg

Both recipes pair sole with spinach and cheese. The light fillets are poached instead of sautéed in butter.

POACHED SOLE FLORENTINE

4 cups water
2 tablespoons white wine vinegar
1½ pounds sole fillets
   Vegetable cooking spray
1 tablespoon reduced-calorie margarine
1 (10-ounce) package frozen chopped
   spinach, thawed and drained
¼ cup plus 1 tablespoon all-purpose flour
¾ cup canned no-salt-added chicken
   broth, undiluted and divided
¾ cup skim milk
½ cup (2 ounces) shredded reduced-fat
   Swiss cheese, divided
½ cup nonfat sour cream alternative
2 tablespoons lemon juice
1 teaspoon minced garlic, divided
⅛ teaspoon salt
¼ teaspoon ground white pepper
¼ cup fine, dry breadcrumbs
1 tablespoon grated Parmesan cheese
2 tablespoons minced fresh parsley
1 tablespoon reduced-calorie margarine,
   melted

Bring water and vinegar to a boil in a Dutch oven. Reduce heat; add fillets. Cover and simmer 1 minute or until opaque. Remove from liquid; discard liquid.

Coat a nonstick skillet with cooking spray; add 1 tablespoon margarine. Place over medium-high heat until margarine melts. Add spinach; sauté 1 minute.

Stir flour into ½ cup broth. Bring remaining ¼ cup broth and milk to a boil. Add flour mixture; cook, stirring constantly, until thickened. Add ¼ cup Swiss cheese, sour cream, lemon juice, ½ teaspoon garlic, salt, and pepper. Stir ½ cup cheese sauce into spinach mixture. Spread in an 11- x 7- x 1½-inch baking dish coated with cooking spray. Arrange fillets over spinach; pour remaining cheese sauce over fillets. Combine remaining ¼ cup Swiss cheese and ½ teaspoon garlic, breadcrumbs, and remaining ingredients. Sprinkle over casserole. Bake at 375° for 15 minutes. Yield: 6 servings.

Per serving: Calories 244 (24% from fat)
Carbohydrate 14.3g Protein 30.7g Fat 6.4g (Sat. Fat 1.9g)
Cholesterol 69mg Sodium 312mg

Sautéed Sole Florentine

1½ pounds sole fillets
½ teaspoon salt, divided
½ teaspoon ground white pepper, divided
½ cup all-purpose flour, divided
1 teaspoon paprika
¼ cup plus 2 tablespoons butter, melted
   and divided
1 (10-ounce) package frozen chopped
   spinach, thawed and drained
¼ cup butter
2 cups half-and-half
1 cup (4 ounces) shredded Swiss cheese,
   divided
1 tablespoon lemon juice
¼ cup fine, dry breadcrumbs
2 tablespoons grated Parmesan cheese
2 tablespoons minced fresh parsley

Rinse fillets, and pat dry; sprinkle with ¼ teaspoon salt and ¼ teaspoon pepper. Combine 3 tablespoons flour and paprika; dredge fillets in flour mixture.

Sauté one-third of fillets in 1 tablespoon butter in a skillet over medium heat 1 minute on each side or until opaque. Remove from skillet. Repeat procedure with remaining fillets and 2 tablespoons butter.

Sauté spinach in 2 tablespoons butter in a skillet over medium heat 1 minute.

Melt ¼ cup butter in a heavy saucepan over medium heat; add remaining ¼ cup plus 1 tablespoon flour. Cook 1 minute, stirring constantly with a wire whisk. Add half-and-half. Cook, stirring constantly, until thickened. Add ½ cup Swiss cheese, lemon juice, and remaining ¼ teaspoon salt and ¼ teaspoon pepper. Stir ¾ cup cheese sauce into spinach mixture. Spread in a greased 11- x 7- x 1½-inch baking dish. Arrange fillets over spinach; pour remaining sauce over fillets.

Combine remaining ½ cup Swiss cheese, breadcrumbs, Parmesan cheese, parsley, and remaining 1 tablespoon melted butter. Sprinkle over casserole. Bake at 375° for 15 minutes. Yield: 6 servings.

Per serving: Calories 527 (61% from fat)
Carbohydrate 18.0g Protein 33.6g Fat 35.9g (Sat. Fat 21.7g)
Cholesterol 162mg Sodium 661mg

Tuna steaks make a perfect choice for grilling. An oil-free marinade with soy sauce and gingerroot lends low-fat Oriental flavor. Cilantro butter provides the crowning touch on the luscious steaks.

ORIENTAL GRILLED TUNA

6 (4-ounce) tuna steaks (¾ inch thick)
½ cup low-sodium soy sauce
½ cup water
¼ cup firmly packed brown sugar
2 tablespoons lemon juice
2 tablespoons peeled, minced gingerroot
2 tablespoons minced green onions
1 tablespoon grated lemon rind
2 teaspoons minced garlic
¼ teaspoon crushed red pepper
   Vegetable cooking spray
   Green onion curls (optional)

Place tuna steaks in a shallow dish. Combine soy sauce and next 8 ingredients in a medium bowl; pour over tuna steaks. Cover and marinate in refrigerator 30 minutes, turning once.

Remove tuna steaks from marinade, reserving marinade. Coat grill rack with cooking spray; place on grill over medium-hot coals (350° to 400°). Place tuna on rack; grill, covered, 4 to 6 minutes on each side or until fish flakes easily when tested with a fork, basting occasionally with reserved marinade. Transfer tuna to serving plates. Garnish with green onion curls, if desired. Yield: 6 servings.

Per serving: Calories 179 (30% from fat)
Carbohydrate 2.6g Protein 26.9g Fat 5.9g (Sat. Fat 1.5g)
Cholesterol 44mg Sodium 176mg

Grilled Tuna with Cilantro Butter

¼ cup plus 2 tablespoons butter, softened
¼ cup fresh cilantro leaves, loosely packed
2 tablespoons plus 2 teaspoons peeled, minced gingerroot, divided
1 teaspoon minced garlic
6 (4-ounce) tuna steaks (¾ inch thick)
½ cup firmly packed brown sugar
½ cup soy sauce
½ cup water
¼ cup dark sesame oil
2 tablespoons minced green onions
2 teaspoons minced garlic
¼ teaspoon crushed red pepper
   Fresh cilantro sprigs (optional)

Position knife blade in food processor bowl; add butter, ¼ cup cilantro, 2 teaspoons gingerroot, and garlic. Process until smooth. Shape mixture into a log. Wrap in wax paper, and chill until firm.

Place tuna steaks in a shallow dish. Combine remaining 2 tablespoons gingerroot, brown sugar, and next 6 ingredients in a medium bowl; pour over tuna steaks. Cover and marinate in refrigerator 30 minutes, turning once.

Remove tuna steaks from marinade, reserving marinade. Place grill rack on grill over medium-hot coals (350° to 400°). Place tuna on rack; grill, covered, 4 to 6 minutes on each side or until fish flakes easily when tested with a fork, basting occasionally with reserved marinade. Transfer tuna to serving plates.

Divide chilled butter mixture into 6 pieces; place 1 piece of butter mixture on each tuna steak. Garnish with fresh cilantro sprigs, if desired. Yield: 6 servings.

Per serving: Calories 310 (57% from fat)
Carbohydrate 5.5g Protein 27.4g Fat 19.5g (Sat. Fat 8.9g)
Cholesterol 75mg Sodium 442mg

Right: *Grilled Tuna with Cilantro Butter*

Enhance the flavor of clams with either a low-fat white sauce or a rich butter sauce.

CLAMS IN LEMON WHITE SAUCE

4   pounds littleneck clams
3   tablespoons cornmeal
1   cup chopped onion
2   tablespoons chopped shallots
1½ cups Chablis or other dry white wine
2   tablespoons reduced-calorie margarine
2   tablespoons all-purpose flour
1   cup 1% low-fat milk
2   teaspoons grated lemon rind
¼   cup fresh lemon juice
2   cloves garlic, minced
2   tablespoons minced fresh parsley
2   tablespoons minced green onions
¼   teaspoon salt
¼   teaspoon ground white pepper

Scrub clams thoroughly, discarding any that are cracked or open. Place clams in a large bowl; cover with cold water, and sprinkle with cornmeal. Let stand 30 minutes. Drain and rinse clams; set aside. Discard cornmeal.

Combine clams, chopped onion, shallots, and wine in a large Dutch oven. Bring to a boil; cover, reduce heat, and simmer 6 minutes or until most clams are open. Remove clams to a serving bowl as they open; keep warm. Discard any unopened clams. Bring remaining liquid to a boil; cook over high heat until reduced to 1 cup. Pour liquid through a sieve, and set aside.

Melt margarine in a heavy saucepan over low heat; add flour, stirring until smooth. Cook 1 minute, stirring constantly. Gradually add milk, reserved 1 cup of clam liquid, lemon rind, lemon juice, and garlic. Cook over medium heat, stirring constantly, until mixture is thickened and bubbly. Remove from heat; stir in parsley, green onions, salt, and pepper. Pour sauce over clams. Serve immediately. Yield: 2 servings.

Per serving: Calories 265 (33% from fat)
Carbohydrate 28.3g Protein 18.6g Fat 9.7g (Sat. Fat 1.9g)
Cholesterol 37mg Sodium 537mg

Clams in Lemon Butter Sauce

4   pounds littleneck clams
3   tablespoons cornmeal
1   cup chopped onion
2   tablespoons chopped shallots
1½ cups Chablis or other dry white wine
2   teaspoons grated lemon rind
¼   cup fresh lemon juice
2   cloves garlic, minced
½   cup butter, cut into pieces
2   tablespoons minced fresh parsley
2   tablespoons minced green onions
¼   teaspoon salt
¼   teaspoon ground white pepper

Scrub clams thoroughly, discarding any that are cracked or open. Place clams in a large bowl; cover with cold water, and sprinkle with cornmeal. Let stand 30 minutes. Drain and rinse clams; set aside. Discard cornmeal.

Combine clams, chopped onion, shallots, and wine in a large Dutch oven. Bring to a boil; cover, reduce heat, and simmer 6 minutes or until most clams are open. Remove clams to a serving bowl as they open; keep warm. Discard any unopened clams. Bring remaining liquid to a boil; cook over high heat until reduced to 1 cup. Pour liquid through a sieve. Pour strained liquid into a medium saucepan.

Bring liquid to a boil; reduce heat to simmer. Stir in lemon rind, lemon juice, and garlic. Remove from heat; add butter and remaining ingredients. Stir with a whisk until butter melts. Pour sauce over clams. Serve immediately. Yield: 2 servings.

Per serving: Calories 531 (80% from fat)
Carbohydrate 16.6g Protein 14.3g Fat 47.1g (Sat. Fat 28.8g)
Cholesterol 156mg Sodium 834mg

Both dishes are full of crabmeat, but the lighter Cheesy Crabmeat Bake uses low-fat milk and cheese.

CHEESY CRABMEAT BAKE

Vegetable cooking spray
1 tablespoon reduced-calorie margarine
1¼ cups canned no-salt-added chicken broth, undiluted and divided
½ pound fresh mushrooms, quartered
1 pound fresh lump crabmeat, drained
¼ teaspoon salt
¼ teaspoon ground white pepper
¼ cup plus 2 tablespoons all-purpose flour
¾ cup 1% low-fat milk, divided
½ cup nonfat sour cream alternative
¼ cup (1 ounce) finely shredded reduced-fat Swiss cheese
1 tablespoon lemon juice
1 teaspoon minced garlic
1 (14-ounce) can artichoke hearts, drained and quartered
2 tablespoons fine, dry breadcrumbs
2 tablespoons freshly grated Parmesan cheese
2 teaspoons reduced-calorie margarine, melted
½ teaspoon paprika

Coat a nonstick skillet with cooking spray; add 1 tablespoon margarine. Place over medium-high heat until margarine melts. Add ½ cup broth and mushrooms; cook over high heat until liquid evaporates. Remove from heat; stir in crabmeat, salt, and pepper.

Combine flour and ¼ cup milk. Combine remaining milk and broth in a saucepan; add flour mixture. Cook over medium heat, stirring constantly, until thick. Remove from heat; stir in sour cream and next 3 ingredients. Stir in crabmeat mixture and artichoke. Spoon into a shallow 2-quart baking dish coated with cooking spray.

Combine breadcrumbs, Parmesan cheese, 2 teaspoons margarine, and paprika. Sprinkle over crabmeat mixture. Bake, uncovered, at 400° for 15 minutes or until lightly browned. Yield: 6 servings.

Per serving: Calories 212 (24% from fat)
Carbohydrate 17.5g Protein 22.0g Fat 5.6g (Sat. Fat 1.6g)
Cholesterol 77mg Sodium 447mg

Creamy Crabmeat au Gratin

½ pound fresh mushrooms, quartered
¼ cup unsalted butter, melted and divided
1 pound fresh lump crabmeat, drained
¼ teaspoon salt
¼ teaspoon ground white pepper
¼ cup unsalted butter
¼ cup all-purpose flour
1 cup whipping cream
¼ cup Chablis or other dry white wine
2 teaspoons fresh lemon juice
¼ teaspoon salt
¼ teaspoon ground white pepper
1 (14-ounce) can artichoke hearts, drained and quartered
¼ cup fine, dry breadcrumbs
¼ cup freshly grated Parmesan cheese
1 teaspoon paprika

Sauté mushrooms in 3 tablespoons butter in a large skillet over high heat 4 minutes or until tender. Remove from heat, and stir in crabmeat, ¼ teaspoon salt, and ¼ teaspoon pepper; set aside.

Melt ¼ cup butter in a heavy saucepan; add flour, stirring until smooth. Cook 1 minute, stirring constantly. Gradually add whipping cream and wine; cook over medium heat, stirring constantly, until thick. Stir in lemon juice, ¼ teaspoon salt, and ¼ teaspoon pepper. Stir in crabmeat mixture and artichoke. Spoon into a buttered shallow 2-quart baking dish.

Combine breadcrumbs, Parmesan cheese, paprika, and remaining 1 tablespoon melted butter. Sprinkle over crabmeat mixture. Bake, uncovered, at 400° for 15 minutes or until lightly browned. Yield: 6 servings.

Per serving: Calories 436 (70% from fat)
Carbohydrate 15.2g Protein 19.9g Fat 33.7g (Sat. Fat 20.1g)
Cholesterol 172mg Sodium 550mg

A spicy curry sauce enhances the sweetness of lobster in both recipes. The only difference in the sauces is that the light one uses margarine instead of butter and evaporated skimmed milk in place of half-and-half.

LOBSTER WITH LIGHT CURRY SAUCE

2   (8-ounce) fresh or frozen lobster tails, thawed
    Vegetable cooking spray
1   tablespoon margarine
2   teaspoons curry powder
1   tablespoon peeled, minced gingerroot
1   teaspoon minced garlic
½   cup evaporated skimmed milk
½   cup clam juice
¼   cup Chablis or other dry white wine
¼   cup ruby port wine
1   tablespoon balsamic vinegar
¼   teaspoon freshly ground pepper
¼   teaspoon crushed red pepper
    Sliced green onions (optional)

Cut lobster tails in half lengthwise, cutting through upper and lower hard shells with an electric knife. Coat a large nonstick skillet with cooking spray; place over medium-high heat until hot. Add lobster tail halves, cut side down. Cook 4 minutes on each side or until lobster is done. Remove lobster from skillet, and keep warm.

Add margarine and curry powder to skillet; heat over medium-high heat until margarine melts. Cook 30 seconds over medium-high heat, stirring constantly. Add gingerroot and garlic; sauté until tender. Add milk and next 6 ingredients; stir well. Cook over medium-high heat, stirring constantly, 10 to 12 minutes until mixture is reduced to ½ cup.

Spoon ¼ cup curry mixture onto each individual serving plate. Place 2 lobster tail halves, cut side down, on each plate. Garnish with green onions, if desired. Yield: 2 servings.

Per serving: Calories 274 (26% from fat)
Carbohydrate 11.6g Protein 38.0g Fat 7.9g (Sat. Fat 1.6g)
Cholesterol 165mg Sodium 581mg

Lobster with Creamy Curry Sauce

2   (8-ounce) fresh or frozen lobster tails, thawed
1   tablespoon butter
1   tablespoon peeled, minced gingerroot
2   teaspoons curry powder
1   teaspoon minced garlic
½   cup half-and-half
½   cup clam juice
¼   cup Chablis or other dry white wine
¼   cup ruby port wine
1   tablespoon balsamic vinegar
¼   teaspoon freshly ground pepper
¼   teaspoon dried crushed red pepper
    Sliced green onions (optional)

Cut lobster tails in half lengthwise, cutting through upper and lower hard shells with an electric knife. Heat butter in a large skillet over medium heat until butter melts. Add lobster tail halves, cut side down. Cook 4 minutes on each side or until lobster is done. Remove lobster from skillet, and keep warm.

Add gingerroot, curry powder, and garlic to skillet. Sauté over medium-high heat 2 to 3 minutes. Add half-and-half and next 6 ingredients; stir well. Cook over medium-high heat, stirring constantly, 10 to 12 minutes or until mixture is reduced to ½ cup.

Spoon ¼ cup curry mixture onto each individual serving plate. Place 2 lobster tail halves, cut side down, on each plate. Garnish with green onions, if desired. Yield: 2 servings.

Per serving: Calories 300 (44% from fat)
Carbohydrate 7.0g Protein 34.7g Fat 14.6g (Sat. Fat 8.3g)
Cholesterol 200mg Sodium 521mg

Left: *Lobster with Light Curry Sauce*

Tender bay scallops take an extravagant turn when drenched with a buttery cream sauce and topped with Swiss cheese. In Scallop and Leek au Gratin, evaporated milk replaces the whipping cream, and reduced-fat cheese substitutes for regular Swiss cheese.

Scallop and Leek au Gratin

    1   cup minced leeks without tops
 1½   cups clam juice
    1   cup Chablis or other dry white wine
 1½   pounds bay scallops
   ¼   cup all-purpose flour
   ½   cup evaporated skimmed milk
   ½   cup (2 ounces) shredded reduced-fat
        Swiss cheese, divided
    2   teaspoons lemon juice
   ½   teaspoon minced garlic
   ¼   teaspoon salt
   ¼   teaspoon ground white pepper
        Vegetable cooking spray

Bring first 3 ingredients to a boil in a large saucepan over medium heat. Reduce heat, and add scallops; simmer 1 minute or until scallops are opaque and slightly firm. Strain scallop mixture, reserving liquid; set scallops and leeks aside. Return liquid to saucepan. Bring to a boil; cook, uncovered, 20 minutes or until liquid is reduced to 1¼ cups.

Combine flour and milk in a small heavy saucepan; stir until smooth. Cook over medium heat, stirring constantly, until thickened. Gradually add reduced liquid, stirring constantly. Cook, stirring constantly, until thickened. Add ¼ cup cheese and next 4 ingredients; stir until cheese melts.

Combine scallop mixture and ¾ cup cheese sauce; stir well. Spoon scallop mixture evenly into 6 individual gratin dishes coated with cooking spray. Spoon remaining 1 cup cheese sauce evenly over scallop mixture. Sprinkle evenly with remaining ¼ cup cheese. Bake at 375° for 15 minutes or until bubbly. Yield: 6 servings.

Per serving: Calories 182 (15% from fat)
Carbohydrate 12.7g Protein 25.0g Fat 3.0g (Sat. Fat 1.1g)
Cholesterol 44mg Sodium 455mg

Creamy Scallops Parisienne

    1   cup clam juice
    1   cup Chablis or other dry white wine
    2   tablespoons minced green onions
 1½   pounds bay scallops
   ¼   cup plus 1 tablespoon butter, divided
   ¼   cup all-purpose flour
   ¾   cup whipping cream
    2   egg yolks, lightly beaten
    2   teaspoons lemon juice
   ½   teaspoon salt
   ¼   teaspoon ground white pepper
   ½   cup (2 ounces) shredded Swiss cheese

Bring first 3 ingredients to a boil in a large saucepan over medium heat. Reduce heat, and add scallops; simmer 1 minute or until scallops are opaque and slightly firm. Strain scallop mixture, reserving liquid; set scallops and onions aside. Return liquid to saucepan. Bring to a boil; cook, uncovered, 15 minutes or until liquid is reduced to 1 cup.

Melt ¼ cup butter in a small, heavy saucepan over medium heat; add flour. Cook 1 minute, stirring constantly with a wire whisk. Gradually add reduced liquid and whipping cream, stirring constantly. Cook, stirring constantly, an additional 2 minutes or until thickened and bubbly. Gradually stir about one-fourth of hot mixture into beaten egg yolks; add to remaining hot mixture, stirring constantly. Cook an additional minute or until thickened. Remove from heat. Add lemon juice, salt, and white pepper; stir well.

Combine scallop mixture and 1 cup sauce; stir well. Spoon scallop mixture evenly into 6 lightly greased individual gratin dishes. Spoon remaining 1 cup sauce evenly over scallop mixture. Sprinkle evenly with cheese. Dot tops evenly with remaining 1 tablespoon butter. Bake at 375° for 15 minutes or until bubbly. Yield: 6 servings.

Per serving: Calories 369 (64% from fat)
Carbohydrate 8.8g Protein 24.2g Fat 26.2g (Sat. Fat 15.4g)
Cholesterol 186mg Sodium 607mg

Light Shrimp Curry offers a low-fat taste of the tropics. Its tomato-based sauce contains jalapeño pepper, gingerroot, and nonfat yogurt. Coconut milk gives the luscious shrimp curry a slightly sweet tropical flavor.

LIGHT SHRIMP CURRY

    3 pounds unpeeled medium-size fresh
       shrimp
       Vegetable cooking spray
    1 tablespoon margarine
    1 cup chopped onion
  1/4 cup minced jalapeño pepper
    2 tablespoons peeled, minced gingerroot
    1 teaspoon minced garlic
    2 tablespoons curry powder
    2 (14½-ounce) cans no-salt-added stewed
       tomatoes, undrained
    1 (8-ounce) carton plain nonfat yogurt
  1/4 teaspoon salt
  1/4 teaspoon ground white pepper
    3 cups cooked long-grain rice (cooked
       without salt or fat)
  1/4 cup chopped green onions
    2 tablespoons minced fresh parsley

Peel and devein shrimp; set aside.

Coat a large nonstick skillet with cooking spray; add margarine. Place over medium-high heat until margarine melts. Add onion; sauté until tender. Stir in jalapeño pepper, gingerroot, and garlic; sauté 2 minutes. Add curry powder; sauté 2 minutes. Add tomato; cook over medium heat 5 minutes or until slightly thickened, stirring frequently. Stir in yogurt, salt, and white pepper. Add shrimp; bring to a boil. Reduce heat, and simmer 5 minutes or until shrimp turn pink.

Place rice on a serving platter; spoon shrimp mixture over rice. Sprinkle with green onions and parsley. Serve immediately. Yield: 6 servings.

Per serving: Calories 331 (12% from fat)
Carbohydrate 42.4g Protein 29.6g Fat 4.5g (Sat. Fat 0.8g)
Cholesterol 173mg Sodium 344mg

Coconut Shrimp Curry

    3 pounds unpeeled medium-size fresh
       shrimp
    1 cup chopped onion
  1/4 cup margarine, melted
  1/4 cup minced jalapeño pepper
    2 tablespoons peeled, minced gingerroot
    1 teaspoon minced garlic
    2 tablespoons curry powder
    1 (14-ounce) can coconut milk
  1/4 teaspoon salt
  1/4 teaspoon ground white pepper
    3 cups cooked long-grain rice
  1/4 cup chopped green onions
    2 tablespoons minced fresh parsley

Peel and devein shrimp; set aside.

Sauté onion in margarine in a large nonstick skillet over medium-high heat until tender. Stir in jalapeño pepper, gingerroot, and garlic; sauté 2 minutes. Add curry powder; sauté 2 minutes. Add coconut milk; bring to a boil. Reduce heat, and simmer 3 minutes or until slightly thickened, stirring frequently. Stir in salt and white pepper. Add shrimp; bring to a boil. Reduce heat, and simmer 5 minutes or until shrimp turn pink.

Place rice on a serving platter; spoon shrimp mixture over rice. Sprinkle with green onions and parsley. Serve immediately. Yield: 6 servings.

Per serving: Calories 473 (49% from fat)
Carbohydrate 34.2g Protein 27.5g Fat 25.8g (Sat. Fat 15.9g)
Cholesterol 172mg Sodium 466mg

Breadcrumbs top light Oysters Florentine; bacon and Cheddar take over in Oysters Rockefeller.

OYSTERS FLORENTINE

1　pound fresh spinach
　　Vegetable cooking spray
2　tablespoons minced shallots
1　clove garlic, minced
¼　teaspoon pepper, divided
½　cup clam juice, divided
1½　teaspoons cornstarch
1½　teaspoons lemon juice
1½　teaspoons minced garlic, divided
¼　cup fine, dry breadcrumbs
¼　cup grated Parmesan cheese
1　tablespoon reduced-calorie margarine,
　　melted
36　oysters on the half shell
1　(4-pound) package rock salt

Remove and discard stems from spinach. Wash leaves; pat dry. Coat a nonstick skillet with cooking spray; place over medium-high heat until hot. Add one-third of spinach; sauté 1 minute or until wilted. Set aside. Repeat procedure twice. Chop spinach.

Coat skillet with cooking spray; place over medium-high heat until hot. Add shallots and 1 clove minced garlic; sauté until tender. Stir in spinach and ⅛ teaspoon pepper.

Combine 1 tablespoon clam juice and cornstarch. Combine remaining clam juice, lemon juice, and ½ teaspoon garlic in a saucepan; bring to a boil. Reduce heat; simmer 1 minute. Stir in cornstarch mixture. Cook, stirring constantly, until mixture is thickened. Stir in remaining ⅛ teaspoon pepper. Combine breadcrumbs, cheese, melted margarine, and remaining 1 teaspoon garlic.

Scrape a knife between oysters and shells to free meat; set shells aside. Place oysters in a colander to drain.

Sprinkle rock salt in two 15- x 10- x 1-inch jelly-roll pans; arrange reserved shells on salt. Place 1 oyster in each half shell. Top with spinach mixture; drizzle with sauce. Sprinkle with breadcrumb mixture. Broil 3 inches from heat (with electric oven door partially opened) 4 minutes. Yield: 6 servings.

Per serving:　Calories 123 (35% from fat)
Carbohydrate 10.4g　Protein 10.3g　Fat 4.8g (Sat. Fat 1.4g)
Cholesterol 50mg　Sodium 309mg

Oysters Rockefeller

1　pound fresh spinach
　　Vegetable cooking spray
2　tablespoons minced shallots
1　clove garlic, minced
2　tablespoons butter, melted
¼　teaspoon salt
¼　teaspoon pepper, divided
3　tablespoons butter
3　tablespoons all-purpose flour
1½　cups half-and-half
1　tablespoon lemon juice
36　oysters on the half shell
1　(4-pound) package rock salt
8　slices bacon, cooked and crumbled
2　cups (8 ounces) shredded sharp
　　Cheddar cheese

Remove and discard stems from spinach. Wash leaves; pat dry. Coat a nonstick skillet with cooking spray; place over medium-high heat until hot. Add one-third of spinach; sauté 1 minute or until wilted. Set aside. Repeat procedure twice. Chop spinach.

Sauté shallots and garlic in 2 tablespoons butter over medium-high heat until tender. Stir in spinach, ¼ teaspoon salt, and ⅛ teaspoon pepper.

Melt 3 tablespoons butter in a heavy saucepan over low heat. Add flour; stir until smooth. Cook 1 minute, stirring constantly. Add half-and-half; cook over medium heat, stirring constantly, until mixture is thickened. Stir in lemon juice and remaining ⅛ teaspoon pepper. Stir in spinach mixture.

Scrape a knife between oysters and shells to free meat; set shells aside. Place oysters in a colander to drain.

Sprinkle rock salt in two 15- x 10- x 1-inch jelly-roll pans; arrange reserved shells on salt. Place 1 oyster in each half shell. Top with spinach mixture; sprinkle with bacon and cheese. Broil 3 inches from heat (with electric oven door partially opened) 4 minutes. Yield: 6 servings.

Per serving:　Calories 489 (71% from fat)
Carbohydrate 12.6g　Protein 24.1g　Fat 38.5g (Sat. Fat 21.3g)
Cholesterol 146mg　Sodium 835mg

Right: *Oysters Rockefeller*

Decrease fat in burritos by using mashed pinto beans instead of refried beans.

SPICY PINTO BEAN BURRITOS

6   (9-inch) flour tortillas
    Vegetable cooking spray
1   teaspoon extra-virgin olive oil
½   cup chopped onion
1   jalapeño pepper, seeded and minced
1   teaspoon minced garlic
2   cups canned pinto beans, drained, rinsed, and mashed
½   cup nonfat process cream cheese product, softened
¼   cup nonfat mayonnaise
½   cup chopped green onions
¼   cup plus 2 tablespoons no-salt-added salsa
½   cup (2 ounces) shredded reduced-fat Cheddar cheese
3   cups finely shredded lettuce
1   cup seeded, chopped tomato
½   cup chopped green pepper
2   tablespoons chopped fresh cilantro

Place a damp paper towel in center of a sheet of aluminum foil. Stack tortillas on paper towel. Cover stack with another damp paper towel; seal foil. Bake at 250° for 10 minutes.

Coat a nonstick skillet with cooking spray; add olive oil. Place over medium heat until hot. Add ½ cup onion; sauté 4 minutes. Add jalapeño and garlic; sauté 1 minute. Add pinto beans; cook 3 minutes or until thoroughly heated, stirring frequently. Combine cream cheese and mayonnaise; stir well.

Spoon about ¼ cup bean mixture down one side of each tortilla. Top evenly with cream cheese mixture, green onions, and salsa. Roll up tortillas; arrange seam side down in a 13- x 9- x 2-inch baking dish coated with cooking spray. Cover and bake at 350° for 20 minutes. Sprinkle with Cheddar cheese; bake, uncovered, 5 minutes or until cheese melts. Place ½ cup lettuce and 1 burrito on each plate. Top burritos evenly with tomato, green pepper, and cilantro. Yield: 6 burritos.

Per burrito: Calories 345 (19% from fat)
Carbohydrate 53.7g   Protein 16.3g   Fat 7.2g (Sat. Fat 1.9g)
Cholesterol 10mg   Sodium 747mg

Cheesy Refried Bean Burritos

6   (9-inch) flour tortillas
½   cup chopped onion
2   tablespoons extra-virgin olive oil
1   jalapeño pepper, seeded and minced
½   teaspoon minced garlic
3   cups canned refried beans
⅛   teaspoon salt
⅛   teaspoon freshly ground pepper
1½   cups (6 ounces) shredded Monterey Jack cheese, divided
¼   cup chopped green onions
¼   cup commercial mild green taco sauce
3   cups finely shredded lettuce
½   cup peeled, chopped avocado
½   cup seeded, chopped tomato
1   tablespoon chopped fresh cilantro
½   cup sour cream

Place a damp paper towel in center of a sheet of aluminum foil. Stack tortillas on paper towel. Cover stack with another damp paper towel; seal foil. Bake at 250° for 10 minutes.

Sauté ½ cup onion in hot olive oil in a large skillet over medium heat 5 minutes or until tender. Add jalapeño and garlic; sauté 1 minute. Add refried beans, salt, and pepper, and cook 4 minutes or until thoroughly heated, stirring frequently.

Spoon about ½ cup bean mixture down one side of each tortilla. Top evenly with 1 cup cheese, green onions, and taco sauce. Roll up tortillas; arrange seam side down in a lightly greased 13- x 9- x 2-inch baking dish. Cover and bake at 350° for 30 minutes. Sprinkle with remaining ½ cup cheese; bake, uncovered, 5 minutes or until cheese melts. Place ½ cup lettuce and 1 burrito on each plate. Top burritos evenly with avocado, tomato, cilantro, and sour cream. Yield: 6 burritos.

Per burrito: Calories 638 (48% from fat)
Carbohydrate 62.9g   Protein 22.5g   Fat 33.7g (Sat. Fat 13.3g)
Cholesterol 41mg   Sodium 1122mg

Right: *Cheesy Refried Bean Burritos*

Chunky vegetables and low-fat cheeses pack the light Vegetable Lasagna with flavor. A rich cream sauce and a heavy hand with cheese give Spinach Lasagna its luscious standing.

VEGETABLE LASAGNA

Vegetable cooking spray
1 cup chopped onion
½ cup chopped green pepper
2 cloves garlic, minced
1½ cups peeled, chopped tomato
1½ cups sliced fresh mushrooms
2 cups no-salt-added tomato sauce
1 cup shredded carrot
¼ cup no-salt-added beef broth, undiluted
1 (6-ounce) can no-salt-added tomato paste
2½ tablespoons chopped fresh basil
1 tablespoon chopped fresh oregano
½ teaspoon dried Italian seasoning
½ teaspoon pepper
1 (10-ounce) package frozen chopped spinach, thawed
1 (15-ounce) carton light ricotta cheese
½ cup nonfat cottage cheese
1 cup (4 ounces) shredded part-skim mozzarella cheese, divided
9 cooked lasagna noodles (cooked without salt or fat)
2 tablespoons grated Parmesan cheese

Coat a Dutch oven with cooking spray; place over medium heat until hot. Add onion, green pepper, and garlic; sauté until tender. Add tomato and next 9 ingredients. Bring to a boil. Cover, reduce heat, and simmer 20 minutes. Add spinach; simmer 5 minutes.

Position blade in food processor; add ricotta and cottage cheeses. Process. Stir in ½ cup mozzarella cheese. Spoon 1 cup vegetable mixture into a 13- x 9- x 2-inch baking dish coated with cooking spray. Layer with 3 noodles, one-third of remaining vegetable mixture, and half of cheese mixture. Repeat layers once. Top with remaining noodles and vegetable mixture. Cover and bake at 350° for 25 minutes. Uncover and sprinkle with remaining ½ cup mozzarella cheese and Parmesan cheese. Bake 10 minutes. Yield: 8 servings.

Per serving: Calories 256 (19% from fat)
Carbohydrate 37.5g Protein 18.4g Fat 5.4g (Sat. Fat 2.9g)
Cholesterol 17mg Sodium 245mg

Spinach Lasagna

1 (10-ounce) package frozen chopped spinach, thawed
2 cups chopped onion
3 tablespoons margarine, melted
1 teaspoon minced garlic
¼ cup minced fresh parsley
¾ teaspoon salt, divided
⅛ teaspoon freshly ground black pepper
⅛ teaspoon ground nutmeg
⅓ cup margarine
⅓ cup all-purpose flour
2 cups half-and-half
1 cup canned ready-to-serve chicken broth
1 tablespoon lemon juice
12 cooked lasagna noodles
2 cups (8 ounces) shredded Monterey Jack cheese, divided
1⅓ cups grated Parmesan cheese, divided

Press spinach between layers of paper towels, squeezing until barely moist. Sauté onion in 3 tablespoons margarine in a skillet over medium heat until tender. Add garlic; sauté 1 minute. Stir in spinach, parsley, ¼ teaspoon salt, pepper, and nutmeg. Remove from heat. Melt ⅓ cup margarine in a saucepan over low heat; add flour, stirring until smooth. Cook 1 minute, stirring constantly. Add half-and-half and broth; cook over medium heat, stirring constantly, until mixture is thickened. Add lemon juice and remaining ½ teaspoon salt.

Spread ¼ cup sauce in a greased 13- x 9- x 2-inch baking dish. Arrange 3 lasagna noodles over sauce. Layer with one-third of spinach mixture, ½ cup Monterey Jack cheese, ⅓ cup Parmesan cheese, ⅔ cup sauce, and 3 lasagna noodles. Repeat layers twice, beginning with spinach mixture. Top with remaining 1 cup sauce, ½ cup Monterey Jack cheese, and ⅓ cup Parmesan cheese. Bake, uncovered, at 350° for 30 minutes. Yield: 8 servings.

Per serving: Calories 562 (57% from fat)
Carbohydrate 38.2g Protein 23.1g Fat 35.4g (Sat. Fat 16.0g)
Cholesterol 59mg Sodium 1436mg

Low-fat substitutes for sour cream, milk, and cheese keep the filling for Onion-Stuffed Potatoes as creamy as the mixture stuffed into the richer version.

ONION-STUFFED POTATOES

6 (10-ounce) baking potatoes
1 cup canned no-salt-added chicken broth, undiluted
1 cup finely chopped onion
1 teaspoon minced garlic
1 cup nonfat sour cream alternative
½ cup evaporated skimmed milk
½ teaspoon freshly ground pepper
½ cup (2 ounces) shredded reduced-fat Cheddar cheese
¼ cup plus 1 tablespoon grated Parmesan cheese, divided
2 tablespoons fine, dry breadcrumbs
½ teaspoon paprika
¼ teaspoon minced garlic
1 teaspoon reduced-calorie margarine, melted

Wash potatoes; bake at 400° for 1 hour or until done. Let cool to touch. Cut a 1-inch lengthwise strip from top of each potato; carefully scoop out pulp, leaving shells intact. Mash pulp in a large bowl, and set aside.

Combine broth, onion, and garlic in a small saucepan. Bring to a boil. Reduce heat, and simmer, uncovered, until all liquid is evaporated.

Combine potato pulp, onion mixture, sour cream, milk, and pepper; stir well. Stir in Cheddar cheese and ¼ cup Parmesan cheese. Spoon potato mixture evenly into shells.

Combine remaining 1 tablespoon Parmesan cheese, breadcrumbs, and remaining ingredients; stir well. Sprinkle potatoes evenly with breadcrumb mixture and bake, uncovered, at 375° for 20 minutes or until thoroughly heated. Yield: 6 servings.

Per serving: Calories 335 (12% from fat)
Carbohydrate 57.0g Protein 16.5g Fat 4.5g (Sat. Fat 2.4g)
Cholesterol 12mg Sodium 276mg

Creamy Stuffed Potatoes

6 (10-ounce) baking potatoes
1 cup (4 ounces) shredded Cheddar cheese
¾ cup sour cream
⅓ cup whole milk
¼ cup minced fresh chives
¼ cup margarine, melted
1 teaspoon minced garlic
½ teaspoon salt
½ teaspoon freshly ground pepper
2 tablespoons minced fresh chives

Wash potatoes; bake at 400° for 1 hour or until done. Let cool to touch. Cut a 1-inch lengthwise strip from top of each potato; carefully scoop out pulp, leaving shells intact. Mash pulp in a large bowl. Add cheese and next 7 ingredients; stir well.

Spoon potato mixture evenly into shells. Bake, uncovered, at 375° for 20 minutes or until thoroughly heated. Sprinkle evenly with 2 tablespoons chives. Yield: 6 servings.

Per serving: Calories 425 (44% from fat)
Carbohydrate 49.6g Protein 12.5g Fat 20.6g (Sat. Fat 9.6g)
Cholesterol 34mg Sodium 443mg

Replacing whole eggs with egg whites and fewer yolks reduces Mexican Souffléed Omelets' cholesterol.

Mexican Souffléed Omelets

6   egg whites
¼   teaspoon cream of tartar
4   egg yolks
2   tablespoons all-purpose flour
½   cup (2 ounces) shredded 40% less-fat
      Cheddar cheese
1   tablespoon grated Parmesan cheese
¼   teaspoon salt
¼   teaspoon freshly ground pepper
      Vegetable cooking spray
2   teaspoons reduced-calorie margarine,
      divided
¼   cup peeled, seeded, and chopped tomato
¼   cup canned chopped green chiles
2   tablespoons sliced ripe olives
2   tablespoons sliced green onions
½   cup nonfat sour cream alternative

Beat egg whites and cream of tartar at high speed of an electric mixer until stiff peaks form. Combine egg yolks and flour in a large bowl; beat until thick and pale. Fold one-third of beaten egg white into egg yolk mixture; fold in remaining egg white. Fold in Cheddar cheese and next 3 ingredients.

Coat a 10-inch ovenproof skillet with cooking spray; add 1 teaspoon margarine. Place over medium heat until margarine melts. Pour half of egg mixture into skillet, smoothing top. Cook 3 to 4 minutes or until browned on bottom. Transfer skillet to oven; bake at 350° for 10 minutes or until puffed and golden. Cut a ¼-inch-deep slit down center of omelet, and top with half each of tomato, chiles, olives, green onions, and sour cream. Loosen omelet with spatula, and carefully fold in half. Slide omelet onto a serving platter, and cut in half. Repeat procedure with remaining 1 teaspoon margarine, egg mixture, and toppings. Yield: 4 servings.

Per serving: Calories 188 (47% from fat)
Carbohydrate 11.2g Protein 13.8g Fat 9.9g (Sat. Fat 3.4g)
Cholesterol 226mg Sodium 453mg

Chile Cheddar Omelets

1   dozen eggs
¼   cup whole milk
¾   cup grated Parmesan cheese
½   teaspoon salt
½   teaspoon freshly ground pepper
1   tablespoon butter, divided
1½ cups (6 ounces) shredded Cheddar
      cheese, divided
½   cup canned chopped green chiles,
      divided
½   cup commercial salsa

Combine first 5 ingredients in a large bowl, stirring well.

Melt 1½ teaspoons butter in a 10-inch ovenproof skillet over medium heat. Pour half of egg mixture into skillet. As mixture begins to cook, gently lift edges of omelet with a spatula, and tilt pan to allow uncooked portions to flow underneath. Cook until browned on bottom. Transfer skillet to oven; broil 5½ inches from heat (with electric oven door partially opened) 1 minute or until top is golden. Cut a ¼-inch-deep slit down center of omelet. Top omelet with ¾ cup cheese and ¼ cup chiles. Loosen omelet with spatula, and carefully fold in half. Slide omelet onto a serving platter, and cut in half.

Repeat procedure with remaining 1½ teaspoons butter, egg mixture, cheese, and chiles. Top each serving with 2 tablespoons salsa just before serving. Yield: 4 servings.

Per serving: Calories 526 (65% from fat)
Carbohydrate 8.2g Protein 37.7g Fat 37.7g (Sat. Fat 18.8g)
Cholesterol 729mg Sodium 1073mg

Left: *Mexican Souffléed Omelets*

The light crust has very little oil; the pastry for the other quiche is made with butter and shortening.

LIGHT SPINACH AND MUSHROOM QUICHE

¾ cup all-purpose flour
¼ teaspoon salt
2 tablespoons vegetable oil
2 tablespoons cold water
    Vegetable cooking spray
2 cups sliced fresh mushrooms
½ cup chopped onion
2 cloves garlic, minced
1 cup nonfat cottage cheese
¾ cup frozen egg substitute,
    thawed
½ cup skim milk
1 tablespoon Dijon mustard
¼ teaspoon pepper
¼ teaspoon ground whole thyme
1 (10-ounce) package frozen chopped
    spinach, thawed and drained
¼ cup plus 2 tablespoons (1½ ounces)
    shredded reduced-fat Swiss cheese

Combine flour and salt. Combine oil and water; stir well. Add oil mixture to dry ingredients, stirring with a fork just until dry ingredients are moistened. Shape into a ball; chill 30 minutes.

Roll dough to ⅛-inch thickness between 2 sheets of heavy-duty plastic wrap. Place in freezer 5 minutes. Remove bottom sheet of plastic wrap. Fit dough into a 10-inch quiche dish; remove top sheet of plastic wrap. Fold edges under and flute, if desired. Prick bottom of pastry shell lightly with a fork. Bake at 400° for 15 minutes or until golden.

Coat a nonstick skillet with cooking spray; place over medium-high heat until hot. Add mushrooms, onion, and garlic; sauté until tender. Combine cottage cheese and next 5 ingredients; stir in spinach and mushroom mixture. Spoon mixture into prepared pastry shell. Bake at 350° for 35 minutes. Remove from oven, and sprinkle with Swiss cheese. Bake 5 minutes or until cheese melts. Let stand 10 minutes before slicing. Yield: 8 servings.

Per serving: Calories 145 (30% from fat)
Carbohydrate 14.8g Protein 11.2g Fat 4.9g (Sat. Fat 1.2g)
Cholesterol 5mg Sodium 312mg

Leek and Onion Quiche

1½ cups all-purpose flour
½ teaspoon salt
¼ cup plus 2 tablespoons butter
3 tablespoons shortening
4 tablespoons cold water
1 cup chopped onion
1 cup chopped leeks (white portion only)
2 teaspoons minced garlic
2 tablespoons butter, melted
½ teaspoon dried whole tarragon
1 cup (4 ounces) shredded Gruyère
    cheese, divided
4 eggs, lightly beaten
2 cups whipping cream
½ teaspoon salt
¼ teaspoon ground white pepper

Combine flour and ½ teaspoon salt; cut in butter and shortening with pastry blender until mixture is crumbly. Sprinkle water (1 tablespoon at a time) over surface, stirring with a fork until dry ingredients are moistened. Shape into a ball; chill 1 hour.

Roll pastry to a 12-inch circle on a floured surface. Line a 10-inch quiche dish with pastry; trim excess pastry around edges. Chill 30 minutes. Line dish with aluminum foil; add pie weights. Spread pie weights over bottom and up sides of foil-lined pastry. Bake at 425° for 15 minutes. Remove aluminum foil and pie weights. Bake an additional 5 minutes. Let cool completely on a wire rack.

Sauté onion, leeks, and garlic in 2 tablespoons butter in a large skillet over medium-high heat until vegetables are tender. Remove from heat; stir in tarragon. Sprinkle ¼ cup cheese in baked pastry shell. Spoon onion mixture over cheese. Combine eggs and remaining ingredients; stir with a wire whisk. Pour over onion mixture in pastry shell. Sprinkle with remaining ¾ cup cheese. Bake at 350° for 30 minutes or just until set. Let stand 10 minutes before slicing. Yield: 8 servings.

Per serving: Calories 546 (74% from fat)
Carbohydrate 24.7g Protein 11.8g Fat 45.0g (Sat. Fat 25.3g)
Cholesterol 239mg Sodium 517mg

Fresh vegetables accent the light strata; a generous amount of cheese laces the other.

LIGHT VEGETABLE CHEESE STRATA

Vegetable cooking spray
1 teaspoon reduced-calorie margarine
2 tablespoons minced shallots
1 teaspoon minced garlic
1 cup sliced fresh mushrooms
1 cup diced zucchini
1 cup diced green pepper
2½ cups skim milk
2 eggs, beaten
4 egg whites, lightly beaten
¼ teaspoon freshly ground pepper
⅛ teaspoon salt
6 cups cubed French bread
½ cup (2 ounces) shredded reduced-fat Cheddar cheese
¼ cup grated Parmesan cheese

Coat a large nonstick skillet with cooking spray. Add margarine, and place over medium-high heat until margarine melts. Add shallots and garlic; sauté until tender. Add mushrooms; sauté 5 minutes or until tender. Add zucchini and green pepper; sauté 5 minutes or until crisp-tender. Remove from heat, and set aside.

Combine milk, eggs, egg whites, pepper, and salt in a large bowl. Stir in vegetable mixture, bread cubes, and cheeses. Pour mixture into a 13- x 9- x 2-inch baking dish coated with cooking spray. Bake, uncovered, at 325° for 50 to 60 minutes or until lightly browned. Let stand 5 minutes. Cut into rectangles, and serve immediately. Yield: 8 servings.

Per serving: Calories 183 (24% from fat)
Carbohydrate 21.3g Protein 12.5g Fat 4.9g (Sat. Fat 2.2g)
Cholesterol 65mg Sodium 398mg

Mushroom Cheddar Strata

2 tablespoons minced shallots
1 teaspoon minced garlic
3 tablespoons margarine, melted
1 pound fresh mushrooms, sliced
1½ cups whole milk
1 cup half-and-half
4 eggs, beaten
½ teaspoon salt
¼ teaspoon freshly ground pepper
8 (1-ounce) slices white bread
2½ cups (10 ounces) shredded sharp Cheddar cheese

Sauté shallots and garlic in margarine in a large skillet over medium-high heat until tender. Add mushrooms, and cook until mushrooms are tender. Remove from heat, and set aside.

Combine milk, half-and-half, eggs, salt, and pepper in a large bowl. Remove crusts from bread, and reserve for another use. Cut bread slices into cubes, and add to milk mixture. Stir in mushroom mixture and cheese. Pour mixture into a greased 13- x 9- x 2-inch baking dish. Bake, uncovered, at 325° for 50 to 60 minutes or until lightly browned. Let stand 5 minutes. Cut into rectangles, and serve immediately. Yield: 8 servings.

Per serving: Calories 341 (65% from fat)
Carbohydrate 13.6g Protein 16.8g Fat 24.7g (Sat. Fat 12.5g)
Cholesterol 166mg Sodium 555mg

From left: *Antipasto Salad Stack-Up* (page 145),
Hot and Sour Spinach Salad (page 140)

Salads

Neufchâtel cheese, skim milk, and gelatin compose the creamy layer of the light Congealed Waldorf Salad instead of sweetened cream cheese and frozen whipped topping.

CONGEALED WALDORF SALAD

    2   envelopes unflavored gelatin
    2   cups cold water
    3   tablespoons sugar
 1½   cups unsweetened apple juice
  ¼   cup lemon juice
    2   cups coarsely shredded Red Delicious
        apple
  ½   cup diced celery
  ½   cup golden raisins
    3   tablespoons finely chopped dry-roasted
        unsalted cashews
        Vegetable cooking spray
    1   (3-ounce) package lemon-flavored
        gelatin
    1   cup boiling water
    3   ounces Neufchâtel cheese, softened
    1   cup skim milk

Sprinkle unflavored gelatin over 2 cups cold water in a large saucepan; let stand 1 minute. Stir in sugar. Cook over low heat, stirring constantly, until gelatin and sugar dissolve. Remove from heat; stir in juices. Chill gelatin mixture 1½ hours or until consistency of unbeaten egg white.

Fold apple, celery, raisins, and cashews into gelatin mixture. Pour half of mixture into an 11- x 7- x 1½-inch baking dish coated with cooking spray; cover and chill until firm. Keep remaining mixture at room temperature.

Combine lemon-flavored gelatin and boiling water in a small bowl, stirring 2 minutes or until gelatin dissolves; set aside.

Place cheese in a medium bowl; beat at medium speed of an electric mixer until smooth. Gradually add skim milk, beating well. Add lemon-flavored gelatin mixture, and beat well. Let cool to room temperature. Pour over congealed apple-gelatin mixture. Cover and chill just until firm.

Spoon remaining apple-gelatin mixture over cheese mixture. Cover and chill until firm. To serve, cut into rectangles. Yield: 12 servings.

Per serving: Calories 132 (20% from fat)
Carbohydrate 24.0g Protein 3.6g Fat 3.0g (Sat. Fat 1.3g)
Cholesterol 6mg Sodium 73mg

Apple Pretzel Salad

    2   cups chopped pretzels
  ¾   cup margarine, softened
    3   tablespoons sugar
    1   (8-ounce) package cream cheese,
        softened
  ½   cup sugar
    1   (8-ounce) carton frozen whipped
        topping, thawed
    2   (3-ounce) packages lemon-flavored
        gelatin
 2½   cups boiling water
  ½   cup chopped dates
    1   cup lemon-lime carbonated beverage
    2   tablespoons lemon juice
    2   cups diced Red Delicious apple

Combine first 3 ingredients in a bowl; press mixture into a 13- x 9- x 2-inch baking dish. Bake at 400° for 10 minutes. Let cool completely.

Combine cream cheese and ½ cup sugar in a large bowl; beat at medium speed of an electric mixer until smooth. Fold in whipped topping. Spread cream cheese mixture over pretzel mixture. Cover and chill 1 hour or until firm.

Combine gelatin and boiling water in a medium bowl, stirring 2 minutes or until gelatin dissolves; stir in dates. Let cool to room temperature. Slowly pour carbonated beverage and lemon juice into gelatin mixture. Chill 30 minutes or until consistency of unbeaten egg white.

Fold apple into gelatin mixture. Spoon gelatin mixture over cheese mixture. Cover and chill until firm. To serve, cut into rectangles. Yield: 15 servings.

Per serving: Calories 349 (50% from fat)
Carbohydrate 41.9g Protein 3.4g Fat 19.3g (Sat. Fat 8.5g)
Cholesterol 17mg Sodium 351mg

Crisp vegetables plus a nutty crunch make these slaws distinctive. The light Nutty Pineapple Slaw contains a sprinkle of peanuts; the luscious version offers a liberal measure of cashews.

Nutty Pineapple Slaw

2½ cups shredded green cabbage
1½ cups shredded red cabbage
¾ cup chopped sweet red pepper
1 (8-ounce) can crushed pineapple
    in juice, drained
1 cup nonfat sour cream
    alternative
2 tablespoons sugar
1 tablespoon dry mustard
3 tablespoons cider vinegar
⅛ teaspoon salt
2 tablespoons unsalted dry-roasted
    peanuts, chopped

Combine cabbages and red pepper in a large bowl; toss well.

Combine crushed pineapple, sour cream, sugar, mustard, vinegar, and salt in a small bowl, stirring well. Add pineapple mixture to cabbage mixture, and toss until blended. Cover and chill. Sprinkle slaw with peanuts just before serving. Yield: 8 (½-cup) servings.

Per serving: Calories 66 (16% from fat)
Carbohydrate 10.6g Protein 3.2g Fat 1.2g (Sat. Fat 0.2g)
Cholesterol 0mg Sodium 63mg

Cashew Vegetable Slaw

2 cups shredded zucchini
2½ cups shredded cabbage
½ cup shredded carrot
½ cup thinly sliced radishes
¼ cup sliced green onions
¼ cup chopped fresh parsley
⅓ cup vegetable oil
2 tablespoons whipping cream
3 tablespoons cider vinegar
1 tablespoon spicy brown mustard
½ teaspoon salt
1 cup coarsely chopped roasted cashews

Press zucchini between paper towels until barely moist. Combine zucchini and next 5 ingredients in a large bowl; toss well.

Combine oil and whipping cream in a small bowl. Beat at high speed of an electric mixer until blended. Add vinegar, mustard, and salt; beat well. Pour mixture over vegetables; toss gently. Cover and chill. Stir in cashews just before serving. Yield: 10 (½-cup) servings.

Per serving: Calories 167 (81% from fat)
Carbohydrate 7.1g Protein 2.8g Fat 15.1g (Sat. Fat 3.3g)
Cholesterol 4mg Sodium 237mg

Spinach and radicchio provide a colorful base for the luscious salad, with bacon, croutons, and tangy goat cheese adding interesting flavor and crunch. Equally unique, the light hot and sour salad is topped with reduced-fat Monterey Jack cheese that is cut into cubes, breaded, and baked.

HOT AND SOUR SPINACH SALAD

¼ cup fine, dry breadcrumbs
⅛ teaspoon salt
4 ounces reduced-fat Monterey Jack cheese, cubed
1 egg white, lightly beaten
6 cups torn fresh spinach
½ cup sliced green onions
3 tablespoons brown sugar
¼ cup plus 2 tablespoons canned low-sodium chicken broth, undiluted
3 tablespoons balsamic vinegar
½ teaspoon hot sauce
2 large pink grapefruit, peeled and sectioned

Combine breadcrumbs and salt; stir well. Dip cheese in egg white; dredge in breadcrumb mixture. Place cheese on a baking sheet lined with wax paper. Freeze 30 minutes.

Combine spinach and green onions; toss well, and set aside.

Combine brown sugar and next 3 ingredients in a small saucepan; stir well. Bring to a boil; remove from heat, and stir in grapefruit.

Remove prepared cheese from freezer. Remove wax paper, and bake cheese at 400° for 3 to 4 minutes or until cheese begins to soften.

Pour grapefruit mixture over spinach mixture; toss gently. Top evenly with baked cheese. Serve immediately. Yield: 6 servings.

Per serving: Calories 133 (27% from fat)
Carbohydrate 17.1g Protein 8.5g Fat 4.0g (Sat. Fat 2.2g)
Cholesterol 13mg Sodium 246mg

Spinach and Bacon Salad

12 slices bacon
4 (1-ounce) slices French bread, cut into cubes
6 cups fresh spinach leaves
1 small head radicchio, separated into leaves
½ cup sliced green onions
3 ounces goat cheese
⅓ cup red wine vinegar
⅓ cup vegetable oil
1 tablespoon sugar
¾ teaspoon dry mustard
¼ teaspoon salt
¼ teaspoon pepper

Cook bacon in a large skillet until crisp; remove bacon, reserving drippings in skillet. Crumble bacon, and set aside. Cook bread cubes in drippings over medium-high heat, stirring constantly, until crisp. Remove croutons from skillet, using a slotted spoon; drain on paper towels, and set aside.

Arrange spinach, radicchio, and green onions evenly on 6 individual salad plates. Cut goat cheese into 12 slices; cut into decorative shapes, if desired. Top each salad with 2 slices goat cheese.

Combine vinegar and remaining ingredients in a small jar; cover tightly, and shake vigorously to blend. Pour vinegar mixture evenly over salads; top evenly with reserved bacon and croutons. Yield: 6 servings.

Per serving: Calories 416 (77% from fat)
Carbohydrate 15.2g Protein 8.9g Fat 35.7g (Sat. Fat 12.1g)
Cholesterol 34mg Sodium 523mg

Right: *Spinach and Bacon Salad*

If you're a Caesar salad fan who's cutting back on fat, you'll appreciate our light Tangy Caesar Salad. The croutons originate from sliced and baked garlic bagels instead of bread cubes sautéed in butter. Splurge with the traditional version on special occasions.

Tangy Caesar Salad

2　garlic-flavored bagels
　　Butter-flavored vegetable cooking spray
8　cups torn romaine lettuce (about 1 large
　　head)
2　tablespoons freshly grated Parmesan
　　cheese
1　teaspoon coarsely ground pepper
2　tablespoons lemon juice
2　teaspoons low-sodium Worcestershire
　　sauce
1½　teaspoons red wine vinegar
½　teaspoon dry mustard
¼　teaspoon garlic powder
¼　cup plus 2 tablespoons plain nonfat
　　yogurt

Cut each bagel into 2 half-circles using a serrated knife. Cut each half-circle horizontally into ¼-inch-thick slices. Place bagel slices on a baking sheet; coat with cooking spray. Bake at 300° for 25 minutes or until lightly browned and crisp; set aside.

Combine lettuce, cheese, and pepper in a large bowl; toss well. Combine lemon juice and next 4 ingredients, stirring well. Add yogurt; stir well. Add to lettuce mixture; toss gently to coat.

Break bagel chips into small pieces; add to lettuce mixture, and toss gently. Serve immediately. Yield: 8 (1-cup) servings.

Per serving:　Calories 97 (12% from fat)
Carbohydrate 16.6g　Protein 4.6g　Fat 1.3g (Sat. Fat 0.4g)
Cholesterol 1mg　Sodium 186mg

Regal Caesar Salad

¼　cup butter
1　tablespoon olive oil
6　(1-ounce) slices French bread, cut into
　　cubes
8　cups torn romaine lettuce (about 1 large
　　head)
⅔　cup freshly grated Parmesan cheese
1½　teaspoons cracked pepper
½　cup olive oil
1　tablespoon red wine vinegar
1　tablespoon lemon juice
1　tablespoon anchovy paste
1　teaspoon Dijon mustard
1　teaspoon Worcestershire sauce
⅛　teaspoon hot sauce
1　clove garlic, minced

Melt butter in a large skillet over medium heat; add 1 tablespoon olive oil. Add bread cubes, and sauté 3 to 5 minutes or until golden. Remove croutons from skillet, and set aside.

Combine lettuce, cheese, and pepper in a large bowl; toss well. Combine ½ cup olive oil and remaining ingredients in a jar; cover tightly, and shake vigorously to blend. Pour olive oil mixture over lettuce mixture; toss gently to coat. Add croutons, and toss gently. Serve immediately. Yield: 8 (1-cup) servings.

Per serving:　Calories 297 (73% from fat)
Carbohydrate 13.6g　Protein 6.5g　Fat 24.2g (Sat. Fat 7.4g)
Cholesterol 23mg　Sodium 619mg

Balsamic vinegar adds a burst of flavor without fat in our light adaptation of green bean salad. Our luscious Basil Green Bean Salad boasts a generous sprinkling of freshly grated Parmesan cheese and a full-bodied oil-and-vinegar dressing.

BALSAMIC GREEN BEAN SALAD

1	pound fresh green beans
½	cup water
½	cup diced tomato
3	tablespoons balsamic vinegar
2	tablespoons grated Parmesan cheese
1	teaspoon anchovy paste
¼	teaspoon pepper
2	cloves garlic, minced
1	tablespoon pine nuts, toasted

Wash beans; trim ends, and remove strings.

Place ½ cup water in a large Dutch oven; bring to a boil. Add green beans; cover, reduce heat, and simmer 10 minutes or until crisp-tender. Plunge beans immediately into ice water for 5 minutes; drain. Place beans in a large bowl. Add tomato; toss well.

Combine vinegar and next 4 ingredients in a small bowl, stirring well. Pour vinegar mixture over vegetable mixture; toss gently. Cover and marinate in refrigerator at least 3 hours, stirring occasionally. Sprinkle with pine nuts just before serving. Serve with a slotted spoon. Yield: 4 servings.

Per serving: Calories 71 (30% from fat)
Carbohydrate 10.5g Protein 4.4g Fat 2.4g (Sat. Fat 0.7g)
Cholesterol 2mg Sodium 228mg

Basil Green Bean Salad

1	pound fresh green beans
½	cup water
8	sun-dried tomatoes in olive oil, drained and cut into strips
½	cup diced purple onion
½	cup white wine vinegar
⅓	cup vegetable oil
¼	cup minced fresh basil
1	teaspoon sugar
½	cup freshly grated Parmesan cheese

Wash beans; trim ends, and remove strings.

Place ½ cup water in a large Dutch oven; bring to a boil. Add green beans; cover, reduce heat, and simmer 10 minutes or until crisp-tender. Plunge beans immediately into ice water for 5 minutes; drain. Place beans in a large bowl. Add tomato and onion; toss well.

Combine vinegar and next 3 ingredients in a small bowl, stirring well. Pour vinegar mixture over vegetable mixture; toss gently. Cover and marinate in refrigerator at least 3 hours, stirring occasionally. Sprinkle with cheese just before serving. Serve with a slotted spoon. Yield: 4 servings.

Per serving: Calories 276 (72% from fat)
Carbohydrate 13.2g Protein 7.9g Fat 22.1g (Sat. Fat 5.7g)
Cholesterol 10mg Sodium 321mg

A tangy dressing that contains very little fat enhances crisp fresh vegetables in Seven-Layer Italian Salad. Pepperoni and marinated artichoke hearts pack powerful flavor into the luscious antipasto salad.

SEVEN-LAYER ITALIAN SALAD

3   cups shredded iceberg lettuce
1   medium-size sweet red pepper, cut into strips
1   medium cucumber, sliced
2   cups yellow or red teardrop tomatoes, halved
1   medium-size sweet yellow pepper, cut into ½-inch pieces
1   cup thinly sliced celery
¾   cup sliced green onions
¼   cup red wine vinegar
¼   cup water
1   tablespoon vegetable oil
2   teaspoons Dijon mustard
1   teaspoon dried Italian seasoning
1   teaspoon minced fresh garlic
½   teaspoon pepper
¼   teaspoon hot sauce
½   cup (2 ounces) shredded nonfat mozzarella cheese
    Sweet red pepper rings (optional)

Layer first 7 ingredients in a 3-quart bowl. Combine vinegar and next 7 ingredients in a small bowl, stirring with a wire whisk. Pour vinegar mixture over vegetable layers. Sprinkle with cheese. Cover and chill. Garnish with red pepper rings, if desired. Yield: 8 servings.

Per serving: Calories 61 (34% from fat)
Carbohydrate 7.6g Protein 3.8g Fat 2.3g (Sat. Fat 0.4g)
Cholesterol 1mg Sodium 115mg

Antipasto Salad Stack-Up

3   cups shredded romaine lettuce
2   cups cherry tomatoes, halved
1   cup canned garbanzo beans, drained
2   cups thinly sliced zucchini
2   (6-ounce) jars marinated quartered artichoke hearts
6   ounces pepperoni, cut into julienne strips
1   small purple onion, thinly sliced and separated into rings
1   cup mayonnaise
½   cup grated Parmesan cheese
2   tablespoons chopped fresh parsley

Layer first 4 ingredients in a 3-quart bowl. Drain artichoke hearts, reserving marinade. Layer artichoke hearts, pepperoni, and onion over zucchini. Cover and chill.

Combine reserved artichoke marinade, mayonnaise, and cheese in a small bowl; cover and chill. Spread mayonnaise mixture over salad just before serving. Sprinkle with chopped parsley. Yield: 8 servings.

Per serving: Calories 479 (76% from fat)
Carbohydrate 19.6g Protein 12.1g Fat 40.4g (Sat. Fat 9.0g)
Cholesterol 37mg Sodium 805mg

Left: *Seven-Layer Italian Salad*

Olives, green chiles, and Ranch-style dressing give traditional potato salad a bold Southwestern flair. You'll find Salsa Potato Salad just as creamy and spicy but much lower in fat because it uses nonfat mayonnaise and nonfat sour cream.

SALSA POTATO SALAD

10 ounces red potatoes
¼ cup chopped celery
¼ cup diced sweet red pepper
2 tablespoons minced fresh cilantro
¼ cup nonfat mayonnaise
3 tablespoons nonfat sour cream alternative
2 tablespoons commercial hot salsa
¼ teaspoon ground cumin

Wash potatoes. Cook in boiling water to cover 15 minutes or until tender; drain and cool completely. Peel potatoes, and cut into ½-inch cubes. Combine potato, celery, pepper, and cilantro; stir gently.

Combine mayonnaise and remaining ingredients in a small bowl; stir well. Add mayonnaise mixture to potato mixture; toss gently to coat. Cover and chill. Yield: 4 (½-cup) servings.

Per serving: Calories 80 (2% from fat)
Carbohydrate 17.3g Protein 2.5g Fat 0.2g (Sat. Fat 0.0g)
Cholesterol 0mg Sodium 211mg

Southwestern Potato Salad

10 ounces red potatoes
¼ cup sliced, drained ripe olives
¼ cup diced purple onion
¼ cup commercial Southwestern Ranch-style dressing
¼ cup sour cream
¼ teaspoon ground red pepper
1 (4-ounce) can chopped green chiles, drained

Wash potatoes. Cook in boiling water to cover 15 minutes or until tender; drain and cool completely. Peel potatoes, and cut into ½-inch cubes. Combine potato, olives, and onion; stir gently.

Combine Ranch-style dressing and remaining ingredients in a small bowl; stir well. Add dressing mixture to potato mixture; toss gently to coat. Cover and chill. Yield: 4 (½-cup) servings.

Per serving: Calories 162 (54% from fat)
Carbohydrate 16.4g Protein 2.6g Fat 9.8g (Sat. Fat 3.0g)
Cholesterol 12mg Sodium 256mg

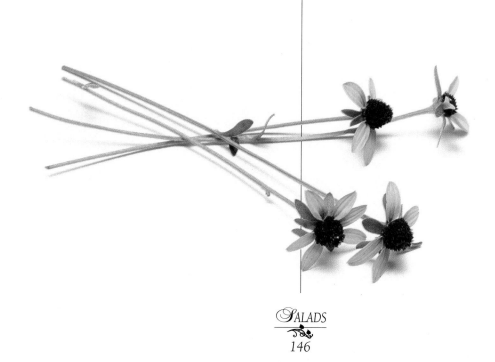

Nonfat yogurt and a reduced amount of cheese and olive oil cut calories and fat from Greek Spinach Rice Salad. Toasted pine nuts, kalamata olives, and a generous amount of feta cheese create the robust flavor of the Mediterranean Rice Salad.

GREEK SPINACH RICE SALAD

2¼ cups water
1 cup long-grain rice, uncooked
2 cups fresh spinach, cut into thin strips
1½ cups peeled, seeded, and chopped tomato
½ cup sliced green onions
2 tablespoons crumbled feta cheese
3 tablespoons lemon juice
1 tablespoon olive oil
1 tablespoon water
1½ tablespoons minced fresh oregano
½ teaspoon garlic powder
¼ teaspoon ground red pepper
½ cup plain nonfat yogurt
6 lettuce leaves (optional)

Bring 2¼ cups water to a boil in a medium saucepan; stir in rice. Cover, reduce heat, and simmer 20 minutes or until rice is tender and liquid is absorbed. Combine rice, spinach, and next 3 ingredients in a large bowl.

Combine lemon juice and next 5 ingredients in a small bowl, stirring well with a wire whisk. Pour lemon juice mixture over rice mixture; toss gently. Cover and chill. Stir in yogurt just before serving. Serve on lettuce leaves, if desired. Yield: 6 (1-cup) servings.

Per serving: Calories 165 (17% from fat)
Carbohydrate 29.7g Protein 4.4g Fat 3.2g (Sat. Fat 0.8g)
Cholesterol 2mg Sodium 54mg

Mediterranean Rice Salad

1½ cups peeled, chopped cucumber
1 teaspoon salt
2¼ cups water
1 cup long-grain rice, uncooked
1 teaspoon salt
¾ cup pitted, slivered kalamata olives
½ cup pine nuts, toasted
¼ cup chopped fresh parsley
1½ tablespoons minced fresh oregano
1 (4-ounce) package feta cheese, crumbled
1 (2-ounce) jar diced pimiento, drained
¼ cup plus 1 tablespoon olive oil
2 tablespoons white wine vinegar
½ teaspoon ground white pepper
6 lettuce leaves (optional)

Sprinkle cucumber with 1 teaspoon salt; cover and let stand 30 minutes. Rinse well.

Bring water to a boil in a medium saucepan; stir in rice and 1 teaspoon salt. Cover, reduce heat, and simmer 20 minutes or until rice is tender and liquid is absorbed. Combine cucumber, rice, olives, and next 5 ingredients in a large bowl.

Combine olive oil, vinegar, and pepper in a small bowl, stirring well with a wire whisk. Pour olive oil mixture over rice mixture; toss gently. Cover and chill. Serve on lettuce leaves, if desired. Yield: 6 (1-cup) servings.

Per serving: Calories 349 (59% from fat)
Carbohydrate 30.9g Protein 8.4g Fat 22.7g (Sat. Fat 5.6g)
Cholesterol 17mg Sodium 844mg

Corn tortillas and commercial salsa help keep fat low in the light salad, while crunchy corn chips and a creamy avocado topping elevate Ultimate Taco Salad to its luscious standing.

TACO CHICKEN SALAD

- 6 (6-inch) corn tortillas
  Vegetable cooking spray
- ½ teaspoon garlic powder
- ¼ teaspoon ground red pepper
- ½ cup chopped onion
- 4 cups shredded cooked chicken breast (skinned before cooking and cooked without salt)
- 2 (10-ounce) cans tomatoes and green chiles, drained and chopped
- ¾ cup nonfat sour cream alternative
- 6 cups torn iceberg lettuce
- ¼ cup plus 2 tablespoons (1½ ounces) shredded reduced-fat sharp Cheddar cheese
- 3 tablespoons minced fresh cilantro
- ¾ cup commercial mild no-salt-added salsa

Place tortillas on a large baking sheet. Bake at 350° for 6 minutes. Remove from oven; turn tortillas over, and coat lightly with cooking spray. Sprinkle garlic powder and red pepper evenly over tortillas. Bake an additional 6 minutes or until tortillas are crisp. Set aside.

Coat a large nonstick skillet with cooking spray; place over medium-high heat until hot. Add onion; sauté until tender. Add chicken and tomato and green chiles; stir well. Cook over medium heat until thoroughly heated, stirring frequently. Remove from heat; stir in sour cream.

Place tortillas on individual serving plates. Top each tortilla with 1 cup lettuce. Spoon chicken mixture evenly over lettuce. Sprinkle salads evenly with Cheddar cheese and cilantro. Serve salads with salsa. Yield: 6 servings.

Per serving: Calories 258 (18% from fat)
Carbohydrate 19.3g Protein 31.0g Fat 5.3g (Sat. Fat 1.7g)
Cholesterol 71mg Sodium 318mg

Ultimate Taco Salad

- 1 pound ground beef
- ½ cup chopped onion
- 1 (16½-ounce) can cream-style corn
- 1 (16-ounce) can red kidney beans, drained
- 1 (1¼-ounce) package taco seasoning mix
- 1 (11-ounce) package corn chips
- 6 cups torn iceberg lettuce
- 2 cups (8 ounces) shredded Cheddar cheese
- 2 cups diced tomato
- 1 (2¼-ounce) can sliced ripe olives, drained
- 1 (3-ounce) package cream cheese, softened
- 1 ripe avocado, peeled and mashed
- ¾ cup sour cream
- 2 tablespoons mayonnaise
- 1½ tablespoons lemon juice
- 1 tablespoon chopped green chiles
- 1 clove garlic, crushed
- ¾ teaspoon chili powder
- ¼ teaspoon salt
- ¼ teaspoon hot sauce

Cook ground beef and onion in a large skillet over medium heat until browned, stirring until meat crumbles. Drain and return to skillet. Add corn, beans, and seasoning mix; stir well.

Layer corn chips, beef mixture, and lettuce evenly on individual serving plates. Top evenly with shredded cheese, tomato, and olives.

Beat cream cheese at medium speed of an electric mixer until light and fluffy. Add avocado and remaining ingredients; beat well. Serve avocado mixture with salad. Yield: 6 servings.

Per serving: Calories 932 (62% from fat)
Carbohydrate 64.4g Protein 32.3g Fat 64.0g (Sat. Fat 21.1g)
Cholesterol 120mg Sodium 1692mg

Right: *Ultimate Taco Salad*

Preparation of the chicken makes a great difference in the fat content of these salads. In light Crispy Chicken Salad, the chicken strips are baked; in the other, the chicken is pan-fried.

CRISPY CHICKEN SALAD

½ cup fine, dry breadcrumbs
¼ teaspoon onion powder
¼ teaspoon garlic powder
¼ teaspoon dried whole thyme
1 egg white, lightly beaten
2 tablespoons skim milk
4 (4-ounce) skinned, boned chicken breast halves, cut into 1-inch strips
   Vegetable cooking spray
2 cups shredded iceberg lettuce
2 cups shredded romaine lettuce
1 cup shredded red cabbage
¾ cup shredded carrot
¼ cup sliced green onions
⅓ cup white wine vinegar
1 tablespoon chopped fresh parsley
1 tablespoon olive oil
1 tablespoon Dijon mustard
1 teaspoon chopped fresh basil
¼ teaspoon freshly ground pepper

Combine first 4 ingredients in a shallow dish; stir well. Combine egg white and milk. Dip chicken in egg white mixture; dredge in breadcrumb mixture. Place chicken on a baking sheet coated with cooking spray. Bake at 350° for 35 minutes or until lightly browned.

Combine lettuces, cabbage, carrot, and green onions; toss well. Combine vinegar and remaining ingredients; pour over lettuce mixture, and toss well. Divide lettuce mixture evenly among individual serving plates. Top evenly with chicken strips. Yield: 4 servings.

Per serving: Calories 246 (22% from fat)
Carbohydrate 15.4g Protein 30.3g Fat 6.1g (Sat. Fat 1.0g)
Cholesterol 67mg Sodium 312mg

Chicken Piccata Salad

⅓ cup fresh lemon juice
2 tablespoons minced fresh parsley
2 tablespoons whipping cream
⅓ cup vegetable oil
4 (4-ounce) skinned, boned chicken breast halves
¼ cup plus 2 tablespoons all-purpose flour
1 teaspoon paprika
¼ teaspoon salt
¼ teaspoon pepper
¼ cup margarine, melted
1 large sweet onion, thinly sliced and separated into rings
2 tablespoons frozen lemonade concentrate, thawed and undiluted
4 cups torn romaine lettuce
⅓ cup slivered almonds, toasted
2 tablespoons capers, drained

Combine first 3 ingredients in a small bowl; stir well. Gradually add oil, stirring well with a wire whisk; set aside.

Cut chicken into 2-inch strips. Combine flour, paprika, salt, and pepper in a shallow bowl; dredge chicken in flour mixture.

Cook chicken in margarine in a large skillet over medium heat 10 minutes or until golden, turning frequently. Remove chicken, and drain on paper towels; keep warm.

Add onion and lemonade concentrate to skillet. Sauté 3 minutes or until tender; remove onion from skillet. Combine onion, lettuce, and almonds in a large bowl; toss gently. Divide lettuce mixture evenly among individual serving plates; top evenly with chicken strips. Drizzle evenly with reserved lemon juice mixture, and sprinkle with capers. Yield: 4 servings.

Per serving: Calories 569 (62% from fat)
Carbohydrate 23.6g Protein 31.7g Fat 39.5g (Sat. Fat 8.1g)
Cholesterol 76mg Sodium 756mg

These creamy, ginger-laced dressings jazz up fresh fruit. Ginger Cream Dressing has no fat because it uses nonfat frozen yogurt instead of cream cheese and whipping cream.

GINGER CREAM DRESSING

1   tablespoon cornstarch
⅔   cup pineapple-orange juice, divided
2   tablespoons minced crystallized ginger
2   tablespoons honey
1   tablespoon lemon juice
¾   cup vanilla nonfat frozen yogurt, softened

Combine cornstarch and 2 tablespoons pineapple-orange juice in a small saucepan; stir until smooth. Add remaining pineapple-orange juice, ginger, honey, and lemon juice; stir well. Cook over medium heat until thickened and bubbly, stirring frequently. Remove from heat, and transfer to a small bowl. Cover and chill.

Stir in yogurt just before serving. Serve with fresh fruit. Yield: 1½ cups.

Per tablespoon: Calories 20 (0% from fat)
Carbohydrate 4.9g Protein 0.2g Fat 0.0g (Sat. Fat 0.0g)
Cholesterol 0mg Sodium 5mg

Fluffy Cream Cheese Dressing

1   (8-ounce) package cream cheese, softened
¼   cup whole milk
¼   cup orange marmalade
½   teaspoon ground ginger
1   cup whipping cream
2   tablespoons sifted powdered sugar

Combine cream cheese and milk in a medium bowl; beat at medium speed of an electric mixer until smooth. Stir in marmalade and ginger.

Beat whipping cream at high speed of an electric mixer until foamy; gradually add powdered sugar, beating until stiff peaks form. Gently fold whipped cream into cream cheese mixture. Serve with fresh fruit. Yield: 3½ cups plus 2 tablespoons.

Per tablespoon: Calories 33 (79% from fat)
Carbohydrate 1.5g Protein 0.4g Fat 2.9g (Sat. Fat 1.8g)
Cholesterol 10mg Sodium 14mg

Rosy Italian Dressing is a dieter's delight at only eight calories and zero grams of fat per tablespoon. Nonfat buttermilk and mayonnaise give this dressing a creamy base. Zesty Italian Dressing offers a more traditional oil-and-vinegar combination.

ROSY ITALIAN DRESSING

½ cup plus 1 tablespoon nonfat buttermilk
¼ cup plus 1 tablespoon nonfat mayonnaise
¼ cup no-salt-added tomato juice
1 tablespoon grated onion
¼ teaspoon dried whole oregano
¼ teaspoon dried whole basil
¼ teaspoon pepper
¼ teaspoon paprika
1 clove garlic, crushed

Combine all ingredients in a small bowl, stirring well with a wire whisk. Cover and chill. Serve with salad greens. Yield: 1 cup plus 2 tablespoons.

Per tablespoon: Calories 8 (0% from fat)
Carbohydrate 1.6g Protein 0.4g Fat 0.0g (Sat. Fat 0.0g)
Cholesterol 0mg Sodium 62mg

ZESTY ITALIAN DRESSING

½ cup plus 2 tablespoons vegetable oil
½ cup white wine vinegar
¼ cup grated Parmesan cheese
1 teaspoon seasoned salt
½ teaspoon dry mustard
¼ teaspoon dried whole oregano
¼ teaspoon dried whole basil
¼ teaspoon paprika
1 clove garlic, crushed

Combine all ingredients in a small jar; cover tightly, and shake vigorously to blend. Serve with salad greens. Yield: 1¼ cups.

Per tablespoon: Calories 66 (97% from fat)
Carbohydrate 0.2g Protein 0.5g Fat 7.1g (Sat. Fat 1.4g)
Cholesterol 1mg Sodium 122mg

A little blue cheese goes a long way in flavor, so the light Creamy Blue Cheese Dressing contains only a small amount of this strongly flavored ingredient. It also uses nonfat yogurt, nonfat mayonnaise, and skim milk instead of mayonnaise and whole milk.

CREAMY BLUE CHEESE DRESSING

½ cup plain nonfat yogurt
½ cup nonfat mayonnaise
¼ cup plus 3 tablespoons skim milk
¼ cup crumbled blue cheese
2 tablespoons lemon juice
½ teaspoon minced fresh garlic
⅛ teaspoon freshly ground pepper
   Dash of hot sauce

Combine all ingredients in a small bowl, stirring well. Cover and chill. Serve with salad greens. Yield: 1½ cups.

Per tablespoon: Calories 13 (28% from fat)
Carbohydrate 1.7g   Protein 0.7g   Fat 0.4g (Sat. Fat 0.2g)
Cholesterol 1mg   Sodium 86mg

Chunky Blue Cheese Dressing

1½ cups crumbled blue cheese
1 cup mayonnaise
3 tablespoons whole milk
2 tablespoons lemon juice
1 teaspoon sugar
¼ teaspoon dry mustard
¼ teaspoon white wine Worcestershire sauce
   Dash of freshly ground pepper
1 clove garlic, minced

Combine all ingredients in a small bowl, stirring well. Cover and chill. Serve with salad greens. Yield: 2¼ cups.

Per tablespoon: Calories 62 (91% from fat)
Carbohydrate 0.6g   Protein 1.1g   Fat 6.3g (Sat. Fat 1.6g)
Cholesterol 7mg   Sodium 102mg

From left: *Bacon Minestrone (page 160),*
All-American Turkey Sub (page 169)

SOUPS & SANDWICHES

Traditional French Onion Soup is richly flavored with Cognac and topped with thick slices of French bread and Gruyère and Parmesan cheeses. The light Cheese Onion Soup keeps the Parmesan and thick slices of bread but uses part-skim mozzarella cheese instead of Gruyère.

CHEESE ONION SOUP

Butter-flavored vegetable cooking spray
1 tablespoon reduced-calorie margarine
3 large onions, halved and thinly sliced
   (about 2 pounds)
1 teaspoon sugar
¼ teaspoon pepper
3 tablespoons all-purpose flour
7¼ cups canned no-salt-added beef broth,
   undiluted
8 (½-inch-thick) slices French bread,
   toasted
1 cup (4 ounces) shredded part-skim
   mozzarella cheese
2 tablespoons grated Parmesan cheese

Coat a Dutch oven with cooking spray; add margarine. Place over medium heat until margarine melts. Add onion; cook 20 to 25 minutes or until golden, stirring frequently. Add sugar and pepper; stir well. Add flour; cook, stirring constantly, 1 minute. Gradually add beef broth. Bring to a boil; cover, reduce heat, and simmer 30 minutes.

Place 8 ovenproof soup bowls on a baking sheet; ladle soup evenly into bowls. Top each with a slice of French bread. Sprinkle cheeses evenly over bread. Broil 5½ inches from heat (with electric oven door partially opened) 3 minutes or until cheese melts. Serve immediately. Yield: 8 (1-cup) servings.

Per serving: Calories 189 (21% from fat)
Carbohydrate 26.7g Protein 8.0g Fat 4.5g (Sat. Fat 1.9g)
Cholesterol 10mg Sodium 239mg

French Onion Soup

3 tablespoons butter
3 large onions, halved and thinly sliced
   (about 2 pounds)
1 teaspoon sugar
¼ teaspoon salt
¼ teaspoon pepper
3 tablespoons all-purpose flour
2½ cups water
2 (10½-ounce) cans beef broth
1 (10-ounce) can beef consommé
¼ cup Cognac
1 tablespoon Worcestershire sauce
8 (½-inch-thick) slices French bread,
   toasted
8 ounces thinly sliced Gruyère cheese
2 tablespoons grated Parmesan cheese

Melt butter in a large Dutch oven. Add onion; cook over medium heat 20 to 25 minutes or until golden, stirring frequently. Add sugar, salt, and pepper; stir well. Add flour; cook, stirring constantly, 1 minute. Gradually add water, beef broth, and consommé. Bring to a boil; cover, reduce heat, and simmer 30 minutes. Stir in Cognac and Worcestershire sauce.

Place 8 ovenproof soup bowls on a baking sheet; ladle soup evenly into bowls. Top each with a slice of French bread. Place cheese slices evenly over bread, and sprinkle evenly with Parmesan cheese. Broil 5½ inches from heat (with electric oven door partially opened) 5 minutes or until cheese melts. Serve immediately. Yield: 8 (1-cup) servings.

Per serving: Calories 280 (46% from fat)
Carbohydrate 18.1g Protein 15.6g Fat 14.2g (Sat. Fat 8.4g)
Cholesterol 65mg Sodium 1015mg

Smoked ham provides the height of flavor for our rich and velvety beer-cheese soup. By simply omitting the ham and substituting low-fat milk and cheese, Vegetable Cheese Soup retains the creaminess desired in a cheese soup with significant reductions in fat and sodium.

VEGETABLE CHEESE SOUP

Vegetable cooking spray
1⅓ cups finely chopped onion
 1 cup thinly sliced carrot
 ½ cup thinly sliced green onions
 ½ cup thinly sliced celery
 2 (10½-ounce) cans low-sodium chicken broth
 2 cups peeled, diced red potato
 ¼ cup long-grain rice, uncooked
 4 ounces reduced-fat process cheese spread, cubed
 2 cups 1% low-fat milk
 2 tablespoons diced pimiento
 ¼ teaspoon salt
 ¼ teaspoon pepper
 ⅛ teaspoon garlic powder
 ⅛ teaspoon ground red pepper

Coat a Dutch oven with cooking spray; place over medium-high heat until hot. Add onion, carrot, green onions, and celery; sauté until tender. Add chicken broth, potato, and rice; bring to a boil. Reduce heat, and simmer 20 minutes or until vegetables are tender. Remove from heat, and let cool 10 minutes.

Transfer mixture, in batches, to container of an electric blender; cover and process until smooth. Return mixture to pan. Stir in cheese and remaining ingredients. Cook over medium heat, stirring constantly, until cheese melts and mixture is smooth. Yield: 7 (1-cup) servings.

Per serving: Calories 158 (22% from fat)
Carbohydrate 23.0g Protein 8.0g Fat 3.9g (Sat. Fat 1.6g)
Cholesterol 11mg Sodium 420mg

Hearty Brew and Cheese Soup

1½ cups diced smoked ham
 1 cup finely chopped onion
 ½ cup thinly sliced celery
 2 tablespoons margarine, melted
 1 (10½-ounce) can condensed chicken broth, divided
 3 cups half-and-half
 1 (12-ounce) can beer
 1 (16-ounce) loaf process cheese spread, cubed
 3 tablespoons all-purpose flour

Sauté ham, onion, and celery in margarine in a Dutch oven over medium heat until vegetables are tender.

Measure ¼ cup chicken broth, and set aside. Add remaining broth, half-and-half, beer, and cheese to ham mixture. Cook over medium heat, stirring constantly, until cheese melts.

Combine reserved ¼ cup broth and flour in a small bowl; stir until smooth. Add flour mixture to mixture in pan, stirring constantly. Cook over medium heat, stirring constantly, until slightly thickened. Yield: 9 (1-cup) servings.

Per serving: Calories 357 (68% from fat)
Carbohydrate 12.7g Protein 16.5g Fat 26.8g (Sat. Fat 12.5g)
Cholesterol 75mg Sodium 1262mg

Savor the flavor of fall with these squash soups, both featuring a succulent combination of apple and butternut squash. The main difference in the two is that Apple Butternut Soup uses low-fat milk and nonfat sour cream, and the luscious soup contains whipping cream and Cheddar cheese.

APPLE BUTTERNUT SOUP

Vegetable cooking spray
1 tablespoon reduced-calorie margarine
1 cup chopped onion
1 clove garlic, minced
1 tablespoon all-purpose flour
1 (10½-ounce) can low-sodium chicken broth
3 cups peeled, seeded, and cubed butternut squash
1⅓ cups peeled, cored, and coarsely chopped cooking apple
¼ teaspoon dried whole thyme
⅛ teaspoon salt
½ cup 1% low-fat milk
Toasted squash seeds (optional)
Fresh thyme sprigs (optional)
Nonfat sour cream alternative (optional)

Coat a Dutch oven with cooking spray; add margarine. Place over medium heat until margarine melts. Add onion and garlic; sauté 5 minutes or until tender. Add flour, stirring until smooth. Stir in chicken broth and next 4 ingredients; bring to a boil. Cover, reduce heat, and simmer 45 minutes or until squash is tender. Let cool.

Position knife blade in food processor bowl; add squash mixture. Process 1 minute or until smooth, scraping sides of processor bowl once.

Return mixture to pan; add milk. Cook over medium heat until thoroughly heated, stirring occasionally. Ladle soup into individual bowls. If desired, garnish with squash seeds, thyme sprigs, and sour cream. Yield: 4 (1-cup) servings.

Per serving: Calories 129 (22% from fat)
Carbohydrate 24.8g Protein 3.4g Fat 3.1g (Sat. Fat 0.7g)
Cholesterol 1mg Sodium 146mg

Creamy Butternut Soup

1 cup chopped onion
1 clove garlic, minced
3 tablespoons margarine, melted
1 tablespoon all-purpose flour
1 (10½-ounce) can ready-to-serve chicken broth
2 cups peeled, seeded, and cubed butternut squash
1⅓ cups peeled, cored, and coarsely chopped cooking apple
¼ teaspoon salt
¼ teaspoon dried whole thyme
1 cup whipping cream
¾ cup (3 ounces) shredded mild Cheddar cheese, divided

Sauté onion and garlic in margarine in a Dutch oven over medium heat 5 minutes or until tender. Add flour, stirring until smooth. Stir in chicken broth and next 4 ingredients; bring to a boil. Cover, reduce heat, and simmer 45 minutes or until squash is tender. Let cool.

Position knife blade in food processor bowl; add squash mixture. Process 1 minute or until smooth, scraping sides of processor bowl once.

Return mixture to pan; add whipping cream and ½ cup cheese. Cook over medium-low heat, stirring constantly, until cheese melts. Ladle soup into individual bowls. Top each serving with 1 tablespoon cheese. Yield: 4 (1-cup) servings.

Per serving: Calories 454 (76% from fat)
Carbohydrate 20.9g Protein 9.4g Fat 38.3g (Sat. Fat 20.0g)
Cholesterol 104mg Sodium 641mg

Left: *Apple Butternut Soup*

Both of these hearty soups are packed with vegetables and macaroni and seasoned with herbs. Italian Minestrone is lower in fat than the luscious soup because it is not topped with crispy bacon.

ITALIAN MINESTRONE

½ pound dried red kidney beans
1 tablespoon olive oil
1 cup thinly sliced leeks
1 cup julienne-cut carrot
½ cup sliced celery
2 tablespoons minced fresh parsley
1 tablespoon minced fresh garlic
1 tablespoon dried whole basil
½ teaspoon dried whole thyme
½ teaspoon dried whole oregano
¼ teaspoon salt
⅛ teaspoon ground red pepper
5 cups water
2 (10½-ounce) cans low-sodium chicken broth
2 (14½-ounce) cans no-salt-added whole tomatoes, undrained and coarsely chopped
1 cup elbow macaroni, uncooked
2 cups coarsely shredded cabbage
1½ cups thinly sliced zucchini
½ (10-ounce) package frozen chopped spinach, thawed
¼ cup freshly grated Parmesan cheese

Sort and wash beans; place in a Dutch oven. Cover with water to a depth of 2 inches above beans; let soak overnight. Drain beans well; set aside.

Add olive oil to pan; place over medium-high heat until hot. Add leeks and next 4 ingredients; sauté until tender. Stir in basil and next 4 ingredients; sauté 1 minute. Stir in beans, 5 cups water, and chicken broth; bring to a boil. Cover, reduce heat, and simmer 1 hour or until beans are tender, stirring occasionally.

Stir in tomato and next 4 ingredients. Bring to a boil; reduce heat, and simmer 15 minutes. Ladle into individual bowls. Top each serving with 1 teaspoon cheese. Yield: 12 (1-cup) servings.

Per serving: Calories 172 (14% from fat)
Carbohydrate 29.6g Protein 9.2g Fat 2.6g (Sat. Fat 0.7g)
Cholesterol 2mg Sodium 142mg

Bacon Minestrone

½ pound dried red kidney beans
8 ounces bacon
1 tablespoon olive oil
1 cup thinly sliced leeks
1 cup julienne-cut carrot
½ cup sliced celery
2 tablespoons chopped fresh parsley
2 tablespoons minced fresh garlic
2 teaspoons dried Italian seasoning
¼ teaspoon salt
2 (10½-ounce) cans chicken broth
5 cups water
2 (14½-ounce) cans whole tomatoes, undrained and coarsely chopped
1 cup elbow macaroni, uncooked
2 cups coarsely shredded cabbage
1½ cups thinly sliced zucchini
½ (10-ounce) package frozen chopped spinach, thawed
¾ cup freshly grated Parmesan cheese

Sort and wash beans; place in a Dutch oven. Cover with water to a depth of 2 inches above beans; let soak overnight. Drain beans well; set aside.

Cook bacon in a Dutch oven over medium heat until crisp; remove bacon, reserving 1 tablespoon drippings in pan. Crumble bacon, and set aside.

Add olive oil to pan; place over medium-high heat until hot. Add leeks and next 4 ingredients; sauté until tender. Stir in Italian seasoning and salt; sauté 1 minute. Stir in beans, chicken broth, and 5 cups water; bring to a boil. Cover, reduce heat, and simmer 1 hour or until beans are tender, stirring occasionally.

Stir in tomato, macaroni, cabbage, zucchini, and spinach. Bring to a boil; reduce heat, and simmer 15 minutes. Ladle into individual bowls. Top each serving with 1 tablespoon cheese and crumbled bacon. Yield: 12 (1-cup) servings.

Per serving: Calories 260 (34% from fat)
Carbohydrate 29.7g Protein 14.4g Fat 9.8g (Sat. Fat 3.7g)
Cholesterol 14mg Sodium 760mg

New England Clam Chowder stays trim by using low-fat milk instead of half-and-half and Canadian bacon in place of regular bacon.

NEW ENGLAND CLAM CHOWDER

Vegetable cooking spray
1 tablespoon reduced-calorie margarine
1½ cups chopped onion
½ cup chopped celery
3 cloves garlic, sliced
2 (6½-ounce) cans minced clams, undrained
3 cups peeled, diced red potato
1 (8-ounce) bottle clam juice
¼ cup all-purpose flour
3 cups 1% low-fat milk
6 (½-ounce) slices Canadian bacon, chopped
½ teaspoon dried whole thyme
⅛ teaspoon ground white pepper
¼ teaspoon hot sauce
2 tablespoons chopped fresh parsley

Coat a Dutch oven with cooking spray, and add margarine. Place over medium-high heat until margarine melts. Add onion, celery, and garlic; sauté until tender.

Drain clams, reserving liquid; set clams aside. Add reserved clam liquid, potato, and bottled clam juice to onion mixture; stir well. Bring to a boil; cover, reduce heat, and simmer 20 minutes or until potato is tender. Let cool slightly.

Position knife blade in food processor bowl; add potato mixture. Process 1 to 2 minutes or until smooth; return mixture to pan.

Place flour in a medium bowl; gradually add milk, stirring with a wire whisk. Add flour mixture to potato mixture; stir well. Stir in reserved clams, Canadian bacon, thyme, pepper, and hot sauce. Cook over medium heat 20 minutes or until thickened and bubbly, stirring frequently. Ladle into individual bowls, and sprinkle with chopped parsley. Yield: 8 (1-cup) servings.

Per serving: Calories 169 (17% from fat)
Carbohydrate 24.1g Protein 11.2g Fat 3.2g (Sat. Fat 1.0g)
Cholesterol 24mg Sodium 547mg

Creamy New England Clam Chowder

6 slices bacon
2 small onions, halved and thinly sliced
1 cup sliced celery
2 cloves garlic, minced
2 (6½-ounce) cans minced clams, undrained
3 cups peeled, diced red potato
1 (8-ounce) bottle clam juice
2 tablespoons butter
2 tablespoons all-purpose flour
3 cups half-and-half
½ teaspoon salt
½ teaspoon dried whole thyme
¼ teaspoon ground pepper
¼ teaspoon hot sauce
2 tablespoons chopped fresh parsley

Cook bacon in a Dutch oven over medium heat until crisp; remove bacon, reserving 2 tablespoons drippings in pan. Crumble bacon, and set aside. Sauté onion, celery, and garlic in reserved bacon drippings until tender.

Drain clams, reserving liquid; set clams aside. Add reserved clam liquid, potato, and bottled clam juice to vegetable mixture; stir well. Bring to a boil; cover, reduce heat, and simmer 20 minutes or until potato is tender. Remove from pan, and let cool slightly.

Add butter to pan; add flour, and stir until smooth. Cook over medium heat, stirring constantly, 1 minute. Gradually add half-and-half; cook over medium heat, stirring constantly, until mixture is thickened and bubbly. Add potato mixture to white sauce in pan. Cook 5 minutes, stirring frequently. Stir in reserved clams, salt, thyme, pepper, and hot sauce; cook 1 minute. Ladle into individual serving bowls; top with crumbled bacon, and sprinkle with chopped parsley. Yield: 8 (1-cup) servings.

Per serving: Calories 303 (59% from fat)
Carbohydrate 21.7g Protein 10.2g Fat 19.7g (Sat. Fat 10.7g)
Cholesterol 64mg Sodium 635mg

We thickened Light Seafood Gumbo with browned flour instead of a traditional roux of flour and oil.

LIGHT SEAFOOD GUMBO

4   (6-ounce) skinned chicken breast halves
2   quarts water
½   cup all-purpose flour
    Vegetable cooking spray
1   tablespoon vegetable oil
2   cups chopped onion
1¾ cups chopped celery
1½ cups chopped green pepper
½   cup chopped green onions
4   cloves garlic, minced
1½ teaspoons dried whole thyme
1   teaspoon dried whole oregano
½   teaspoon pepper
3   bay leaves
1   (13¾-ounce) can no-salt-added chicken
      broth
1   (6-ounce) can no-salt-added tomato paste
½   pound smoked turkey sausage, sliced
1   pound unpeeled medium-size fresh shrimp
6   cups cooked long-grain rice (cooked
      without salt or fat)

Combine chicken and water in a Dutch oven; bring to a boil. Reduce heat; simmer 45 minutes. Cover; chill 8 hours. Remove chicken; skim and discard fat from broth, reserving broth. Bone and chop chicken.

Place flour in a 15- x 10- x 1-inch jellyroll pan. Bake at 350° for 1 hour or until very brown, stirring every 15 minutes. Set aside.

Coat a Dutch oven with cooking spray; add oil. Place over medium heat until hot. Add onion and next 4 ingredients; sauté until tender. Add thyme and next 3 ingredients. Add browned flour; stir until smooth. Add reserved broth, chicken, canned broth, tomato paste, and sausage. Bring to a boil; reduce heat, and simmer, uncovered, 1 hour. Peel and devein shrimp; add to broth mixture. Cover and simmer 10 minutes or until shrimp turn pink. Discard bay leaves. Serve over rice. Yield: 12 (1½-cup) servings.

Per serving: Calories 289 (21% from fat)
Carbohydrate 35.1g Protein 20.4g Fat 6.8g (Sat. Fat 1.9g)
Cholesterol 84mg Sodium 228mg

Left: *Light Seafood Gumbo*

Cajun Gumbo

1   (3-pound) broiler-fryer, skinned
1   cup all-purpose flour
1   cup vegetable oil
2   cups chopped onion
2   cups chopped celery
2   cups chopped green pepper
1   cup chopped green onions
6   cloves garlic, minced
2   teaspoons salt
2   teaspoons dried whole thyme
1½ teaspoons paprika
1   teaspoon dried whole oregano
¼   teaspoon pepper
¼   teaspoon ground red pepper
3   bay leaves
2   (10-ounce) packages frozen
      sliced okra
1   (8-ounce) can tomato paste
1   pound andouille sausage, sliced
1   pound unpeeled medium-size fresh shrimp
1   (12-ounce) container fresh Standard
      oysters, drained
10 cups cooked long-grain rice

Place broiler-fryer in a Dutch oven; cover with water. Bring to a boil; cover, reduce heat, and simmer 1 hour. Remove chicken, reserving 9 cups broth. Bone and chop chicken.

Combine flour and oil in a Dutch oven; cook over medium heat, stirring constantly, until mixture is chocolate colored (about 30 minutes).

Add 2 cups onion and next 4 ingredients; sauté 5 minutes or until tender. Add salt and next 6 ingredients; sauté 2 minutes. Add reserved 9 cups broth, chicken, okra, tomato paste, and sausage. Bring to a boil; cover, reduce heat, and simmer 1½ hours, stirring occasionally. Discard bay leaves.

Peel and devein shrimp. Add shrimp and oysters to broth mixture; simmer an additional 10 minutes or until shrimp turn pink and edges of oysters begin to curl. Serve over rice. Yield: 20 (1½-cup) servings.

Per serving: Calories 452 (43% from fat)
Carbohydrate 38.5g Protein 23.8g Fat 21.8g (Sat. Fat 5.4g)
Cholesterol 82mg Sodium 908mg

Lower-fat turkey sausage replaces kielbasa sausage and bacon in Italian Sausage Black Bean Soup. Using nonfat sour cream in the light version also helps reduce the fat content.

ITALIAN SAUSAGE BLACK BEAN SOUP

6 ounces Italian-flavored turkey sausage
¾ cup chopped onion
½ cup chopped carrot
⅓ cup chopped celery
2 cloves garlic, minced
3 (15-ounce) cans black beans, drained
2 (10½-ounce) cans low-sodium chicken broth
1 (14½-ounce) can no-salt-added whole tomatoes, drained and coarsely chopped
⅓ cup chopped fresh cilantro
2 tablespoons no-salt-added tomato paste
1 tablespoon fresh lime juice
1 teaspoon ground cumin
¼ teaspoon salt
⅛ teaspoon ground red pepper
½ cup nonfat sour cream alternative
Fresh cilantro leaves (optional)

Crumble sausage in a Dutch oven; add onion, carrot, celery, and garlic. Cook over medium-high heat 5 minutes or until sausage is browned and vegetables are tender, stirring frequently. Add 2 cans black beans, chicken broth, and next 7 ingredients.

Place remaining 1 can black beans in a bowl; mash with a fork, and add to soup mixture. Bring to a boil; reduce heat, and simmer, uncovered, 30 minutes or until thickened. Ladle soup into individual bowls. Top each serving with 1 tablespoon sour cream. Garnish with fresh cilantro leaves, if desired. Yield: 8 (1-cup) servings.

Per serving: Calories 223 (23% from fat)
Carbohydrate 29.9g Protein 14.5g Fat 5.7g (Sat. Fat 1.8g)
Cholesterol 19mg Sodium 553mg

Bacon and Sausage Black Bean Soup

4 slices bacon
1 cup chopped onion
½ cup chopped carrot
½ cup chopped celery
2 cloves garlic, minced
3 (15-ounce) cans black beans, drained
2 (10½-ounce) cans condensed chicken broth
1 (14½-ounce) can whole tomatoes, drained and coarsely chopped
½ pound kielbasa sausage, sliced
⅓ cup chopped fresh cilantro
2 tablespoons tomato paste
1 tablespoon fresh lime juice
1 teaspoon ground cumin
⅛ teaspoon ground red pepper
⅛ teaspoon pepper
½ cup plus 1 tablespoon sour cream
Fresh cilantro leaves (optional)

Cook bacon in a Dutch oven over medium heat until crisp; remove bacon, and set aside, reserving drippings in pan. Sauté onion, carrot, celery, and garlic in drippings 3 minutes or until tender.

Position knife blade in food processor bowl; add bacon and vegetable mixture. Process 1½ minutes or until smooth. Wipe pan with a paper towel; add bacon mixture, 2 cans black beans, chicken broth, and next 8 ingredients.

Place remaining 1 can black beans in a bowl; mash with a fork, and add to soup mixture. Bring to a boil; reduce heat, and simmer, uncovered, 30 minutes or until thickened. Ladle soup into individual bowls. Top each serving with 1 tablespoon sour cream. Garnish with fresh cilantro leaves, if desired. Yield: 9 (1-cup) servings.

Per serving: Calories 292 (47% from fat)
Carbohydrate 26.7g Protein 14.1g Fat 15.1g (Sat. Fat 6.1g)
Cholesterol 28mg Sodium 821mg

For a low-fat, low-sodium alternative to piquant beef and sausage chili, try a steaming bowl of our Spicy Vegetable Chili brimming with carrot, green pepper, potato, corn, and beans.

SPICY VEGETABLE CHILI

Vegetable cooking spray
2 teaspoons vegetable oil
1 cup thinly sliced carrot
1 cup chopped onion
½ cup chopped green pepper
3 cloves garlic, minced
2 cups peeled, cubed red potato
1 cup canned no-salt-added beef broth, undiluted
1 cup water
1 cup frozen whole kernel corn, thawed
1 cup commercial chunky salsa
1 (15-ounce) can no-salt-added tomato sauce
1½ tablespoons chili powder
¾ teaspoon ground cumin
¼ teaspoon pepper
1 (15-ounce) can red kidney beans, drained
½ cup (2 ounces) shredded reduced-fat Cheddar cheese
Nonfat sour cream alternative (optional)
Chopped green onions (optional)

Coat a large Dutch oven with cooking spray; add oil, and place over medium-high heat until hot. Add carrot, 1 cup onion, green pepper, and garlic; sauté until tender. Add potato and next 8 ingredients; bring to a boil. Reduce heat; simmer, uncovered, 30 minutes. Cover and simmer an additional 30 minutes or until potato is tender. Add beans, and cook, uncovered, an additional 5 minutes.

Spoon chili into individual serving bowls; sprinkle each serving with 1 tablespoon cheese. If desired, top with sour cream and green onions. Yield: 8 (1-cup) servings.

Per serving: Calories 157 (18% from fat)
Carbohydrate 26.6g Protein 7.5g Fat 3.1g (Sat. Fat 1.1g)
Cholesterol 5mg Sodium 149mg

Southwestern Chili

1 pound mild pork sausage
1 pound ground chuck
2 cups chopped onion
1 cup chopped green pepper
3 cloves garlic, minced
1 (15-ounce) can tomato sauce
1 cup canned ready-to-serve beef broth
1 cup water
1 cup commercial chunky salsa
2 tablespoons chili powder
¼ teaspoon ground cumin
¼ teaspoon salt
¼ teaspoon pepper
2 (15-ounce) cans red kidney beans, drained
1 (1-ounce) square unsweetened chocolate, grated
Shredded Cheddar cheese (optional)
Sour cream (optional)
Chopped green onions (optional)
Sliced ripe olives (optional)
Commercial chunky salsa (optional)

Combine first 5 ingredients in a large Dutch oven. Cook over medium heat until meat is done and vegetables are tender, stirring until meat crumbles. Drain well, and return to pan. Add tomato sauce and next 7 ingredients; bring to a boil. Reduce heat; cover and simmer 30 minutes. Stir in beans and grated chocolate; cook, uncovered, an additional 5 minutes.

Spoon chili into individual serving bowls. If desired, top with cheese, sour cream, green onions, olives, and salsa. Yield: 11 (1-cup) servings.

Per serving: Calories 307 (51% from fat)
Carbohydrate 19.5g Protein 19.9g Fat 17.3g (Sat. Fat 6.5g)
Cholesterol 54mg Sodium 953mg

Both sandwiches feature a creamy spread—one uses nonfat yogurt, the other, cream cheese.

CUCUMBER TEA SANDWICHES

1 (8-ounce) carton plain nonfat yogurt
1/3 cup light process cream cheese product
1 cup peeled, seeded, and shredded
      cucumber
3 tablespoons shredded onion
1/8 teaspoon salt
      Dash of ground white pepper
16 (1-ounce) slices white sandwich bread
16 (1-ounce) slices whole wheat bread
32 thin cucumber slices
      Fresh parsley sprigs (optional)

Line a colander or sieve with a double layer of cheesecloth that has been rinsed out and squeezed dry; allow cheesecloth to extend over edge of colander. Spoon yogurt into colander; fold edges of cheesecloth over to cover yogurt. Place colander in a bowl; refrigerate 12 hours. Scrape yogurt into a bowl, using a rubber spatula; discard liquid.

Beat yogurt and cream cheese at medium speed of an electric mixer until smooth. Press shredded cucumber and onion between paper towels to remove excess moisture. Add vegetables to yogurt mixture; stir well. Stir in salt and pepper. Set aside.

Cut 2 (1¾-inch) rounds out of each bread slice, using a cookie cutter. Spread 1½ teaspoons yogurt mixture on one side of each of 16 white bread rounds; top each with a cucumber slice and a whole wheat round. Repeat procedure, spreading yogurt mixture on 16 whole wheat rounds, and topping each with a cucumber slice and a white bread round. Reserve remaining yogurt mixture.

Transfer sandwiches to a serving platter. Cover with plastic wrap; chill until ready to serve. Dollop remaining yogurt mixture on sandwiches. Garnish with parsley sprigs, if desired. Yield: 32 sandwiches.

Per sandwich: Calories 47 (17% from fat)
Carbohydrate 8.1g Protein 2.1g Fat 0.9g (Sat. Fat 0.3g)
Cholesterol 2mg Sodium 102mg

*Left: Avocado Cucumber Party Sandwiches
and Cucumber Tea Sandwiches*

Avocado Cucumber Party Sandwiches

1 small ripe avocado, peeled and chopped
1/4 cup minced onion
2 tablespoons butter, softened
1 tablespoon lemon juice
      Dash of salt
      Dash of ground red pepper
1 (8-ounce) package cream cheese, softened
2 tablespoons mayonnaise
1¼ cups peeled, seeded, and shredded
      cucumber
1/4 cup shredded onion
1/8 teaspoon salt
1/8 teaspoon ground red pepper
1/2 cup butter, softened
20 (1-ounce) slices white sandwich bread
10 (1-ounce) slices whole wheat bread
      Cucumber wedges (optional)

Position knife blade in food processor bowl; add first 6 ingredients. Process until smooth; set aside.

Beat cream cheese and mayonnaise at medium speed of an electric mixer until smooth. Press shredded cucumber and onion between paper towels. Add cucumber and onion to cream cheese mixture. Stir in 1/8 teaspoon salt and 1/8 teaspoon red pepper. Set aside.

Spread butter on one side of each bread slice. Spread 1 tablespoon plus 1 teaspoon avocado mixture on buttered side of each of 10 white bread slices; top each with 1 whole wheat slice, buttered side down. Reserve remaining avocado mixture. Spread about 3 tablespoons cucumber mixture on each stack; top each with 1 white bread slice, buttered side down. Wrap in plastic wrap; chill. Spoon remaining avocado mixture into a decorating bag fitted with metal tip No. 21.

Unwrap sandwiches, and remove crusts, using an electric knife; discard crusts. Cut each sandwich into fourths, using electric knife. Pipe a rosette of avocado mixture onto each sandwich. Garnish with cucumber wedges, if desired. Yield: 40 sandwiches.

Per sandwich: Calories 86 (67% from fat)
Carbohydrate 6.4g Protein 1.6g Fat 6.4g (Sat. Fat 3.3g)
Cholesterol 15mg Sodium 116mg

English muffins provide the perfect base for these baked sandwiches. The lighter mini-pizzas are topped with no-salt-added spaghetti sauce and fresh basil, while the crostini's unique flavor comes from olive oil, pesto, and ripe olives.

TOMATO CHEESE MINI-PIZZAS

½ cup commercial no-salt-added spaghetti sauce
4 English muffins, split and toasted
2 tablespoons grated Parmesan cheese
16 (¼-inch-thick) slices ripe plum tomato
4 (½-ounce) slices Canadian bacon, quartered
1 tablespoon minced fresh basil
¼ cup (1 ounce) finely shredded part-skim mozzarella cheese

Spread 1 tablespoon spaghetti sauce over each muffin half; sprinkle evenly with Parmesan cheese. Top evenly with tomato slices and Canadian bacon. Sprinkle muffin halves evenly with basil and mozzarella cheese.

Bake at 400° for 8 minutes or just until cheese melts and pizzas are thoroughly heated. Yield: 8 pizzas.

Per pizza: Calories 146 (19% from fat)
Carbohydrate 23.4g Protein 6.6g Fat 3.1g (Sat. Fat 0.9g)
Cholesterol 7mg Sodium 325mg

Tomato Olive Crostini

4 English muffins, split
2 tablespoons olive oil, divided
¼ cup commercial pesto
½ cup minced ripe olives
2 (1½-ounce) slices mozzarella cheese, each cut into 4 pieces
16 (¼-inch-thick) slices ripe plum tomato
¼ teaspoon salt
¼ teaspoon freshly ground pepper

Drizzle cut sides of muffin halves evenly with 1 tablespoon olive oil. Broil 5½ inches from heat (with electric oven door partially opened) until lightly toasted; let cool.

Spread 1½ teaspoons pesto over each muffin half; sprinkle each with 1 tablespoon minced olives. Top each muffin half with 1 piece of mozzarella cheese and 2 tomato slices.

Sprinkle muffin halves evenly with salt and pepper. Drizzle remaining 1 tablespoon olive oil evenly over muffin halves. Bake at 400° for 8 minutes or just until cheese melts and crostini are thoroughly heated. Yield: 8 crostini.

Per crostini: Calories 204 (51% from fat)
Carbohydrate 20.5g Protein 6.0g Fat 11.5g (Sat. Fat 2.8g)
Cholesterol 9mg Sodium 460mg

It's not just what you stack on a sandwich that affects its fat content—it's what you spread on the bread. Nonfat cream cheese and nonfat mayonnaise reduce fat significantly in the turkey sub; Italian dressing and mayonnaise complement the pastrami and ham in Meat-Lover's Hero.

ALL-AMERICAN TURKEY SUB

2 tablespoons nonfat cream cheese
2 tablespoons nonfat mayonnaise
1/4 teaspoon minced chives
1/8 teaspoon onion powder
4 (2-ounce) whole wheat submarine rolls, split
4 curly leaf lettuce leaves
2 tablespoons commercial oil-free Italian dressing
8 ounces thinly-sliced cooked turkey breast
8 (1/4-inch-thick) slices tomato
4 (3/4-ounce) slices low-fat process American cheese
4 thin slices green pepper
4 thin slices sweet red pepper
4 thin slices sweet yellow pepper

Combine first 4 ingredients in a small bowl; stir well. Spread cream cheese mixture evenly on bottom halves of rolls. Combine lettuce and Italian dressing, tossing to coat. Top cream cheese mixture evenly with lettuce leaves, turkey, tomato, process cheese, and pepper slices; top with remaining halves of rolls. Yield: 4 sandwiches.

Per sandwich: Calories 353 (22% from fat)
Carbohydrate 39.3g Protein 28.5g Fat 8.5g (Sat. Fat 1.4g)
Cholesterol 59mg Sodium 725mg

Meat-Lover's Hero

1/4 cup plus 2 tablespoons commercial Italian dressing
1 medium onion, halved and thinly sliced into half rings
1 small green pepper, thinly sliced into rings
4 (2-ounce) submarine rolls, split
1/4 cup prepared mustard
6 ounces thinly sliced pastrami
6 ounces thinly sliced provolone cheese
10 pepperoncini peppers, trimmed and sliced
6 ounces thinly sliced smoked ham
1/4 cup mayonnaise

Combine Italian dressing, onion, and green pepper in a small saucepan; bring to a boil. Reduce heat, and simmer, uncovered, until onion is tender. Set aside to cool.

Scoop out bottom half of each roll, leaving a 1/2-inch shell. Discard excess bread. Spread mustard evenly in bottoms of rolls. Top with pastrami, onion mixture, cheese, pepperoncini peppers, and ham. Spread mayonnaise evenly on cut sides of top halves of rolls; place on top of the bottom halves of rolls. Wrap each roll in aluminum foil, and place on a baking sheet. Bake at 375° for 15 minutes or until thoroughly heated. Yield: 4 sandwiches.

Per sandwich: Calories 681 (58% from fat)
Carbohydrate 38.3g Protein 33.4g Fat 43.9g (Sat. Fat 10.4g)
Cholesterol 99mg Sodium 2570mg

For a leaner barbecue sandwich, start with lean rump roast instead of Boston butt.

Barbecue Beefwiches

1 (3-pound) lean beef rump roast
  Vegetable cooking spray
1½ cups reduced-calorie catsup
¼ cup plus 2 tablespoons red wine vinegar
⅓ cup firmly packed dark brown sugar
1 tablespoon dried onion flakes
1 teaspoon liquid smoke
½ teaspoon salt
½ teaspoon pepper
⅛ teaspoon garlic powder
2½ cups finely shredded cabbage
½ cup finely shredded carrot
2 tablespoons white vinegar
2 tablespoons minced sweet pickle
1½ tablespoons sugar
1½ teaspoons vegetable oil
⅛ teaspoon celery seeds
12 hamburger buns, split and toasted

Trim fat from roast. Coat a Dutch oven with cooking spray; place over medium heat until hot. Add roast; cook until browned on all sides, turning frequently. Remove roast from pan; wipe drippings from pan with a paper towel.

Combine catsup and next 7 ingredients, stirring well. Return roast to pan, and pour catsup mixture over roast. Bring to a boil. Cover, reduce heat, and simmer 4 hours or until meat is tender. Remove roast from pan, reserving sauce in pan. Let roast cool slightly. Shred meat with 2 forks, and return to pan. Cover and cook over medium heat until thoroughly heated, stirring occasionally.

Combine cabbage and carrot. Combine vinegar and next 4 ingredients in a saucepan; bring to a boil, stirring occasionally. Boil 1 minute. Pour over cabbage mixture, and toss gently. Spoon about ½ cup meat mixture on bottom half of each bun; top each with ¼ cup cabbage mixture and a remaining bun half. Yield: 12 sandwiches.

Per sandwich: Calories 325 (22% from fat)
Carbohydrate 39.9g Protein 21.1g Fat 8.0g (Sat. Fat 1.9g)
Cholesterol 60mg Sodium 298mg

Left: *Barbecue Beefwich*

Barbecue Porkies

1 cup finely chopped onion
3 tablespoons margarine, melted
2 cups catsup
½ cup firmly packed brown sugar
½ cup cider vinegar
3 tablespoons Worcestershire sauce
1 tablespoon prepared mustard
2 teaspoons chili powder
1 (5-pound) Boston butt pork roast
1 teaspoon salt
¾ teaspoon pepper
2 tablespoons vegetable oil
3 cups finely shredded cabbage
½ cup shredded carrot
2 tablespoons chopped green onions
⅓ cup mayonnaise
1 tablespoon sugar
1 tablespoon white vinegar
¼ teaspoon dry mustard
⅛ teaspoon celery seeds
12 hamburger buns, split and toasted

Sauté 1 cup onion in margarine in a large saucepan until onion is tender. Add catsup and next 5 ingredients; bring to a boil. Reduce heat, and simmer 10 minutes.

Sprinkle roast with salt and pepper. Cook in hot oil in a Dutch oven until browned on all sides, turning occasionally. Drain. Return roast to pan; pour half of catsup mixture over roast. Bring to a boil. Cover, reduce heat, and simmer 3 hours and 45 minutes or until meat is tender, turning occasionally. Drain and cool slightly. Shred meat with 2 forks; return to pan. Add remaining catsup mixture. Bring to a boil; cover, reduce heat, and simmer 1 hour, stirring occasionally.

Combine cabbage, carrot, and green onions. Combine mayonnaise and next 4 ingredients; add to cabbage mixture. Spoon about ½ cup meat mixture on bottom half of each bun; top each with ¼ cup cabbage mixture and a remaining bun half. Yield: 12 sandwiches.

Per sandwich: Calories 523 (44% from fat)
Carbohydrate 51.7g Protein 21.7g Fat 25.5g (Sat. Fat 6.2g)
Cholesterol 85mg Sodium 981mg

Piled with shredded cabbage and roast beef, Polish Aristocrat provides a healthy alternative to the traditional Reuben sandwich with corned beef, Russian dressing, and sauerkraut. Nonfat mayonnaise and reduced-fat Swiss cheese also lower the fat content.

POLISH ARISTOCRAT

2 cups shredded cabbage
½ cup shredded red cabbage
2 tablespoons sugar
3 tablespoons white wine vinegar
1 tablespoon water
2 teaspoons vegetable oil
2 tablespoons plus 1 teaspoon Dijon mustard, divided
⅛ teaspoon pepper
2 tablespoons nonfat mayonnaise
8 (1-ounce) slices rye bread without caraway seeds, toasted
½ pound cooked roast beef, sliced
2 ounces thinly sliced reduced-fat Swiss cheese

Combine cabbages in a medium bowl; toss well. Combine sugar, vinegar, water, oil, 1 teaspoon mustard, and pepper in a small saucepan; bring to a boil. Pour vinegar mixture over cabbage mixture, and toss gently. Cover and chill at least 2 hours.

Drain cabbage mixture, and set aside.

Combine mayonnaise and remaining 2 tablespoons mustard; stir well. Spread mayonnaise mixture evenly on 4 bread slices. Divide roast beef, Swiss cheese, and cabbage mixture evenly among prepared bread slices. Top with remaining 4 bread slices. Serve immediately. Yield: 4 sandwiches.

Per sandwich: Calories 384 (23% from fat)
Carbohydrate 45.4g Protein 29.4g Fat 9.6g (Sat. Fat 3.1g)
Cholesterol 57mg Sodium 788mg

Reuben Classic

½ cup commercial Russian dressing
8 (1-ounce) slices rye bread without caraway seeds
4 (1-ounce) slices Swiss cheese
1 (8-ounce) can sauerkraut, drained
¾ pound thinly sliced corned beef
2 tablespoons Dijon mustard
¼ cup butter, softened

Spread 2 tablespoons Russian dressing on one side of each of 4 slices of bread. Place 1 cheese slice on each bread slice. Divide sauerkraut and corned beef among sandwiches. Spread mustard on remaining 4 slices of bread, and place on top of sandwiches, mustard side down.

Spread half of butter evenly on tops of sandwiches; place sandwiches on a hot griddle or skillet, buttered side down. Cook until bread is golden. Spread remaining butter evenly on ungrilled sides of sandwiches; turn carefully, and cook until bread is golden and cheese is slightly melted. Serve immediately. Yield: 4 sandwiches.

Per sandwich: Calories 613 (57% from fat)
Carbohydrate 40.7g Protein 29.6g Fat 39.1g (Sat. Fat 15.5g)
Cholesterol 103mg Sodium 2246mg

Dip the light sandwich in an egg mixture containing skim milk instead of half-and-half and cook with vegetable cooking spray instead of butter. It's the Monte Cristo you've always loved, but with one-fourth the fat.

MONTE CRISTO LIGHT

¼ cup plus 2 tablespoons low-sugar
    strawberry spread
12 (1-ounce) slices Vienna sandwich bread
6 ounces thinly sliced turkey breast
    (skinned before cooking and cooked
    without salt)
6 (¾-ounce) slices low-fat process Swiss
    cheese
2 eggs, lightly beaten
1 egg white, lightly beaten
½ cup skim milk
2 tablespoons yellow cornmeal
    Butter-flavored vegetable cooking spray
1 tablespoon sifted powdered sugar

Spread 1 tablespoon strawberry spread on one side of each of 6 bread slices. Place 1 ounce of turkey and 1 slice of cheese over strawberry spread on each bread slice; top with remaining 6 bread slices.

Combine eggs, egg white, and milk; stir well with a wire whisk. Carefully dip sandwiches into egg mixture, allowing excess to drip off. Sprinkle both sides of each sandwich evenly with cornmeal.

Coat a large nonstick skillet with cooking spray; place over medium-low heat until hot. Place 3 sandwiches in skillet; cook sandwiches 6 to 8 minutes on each side or until bread is golden and cheese melts. Remove from skillet, and sprinkle sandwiches evenly with half of powdered sugar. Repeat procedure with remaining 3 sandwiches and remaining powdered sugar. Serve immediately. Yield: 6 sandwiches.

Per sandwich: Calories 314 (14% from fat)
Carbohydrate 43.3g Protein 22.4g Fat 4.9g (Sat. Fat 0.9g)
Cholesterol 94mg Sodium 635mg

Classic Monte Cristo

6 ounces thinly sliced turkey breast
6 ounces thinly sliced cooked ham
6 ounces thinly sliced Swiss cheese
12 (1-ounce) slices Vienna sandwich bread
4 eggs, lightly beaten
⅓ cup half-and-half
2 tablespoons butter, divided
1½ tablespoons sifted powdered sugar
¼ cup plus 2 tablespoons sour cream
¼ cup plus 2 tablespoons strawberry
    preserves

Place 1 ounce each of turkey, ham, and cheese on each of 6 bread slices; top with remaining 6 bread slices.

Combine eggs and half-and-half; stir well with a wire whisk. Carefully dip sandwiches into egg mixture, allowing excess to drip off.

Melt 1 tablespoon butter in a large nonstick skillet or griddle over medium-low heat. Place 3 sandwiches in skillet; cook 6 to 8 minutes on each side or until bread is golden and cheese melts. Remove from skillet, and sprinkle sandwiches evenly with half of powdered sugar. Repeat procedure with remaining 1 tablespoon butter, 3 sandwiches, and remaining powdered sugar.

Top sandwiches evenly with sour cream and strawberry preserves. Serve immediately. Yield: 6 sandwiches.

Per sandwich: Calories 522 (37% from fat)
Carbohydrate 50.7g Protein 29.2g Fat 21.6g (Sat. Fat 11.7g)
Cholesterol 215mg Sodium 1136mg

From top left: *Country Green Beans (page 177),
Orange Sweet Potato Cups (page 189), Mushroom
Pesto Pasta (page 193)*

VEGETABLES & SIDE DISHES

A creamy dill sauce accents both recipes, but the light version uses evaporated skimmed milk instead of half-and-half. The phyllo packets in Asparagus Strudel glisten with butter.

LIGHT ASPARAGUS STRUDEL

1 pound fresh asparagus spears
   Butter-flavored vegetable cooking spray
2 tablespoons minced shallots
3 tablespoons all-purpose flour
1 cup evaporated skimmed milk
1 teaspoon lemon juice
½ teaspoon dried whole dillweed
¼ teaspoon salt
¼ teaspoon ground white pepper
¼ teaspoon ground nutmeg
⅛ teaspoon hot sauce
8 sheets commercial frozen phyllo pastry, thawed

Snap off tough ends of asparagus. Remove scales from stalks with a knife or vegetable peeler, if desired. Cut stalks in half; arrange in a vegetable steamer over boiling water. Cover and steam 5 minutes. Place asparagus in ice water; set aside.

Coat a small nonstick skillet with cooking spray; place over medium-high heat until hot. Add shallots; sauté until tender. Set aside.

Combine flour and milk in a saucepan; stir until smooth. Cook over medium heat, stirring constantly, until mixture is thickened. Remove from heat; stir in shallots, lemon juice, and next 5 ingredients.

Place 1 sheet of phyllo on a damp towel (keep remaining phyllo covered). Coat with cooking spray. Layer second sheet of phyllo on first sheet; coat with cooking spray. Cut stack in half lengthwise, making 2 rectangles. Drain asparagus. Place one-eighth of asparagus at short end of each rectangle; spoon one-eighth of sauce mixture over asparagus on each rectangle. Fold ends of rectangles over asparagus; roll up jellyroll fashion. Repeat with remaining phyllo, asparagus, and sauce mixture. Coat phyllo packets with cooking spray; place on a baking sheet coated with cooking spray. Bake at 350° for 30 minutes. Yield: 8 servings.

Per serving: Calories 105 (15% from fat)
Carbohydrate 17.4g Protein 4.9g Fat 1.8g (Sat. Fat 0.3g)
Cholesterol 1mg Sodium 206mg

Asparagus Strudel

1 pound fresh asparagus spears
2 tablespoons minced shallots
2 tablespoons butter, melted
2 tablespoons all-purpose flour
1 cup half-and-half
1 teaspoon lemon juice
½ teaspoon dried whole dillweed
½ teaspoon salt
¼ teaspoon ground white pepper
¼ teaspoon ground nutmeg
⅛ teaspoon hot sauce
8 sheets commercial frozen phyllo pastry, thawed
½ cup butter, melted and divided

Snap off tough ends of asparagus. Remove scales from stalks with a knife or vegetable peeler, if desired. Cut stalks in half; arrange in a vegetable steamer over boiling water. Cover and steam 5 minutes. Place asparagus in ice water; set aside.

Sauté shallots in 2 tablespoons butter in a heavy saucepan over medium heat until tender. Add flour, stirring until smooth. Cook, stirring constantly, 1 minute. Gradually add half-and-half; cook over medium heat, stirring constantly, until mixture is thickened. Stir in lemon juice and next 5 ingredients.

Place 1 sheet of phyllo on a damp towel (keep remaining phyllo covered). Brush with 2 teaspoons melted butter. Layer second sheet of phyllo on first sheet; brush with 2 teaspoons butter. Cut stack in half lengthwise, making 2 rectangles. Drain asparagus. Place one-eighth of asparagus at short end of each rectangle; spoon one-eighth of sauce mixture over asparagus on each rectangle. Fold ends of rectangles over asparagus; roll up jellyroll fashion. Repeat with remaining phyllo, butter, asparagus, and sauce mixture. Brush phyllo packets with remaining melted butter; place on a greased baking sheet. Bake at 350° for 30 minutes. Yield: 8 servings.

Per serving: Calories 236 (72% from fat)
Carbohydrate 14.4g Protein 3.2g Fat 18.9g (Sat. Fat 11.2g)
Cholesterol 49mg Sodium 398mg

Pair green beans with ham and tomatoes for a variation on a familiar side dish. Flavor Country Green Beans with reduced-fat, low-salt ham instead of a ham hock.

COUNTRY GREEN BEANS

1 pound fresh green beans
1¾ cups peeled, seeded, and coarsely chopped tomato
⅓ cup canned no-salt-added beef broth, undiluted
2 ounces reduced-fat, low-salt ham, diced
1 teaspoon minced garlic
2 tablespoons chopped fresh parsley
1 teaspoon dried whole thyme
¼ teaspoon pepper

Wash beans; trim ends, and remove strings. Arrange beans in a vegetable steamer over boiling water; cover and steam 10 minutes. Rinse beans under cold water until cool; drain. Set aside.

Combine tomato, broth, ham, and garlic in a large saucepan. Cook, uncovered, over medium heat 3 minutes, stirring frequently. Stir in beans, parsley, thyme, and pepper. Cover and cook over low heat 10 minutes or until beans are tender. Yield: 4 servings.

Per serving: Calories 74 (13% from fat)
Carbohydrate 12.8g   Protein 5.4g   Fat 1.1g (Sat. Fat 0.3g)
Cholesterol 7mg   Sodium 126mg

Green Beans with Ham Hock

1 pound fresh green beans
1 small ham hock
1 cup water
1¾ cups peeled, seeded, and coarsely chopped tomato
⅓ cup canned ready-to-serve chicken broth
⅓ cup Chablis or other dry white wine
2 tablespoons chopped fresh parsley
1 teaspoon minced garlic
1 teaspoon dried whole thyme
½ teaspoon salt
¼ teaspoon pepper

Wash beans; trim ends, and remove strings. Combine beans, ham hock, and water in a large saucepan. Bring to a boil; cover, reduce heat, and simmer 20 minutes. Stir in tomato and remaining ingredients. Cover and cook over low heat 10 minutes or until beans are tender. Yield: 4 servings.

Per serving: Calories 107 (27% from fat)
Carbohydrate 12.2g   Protein 9.6g   Fat 3.1g (Sat. Fat 1.0g)
Cholesterol 17mg   Sodium 799mg

Skim fat grams from the Lean Feta Sauce by using evaporated skimmed milk and omitting the butter. Dress up the other broccoli with a rich feta sauce made with butter and half-and-half. Drizzle melted butter over this broccoli for extra flavor.

BROCCOLI WITH LEAN FETA SAUCE

Vegetable cooking spray
2 tablespoons minced onion
1½ cups evaporated skimmed milk
1½ tablespoons cornstarch
2 tablespoons water
2 ounces feta cheese, crumbled
⅛ teaspoon salt
2 tablespoons lemon juice
½ teaspoon dried whole dillweed
4 cups broccoli flowerets
Lemon zest (optional)

Coat a saucepan with cooking spray; place over medium-high heat until hot. Add onion; sauté 3 minutes or until tender. Gradually stir in milk, and cook 5 minutes (do not boil). Combine cornstarch and water, stirring until smooth; stir into warm milk mixture. Cook, stirring constantly, until slightly thickened. Stir in cheese and salt. Cook, stirring constantly, until thoroughly heated. Remove from heat, and stir in lemon juice and dillweed. Cover and keep warm.

Arrange broccoli in a vegetable steamer over boiling water. Cover and steam 5 minutes or until crisp-tender. Transfer broccoli to a serving dish. Spoon sauce evenly over broccoli. Garnish with lemon zest, if desired. Yield: 4 (1-cup) servings.

Per serving: Calories 147 (22% from fat)
Carbohydrate 18.7g Protein 11.3g Fat 3.6g (Sat. Fat 2.3g)
Cholesterol 16mg Sodium 360mg

Broccoli with Creamy Feta Sauce

2 tablespoons minced onion
3 tablespoons butter, melted
3 tablespoons all-purpose flour
1½ cups half-and-half
2 ounces feta cheese, crumbled
½ teaspoon salt
2 tablespoons lemon juice
½ teaspoon dried whole dillweed
4 cups broccoli flowerets
2 tablespoons butter, melted
Lemon zest (optional)

Sauté onion in 3 tablespoons butter in a saucepan over medium-high heat until tender. Add flour, stirring until smooth. Cook, stirring constantly, 1 minute. Gradually add half-and-half; cook over medium heat, stirring constantly, until mixture is thickened and bubbly. Stir in cheese and salt. Cook, stirring constantly, until thoroughly heated. Remove from heat, and stir in lemon juice and dillweed. Cover and keep warm.

Arrange broccoli in a vegetable steamer over boiling water. Cover and steam 5 minutes or until crisp-tender. Transfer broccoli to a serving dish; drizzle with 2 tablespoons melted butter. Spoon sauce evenly over broccoli. Garnish with lemon zest, if desired. Yield: 4 (1-cup) servings.

Per serving: Calories 326 (78% from fat)
Carbohydrate 13.5g Protein 7.5g Fat 28.1g (Sat. Fat 17.6g)
Cholesterol 85mg Sodium 653mg

Right: *Broccoli with Creamy Feta Sauce*

Carrots may become the favorite vegetable in your home when you add a sweet glaze. Orange juice and ginger flavor the light carrots without adding fat. The luscious version features a sweet and buttery bourbon glaze.

ORANGE GLAZED CARROTS

1 pound carrots, scraped and cut into ¼-inch-thick slices
¾ cup canned no-salt-added chicken broth, undiluted
2 tablespoons frozen orange juice concentrate, thawed and undiluted
2 teaspoons sugar
¼ teaspoon ground ginger

Combine carrot and chicken broth in a medium saucepan; bring to a boil. Cover, reduce heat, and simmer 10 minutes. Uncover and cook over high heat 5 minutes.

Add orange juice concentrate and remaining ingredients to carrot mixture, stirring well. Cook over medium heat an additional 2 to 3 minutes or until carrot is tender. Yield: 4 (½-cup) servings.

Per serving: Calories 69 (3% from fat)
Carbohydrate 16.0g   Protein 1.3g   Fat 0.2g (Sat. Fat 0.0g)
Cholesterol 0mg   Sodium 36mg

Bourbon Glazed Carrots

1 pound carrots, scraped and cut into ¼-inch-thick slices
¾ cup canned ready-to-serve chicken broth
2 tablespoons bourbon
1 tablespoon sugar
½ teaspoon ground ginger
2 tablespoons margarine

Combine carrot, broth, and bourbon in a medium saucepan; bring to a boil. Cover, reduce heat, and simmer 10 minutes. Uncover and cook over high heat 5 minutes.

Add sugar and remaining ingredients to carrot mixture, stirring well. Cook over medium heat an additional 2 to 3 minutes or until carrot is tender. Yield: 4 (½-cup) servings.

Per serving: Calories 115 (48% from fat)
Carbohydrate 13.9g   Protein 2.0g   Fat 6.1g (Sat. Fat 1.2g)
Cholesterol 0mg   Sodium 248mg

Mexi-Corn Pudding is full of color and flavor but has almost no fat because it uses egg substitute and evaporated skimmed milk. Full of farm-fresh goodness, the luscious version contains whole milk, half-and-half, eggs, and Cheddar cheese.

MEXI-CORN PUDDING

2 cups frozen Mexican-style corn, thawed
1½ tablespoons all-purpose flour
2 tablespoons diced green pepper
2 teaspoons sugar
¼ teaspoon salt
⅛ teaspoon ground cumin
⅛ teaspoon ground red pepper
½ cup frozen egg substitute, thawed
1 cup evaporated skimmed milk
Vegetable cooking spray

Combine first 7 ingredients in a medium bowl; stir well. Combine egg substitute and milk; add to corn mixture, stirring to combine.

Pour mixture into a 1-quart baking dish coated with cooking spray. Place dish in a 13- x 9- x 2-inch pan; pour hot water into pan to a depth of 1 inch. Bake, uncovered, at 350° for 1 hour or until a knife inserted in center comes out clean. Yield: 6 (½-cup) servings.

Per serving: Calories 95 (4% from fat)
Carbohydrate 16.1g   Protein 6.5g   Fat 0.4g (Sat. Fat 0.1g)
Cholesterol 2mg   Sodium 179mg

Cheesy Corn Pudding

2 tablespoons chopped green pepper
2 tablespoons chopped green onions
2 tablespoons margarine, melted and divided
2 cups frozen whole kernel corn, thawed
3 eggs, lightly beaten
1 cup (4 ounces) shredded Cheddar cheese
¼ cup all-purpose flour
1 tablespoon sugar
½ teaspoon salt
¼ teaspoon ground red pepper
1 cup half-and-half
1 cup whole milk
1 (4-ounce) can green chiles, drained
1 (2-ounce) jar diced pimiento, drained

Sauté green pepper and onions in 1 tablespoon margarine over medium-high heat until tender. Combine corn, eggs, cheese, and green pepper mixture in a large bowl; stir well with a wire whisk.

Combine flour and next 3 ingredients; add to corn mixture. Stir in remaining 1 tablespoon margarine, half-and-half, and remaining ingredients. Pour mixture into a lightly greased shallow 1½-quart baking dish. Place dish in a 13- x 9- x 2-inch pan; pour hot water into pan to a depth of 1 inch. Bake, uncovered, at 325° for 1 hour or until a knife inserted in center comes out clean. Yield: 10 (½-cup) servings.

Per serving: Calories 184 (55% from fat)
Carbohydrate 14.1g   Protein 7.8g   Fat 11.3g (Sat. Fat 5.6g)
Cholesterol 91mg   Sodium 269mg

The recipe for spicy Mexican Black-Eyes uses low-sodium ingredients and has no added fat.
Spike Hoppin' José with onions, garlic, tomatoes, and spices, and top
with sour cream and Cheddar cheese.

MEXICAN BLACK-EYES

1 (10-ounce) package frozen black-eyed
 peas, thawed
 Olive oil-flavored vegetable cooking
 spray
½ cup chopped onion
¼ cup chopped green onions
¼ cup chopped green pepper
1 teaspoon minced garlic
1 cup cooked long-grain rice (cooked
 without salt or fat)
1 (14½-ounce) can no-salt-added stewed
 tomatoes, undrained and chopped
1 (4-ounce) can chopped green chiles,
 undrained
2 teaspoons low-sodium Worcestershire
 sauce
¼ teaspoon pepper
¼ teaspoon dried whole oregano
¼ teaspoon dried whole thyme
⅛ teaspoon salt
⅛ teaspoon hot sauce
2 tablespoons chopped fresh parsley
 No-oil baked tortilla chips (optional)

Cook black-eyed peas according to package directions, omitting salt and fat. Drain and set aside.

Coat a large nonstick skillet with cooking spray;
place over medium-high heat until hot. Add chopped
onion, green onions, green pepper, and garlic; sauté
until tender. Add peas, rice, and next 8 ingredients
to onion mixture; stir well. Spoon mixture into a
1½-quart casserole coated with cooking spray. Bake,
uncovered, at 350° for 30 minutes. Sprinkle with
parsley. To serve, spoon mixture into individual serving dishes. If desired, place tortilla chips around edge
of each dish, and sprinkle with crushed chips. Yield:
10 (½-cup) servings.

Per serving: Calories 83 (3% from fat)
Carbohydrate 16.9g Protein 3.7g Fat 0.3g (Sat. Fat 0.1g)
Cholesterol 0mg Sodium 56mg

Left: *Mexican Black-Eyes*

Hoppin' José

1 (10-ounce) package frozen black-eyed
 peas, thawed
¾ cup chopped onion
½ cup chopped green onions
½ cup chopped green pepper
1 teaspoon minced garlic
1 tablespoon olive oil
1 cup cooked long-grain rice
1 (14½-ounce) can Mexican-style stewed
 tomatoes, drained and chopped
½ cup spicy Bloody Mary mix
¼ teaspoon dried whole oregano
⅛ teaspoon dried whole thyme
½ cup sour cream
½ cup (2 ounces) shredded sharp
 Cheddar cheese
¼ cup chopped fresh parsley
 Tortilla chips (optional)

Cook black-eyed peas according to package directions. Drain and set aside.

Sauté chopped onion, green onions, green pepper, and garlic in hot olive oil in a large skillet over
medium-high heat until tender. Add peas, rice, and
next 4 ingredients to onion mixture; stir well. Spoon
mixture into a greased 1½-quart casserole. Bake, uncovered, at 350° for 30 minutes. Top with sour
cream, cheese, and parsley. If desired, place tortilla
chips around edge of casserole, and sprinkle with
crushed chips. Yield: 10 (½-cup) servings.

Per serving: Calories 144 (37% from fat)
Carbohydrate 15.5g Protein 5.1g Fat 5.9g (Sat. Fat 2.9g)
Cholesterol 11mg Sodium 296mg

Eggplant is steamed in the light casserole and fried in the other version; tomato sauce and cheese top both.

ITALIAN EGGPLANT CASSEROLE

1½ pounds eggplant (about 2 small)
¼ cup canned no-salt-added chicken broth, undiluted
¾ cup sliced fresh mushrooms
½ cup chopped onion
½ cup chopped celery
¼ cup chopped green onions
¼ cup chopped green pepper
2 (8-ounce) cans no-salt-added tomato sauce
¼ cup no-salt-added tomato paste
2 tablespoons chopped fresh parsley
¾ teaspoon minced fresh thyme
¾ teaspoon minced fresh oregano
½ teaspoon pepper
¼ teaspoon hot sauce
 Vegetable cooking spray
½ cup (2 ounces) shredded part-skim mozzarella cheese, divided
2 tablespoons freshly grated Parmesan cheese

Cut eggplant into ¼-inch-thick slices. Arrange eggplant, in batches, in a vegetable steamer over boiling water. Cover and steam 8 to 10 minutes or until tender. Drain on paper towels, and set aside.

Heat chicken broth in a large saucepan over medium-high heat until hot. Add mushrooms, onion, celery, green onions, and green pepper. Sauté until vegetables are tender. Remove from heat; add tomato sauce and next 6 ingredients, stirring well. Set aside.

Arrange half of eggplant slices in an 11- x 7- x 1½-inch baking dish coated with cooking spray. Spoon half of tomato mixture over eggplant; sprinkle ¼ cup mozzarella cheese over tomato mixture. Repeat procedure with remaining eggplant, tomato mixture, and mozzarella cheese. Top with Parmesan cheese. Bake, uncovered, at 350° for 30 minutes or until thoroughly heated. Yield: 8 servings.

Per serving: Calories 81 (20% from fat)
Carbohydrate 13.1g Protein 4.5g Fat 1.8g (Sat. Fat 1.0g)
Cholesterol 5mg Sodium 89mg

Eggplant Parmigiana

2 pounds eggplant (about 2 medium)
1 cup whole milk
1 egg, lightly beaten
1 tablespoon olive oil
1 cup all-purpose flour
 Vegetable oil
1 (14½-ounce) can stewed tomatoes
1 (15-ounce) can tomato sauce
1 (12-ounce) can tomato paste
1 tablespoon minced fresh oregano
1 teaspoon minced fresh basil
½ teaspoon minced fresh thyme
¼ teaspoon pepper
2 (8-ounce) packages mozzarella cheese slices
¼ cup freshly grated Parmesan cheese

Peel and cut eggplant into ½-inch-thick slices. Combine milk, egg, and olive oil; stir well. Gradually stir in flour. Dredge eggplant slices in flour mixture, coating well.

Pour vegetable oil to a depth of 1 inch into a large heavy skillet. Fry eggplant, in batches, in hot oil over medium heat until golden. Drain on paper towels, and set aside.

Drain stewed tomatoes, reserving ½ cup liquid. Chop tomatoes. Combine chopped tomato, reserved ½ cup tomato liquid, tomato sauce, and next 5 ingredients in a medium saucepan, stirring well. Bring mixture to a boil; cover, reduce heat, and simmer 10 minutes.

Arrange half of eggplant slices in a lightly greased 13- x 9- x 2-inch baking dish. Layer half of mozzarella cheese over eggplant, and spoon half of tomato mixture over cheese. Repeat procedure with remaining eggplant, mozzarella cheese, and tomato mixture. Top with Parmesan cheese. Bake, uncovered, at 350° for 30 minutes or until thoroughly heated. Yield: 8 servings.

Per serving: Calories 487 (57% from fat)
Carbohydrate 36.2g Protein 19.6g Fat 31.0g (Sat. Fat 11.7g)
Cholesterol 79mg Sodium 776mg

Egg substitute and reduced-fat cheese make the squash bake a healthy version of squash casserole.

SUMMER SQUASH BAKE

2   pounds yellow squash, cut into
    ¼-inch-thick slices
½   cup chopped onion
½   cup shredded carrot
½   cup (2 ounces) shredded reduced-fat
    Cheddar cheese
½   cup frozen egg substitute with cheese,
    thawed
1   (4-ounce) jar diced pimiento, drained
1   teaspoon low-sodium Worcestershire
    sauce
¼   teaspoon salt
¼   teaspoon pepper
    Vegetable cooking spray
3   tablespoons fine, dry breadcrumbs
1   tablespoon chopped fresh parsley
2   teaspoons chopped fresh oregano
¼   teaspoon paprika

Place squash, onion, and carrot in a vegetable steamer over boiling water; cover and steam 12 to 15 minutes or until vegetables are tender. Combine steamed vegetables, cheese, and next 5 ingredients in a medium bowl; stir well. Spoon mixture into a shallow 2-quart casserole coated with cooking spray.

Combine breadcrumbs and remaining ingredients in a small bowl; stir well. Sprinkle over squash mixture. Bake, uncovered, at 350° for 25 to 30 minutes or until thoroughly heated. Yield: 10 servings.

Per serving: Calories 62 (30% from fat)
Carbohydrate 7.1g Protein 4.6g Fat 2.1g (Sat. Fat 0.8g)
Cholesterol 4mg Sodium 164mg

Country Club Squash Gratin

1   pound yellow squash, cut into
    ¼-inch-thick slices
1   cup chopped onion
1   cup shredded carrot
1   (8-ounce) can sliced water chestnuts,
    drained
1   (2-ounce) jar diced pimiento, drained
2   tablespoons butter
2   tablespoons all-purpose flour
1   cup half-and-half
½   teaspoon salt
⅛   teaspoon ground white pepper
⅛   teaspoon pepper
⅛   teaspoon ground nutmeg
⅛   teaspoon hot sauce
½   cup sour cream
2   cups (8 ounces) shredded Cheddar
    cheese
1   egg, lightly beaten
½   cup herb-seasoned stuffing mix
2   tablespoons butter, melted

Place squash and onion in a medium saucepan; add water to cover. Bring to a boil; reduce heat, and simmer, uncovered, 15 minutes or until squash is tender. Drain squash and onion; add carrot, water chestnuts, and pimiento.

Melt 2 tablespoons butter in a heavy saucepan over low heat; add flour, stirring until smooth. Cook, stirring constantly, 1 minute. Gradually add half-and-half, stirring constantly; cook over medium heat, stirring constantly, until mixture is thickened and bubbly. Stir in salt, peppers, nutmeg, and hot sauce. Gradually stir in sour cream, cheese, and egg.

Combine sauce mixture and vegetable mixture, stirring well. Spoon mixture into a lightly greased shallow 2-quart casserole. Combine stuffing mix and melted butter; sprinkle over squash mixture. Bake, uncovered, at 350° for 45 minutes or until thoroughly heated. Yield: 10 servings.

Per serving: Calories 248 (67% from fat)
Carbohydrate 12.5g Protein 9.0g Fat 18.5g (Sat. Fat 11.4g)
Cholesterol 73mg Sodium 401mg

Fill Fruited Acorn Squash with a sweetened pineapple-orange mixture before baking. For the luscious maple-pecan version, mix the squash with pecans, maple syrup, margarine, and spices. Top with marshmallows, and sprinkle with additional pecans.

FRUITED ACORN SQUASH

2   medium acorn squash (about 2
      pounds)
    Vegetable cooking spray
¾   cup canned crushed pineapple in juice,
      drained
¾   cup chopped orange
3   tablespoons brown sugar
½   teaspoon ground cinnamon
    Orange rind curls (optional)
    Cinnamon sticks (optional)

Cut each squash in half crosswise; remove and discard seeds. Place squash halves, cut side down, in a 15- x 10- x 1-inch jellyroll pan lightly coated with cooking spray. Bake, uncovered, at 350° for 35 minutes.

Combine pineapple, orange, and brown sugar; spoon evenly into squash halves. Sprinkle with cinnamon. Bake, uncovered, an additional 10 to 15 minutes or until fruit mixture is thoroughly heated. If desired, garnish with orange rind curls and cinnamon sticks. Yield: 4 servings.

Per serving: Calories 167 (2% from fat)
Carbohydrate 43.1g   Protein 2.4g   Fat 0.4g (Sat. Fat 0.1g)
Cholesterol 0mg   Sodium 10mg

Maple Pecan Squash

2   medium acorn squash (about 2
      pounds)
½   cup plus 2 tablespoons chopped
      pecans, divided
¼   cup maple-flavored syrup
2   tablespoons margarine, melted
¼   teaspoon salt
¼   teaspoon ground cinnamon
¼   teaspoon ground nutmeg
¼   cup miniature marshmallows

Cut each squash in half crosswise; remove and discard seeds. Place squash halves, cut side down, in a lightly greased 15- x 10- x 1-inch jellyroll pan. Bake, uncovered, at 350° for 35 minutes.

Scoop out pulp; discard shells. Mash pulp in a medium bowl. Add ½ cup pecans and next 5 ingredients; stir well. Spoon mixture evenly into 4 (6-ounce) lightly greased baking dishes. Top evenly with marshmallows and remaining 2 tablespoons chopped pecans. Bake, uncovered, at 350° for 15 minutes or until lightly browned. Yield: 4 servings.

Per serving: Calories 324 (50% from fat)
Carbohydrate 43.3   Protein 3.3g   Fat 18.0g (Sat. Fat 2.2g)
Cholesterol 0mg   Sodium 223mg

Left: *Fruited Acorn Squash*

Keep potato casserole on the light side by using skim milk, reduced-calorie margarine, and reduced-fat Monterey Jack cheese. When the occasion calls for a luscious treat, bake potato slices with whipping cream, whole milk, and generous amounts of two cheeses.

MONTEREY JACK POTATO GRATIN

3 tablespoons all-purpose flour
2 cups skim milk, divided
½ cup instant nonfat dry milk powder
2 tablespoons reduced-calorie margarine, melted
½ teaspoon salt
½ teaspoon ground white pepper
¼ teaspoon ground nutmeg
2 teaspoons minced garlic
Vegetable cooking spray
1 cup thinly sliced onion, separated into rings
2 pounds red potatoes, peeled and thinly sliced
1 (9-ounce) package frozen artichoke hearts, thawed and drained
¼ cup grated Parmesan cheese
½ cup (2 ounces) shredded reduced-fat Monterey Jack cheese

Combine flour and ½ cup milk in a medium saucepan; stir until smooth. Stir in remaining 1½ cups milk, milk powder, and margarine. Cook over medium heat, stirring constantly with a wire whisk, until mixture is thickened and bubbly. Stir in salt, pepper, and nutmeg.

Sprinkle garlic in a 13- x 9- x 2-inch baking dish coated with cooking spray. Arrange half of onion rings over garlic; top with half of potato slices. Arrange artichoke hearts over potato. Repeat layers with remaining onion and potato slices. Pour sauce mixture over potato slices, and sprinkle with Parmesan cheese. Bake, uncovered, at 350° for 40 minutes. Sprinkle evenly with Monterey Jack cheese. Bake an additional 20 minutes or until potato is tender. Let stand 10 minutes before serving. Yield: 10 servings.

Per serving: Calories 154 (21% from fat)
Carbohydrate 22.0g Protein 9.8g Fat 3.6g (Sat. Fat 1.3g)
Cholesterol 8mg Sodium 292mg

Blue Cheese and Cheddar Potato Gratin

¼ cup margarine
¼ cup all-purpose flour
1 cup whipping cream
1 cup whole milk
½ teaspoon salt
½ teaspoon ground white pepper
¼ teaspoon ground nutmeg
½ cup crumbled blue cheese
2 teaspoons minced garlic
1 cup thinly sliced onion, separated into rings
2 pounds red potatoes, peeled and thinly sliced
1 (9-ounce) package frozen artichoke hearts, thawed and drained
1 cup (4 ounces) shredded white Cheddar cheese

Melt margarine in a heavy saucepan over low heat; add flour, stirring until smooth. Cook, stirring constantly, 1 minute. Gradually add cream and milk; cook over medium heat, stirring constantly, until mixture is thickened and bubbly. Stir in salt, pepper, and nutmeg.

Sprinkle blue cheese and garlic in a lightly greased 13- x 9- x 2-inch baking dish. Arrange half of onion rings over blue cheese and garlic; top with half of potato slices. Arrange artichoke hearts over potato slices. Pour half of sauce mixture over artichoke hearts. Repeat layers with remaining onion, potato slices, and sauce mixture. Bake, covered, at 350° for 1 hour. Sprinkle evenly with Cheddar cheese. Bake, uncovered, an additional 15 minutes or until potato is tender. Let stand 10 minutes before serving. Yield: 10 servings.

Per serving: Calories 277 (66% from fat)
Carbohydrate 17.2g Protein 8.4g Fat 20.2g (Sat. Fat 10.5g)
Cholesterol 52mg Sodium 365mg

Both of these presentations make sweet potatoes special. The light soufflé is made with egg substitute and delicately flavored spices. The sweet potato cups offer a twist on the light casserole with a splash of orange liqueur and a streusel topping.

ORANGE SWEET POTATO SOUFFLÉ

2	cups peeled, cubed sweet potato
¾	cup evaporated skimmed milk
½	cup frozen egg substitute, thawed
¼	cup firmly packed brown sugar
1	tablespoon frozen orange juice concentrate, thawed and undiluted
1	tablespoon Triple Sec or other orange-flavored liqueur
½	teaspoon ground cinnamon
½	teaspoon ground allspice
¼	teaspoon salt
¼	teaspoon ground nutmeg
3	egg whites

Cook sweet potato in boiling water to cover 15 minutes or until tender; drain. Transfer sweet potato to a large bowl. Beat at medium speed of an electric mixer until smooth. Add milk and next 8 ingredients; beat at low speed until blended.

Beat egg whites at high speed of an electric mixer until stiff peaks form. Fold one-third of beaten egg whites into sweet potato mixture; fold in remaining egg whites. Spoon mixture into an ungreased 2-quart soufflé dish. Bake, uncovered, at 325° for 55 minutes or until golden. Serve immediately. Yield: 6 servings.

Per serving: Calories 132 (2% from fat)
Carbohydrate 25.8g Protein 6.9g Fat 0.3g (Sat. Fat 0.1g)
Cholesterol 1mg Sodium 200mg

Orange Sweet Potato Cups

4½	cups peeled, cubed sweet potato
3	tablespoons margarine
½	cup unsweetened orange juice
¼	cup whipping cream
1	tablespoon brown sugar
1	tablespoon Triple Sec or other orange-flavored liqueur
¼	teaspoon salt
¼	teaspoon ground nutmeg
¼	cup firmly packed brown sugar
1½	tablespoons all-purpose flour
1½	tablespoons margarine, softened
¼	cup finely chopped pecans

Cook sweet potato in boiling water to cover 15 minutes or until tender; drain. Combine sweet potato and 3 tablespoons margarine in a large bowl; mash. Add orange juice and next 5 ingredients; stir well. Spoon mixture into 4 lightly greased 8-ounce ramekins; set aside.

Combine ¼ cup brown sugar, flour, 1½ tablespoons margarine, and chopped pecans; sprinkle evenly over sweet potato mixture in ramekins. Bake, uncovered, at 350° for 20 minutes or until bubbly. Yield: 4 servings.

Per serving: Calories 464 (47% from fat)
Carbohydrate 58.7g Protein 3.8g Fat 24.1g (Sat. Fat 6.5g)
Cholesterol 20mg Sodium 330mg

Transform plain grits into an appealing side dish with garlic and cheese. The light zippy grits contain skim milk and reduced-fat Cheddar cheese. The creamy grits are prepared with whole milk, margarine, sharp Cheddar cheese, and whipping cream.

ZIPPY GARLIC CHEESE GRITS

4 cups water
½ cup skim milk
1 cup quick-cooking grits, uncooked
1 teaspoon minced garlic
¼ teaspoon salt
2 teaspoons low-sodium Worcestershire sauce
¼ teaspoon hot sauce
1½ cups (6 ounces) shredded reduced-fat Cheddar cheese

Combine water and milk in a medium saucepan; bring to a boil. Stir in grits and next 4 ingredients. Cover, reduce heat, and simmer 10 to 12 minutes or until creamy, stirring occasionally. Stir in cheese. Cook, uncovered, over medium heat, stirring frequently, 12 to 15 minutes or until grits are thickened. Yield: 10 (½-cup) servings.

Per serving: Calories 111 (27% from fat)
Carbohydrate 13.4g Protein 6.9g Fat 3.3g (Sat. Fat 1.9g)
Cholesterol 11mg Sodium 196mg

Creamy Garlic Cheese Grits

2 cups water
2 cups whole milk
¼ cup margarine
1 teaspoon minced garlic
1 cup quick-cooking grits, uncooked
1 teaspoon salt
1½ cups (6 ounces) shredded sharp Cheddar cheese
½ cup whipping cream

Combine water and milk in a medium saucepan; bring to a boil. Add margarine and garlic; stir until margarine melts. Stir in grits and salt; cover, reduce heat, and simmer 15 minutes or until creamy, stirring occasionally. Stir in cheese and whipping cream. Cook, uncovered, over medium heat, stirring frequently, 12 to 15 minutes or until grits are thickened. Yield: 10 (½-cup) servings.

Per serving: Calories 235 (62% from fat)
Carbohydrate 15.1g Protein 7.5g Fat 16.3g (Sat. Fat 8.2g)
Cholesterol 41mg Sodium 422mg

Macaroni and cheese is everyone's favorite, and it's even better with the addition of green pepper, celery, mushrooms, and a breadcrumb topping. Sour cream and mayonnaise give each casserole an extra-creamy base, but Light Macaroni Casserole uses nonfat versions of these products.

LIGHT MACARONI CASSEROLE

1   cup elbow macaroni, uncooked
    Vegetable cooking spray
⅓   cup chopped green pepper
⅓   cup chopped celery
⅓   cup chopped onion
¼   cup canned no-salt-added chicken
        broth, undiluted
2   ounces nonfat process cheese spread
        loaf, cubed
1   cup nonfat mayonnaise
1   (8-ounce) carton nonfat sour cream
        alternative
1   (4-ounce) can sliced mushrooms,
        drained
1   (4-ounce) jar diced pimiento, drained
¼   teaspoon black pepper
⅛   teaspoon ground red pepper
¼   cup soft whole wheat breadcrumbs
¼   teaspoon paprika

Cook macaroni according to package directions, omitting salt and fat. Drain and set aside.

Coat a medium nonstick skillet with cooking spray; place over medium-high heat until hot. Add green pepper, celery, onion, and chicken broth; sauté over medium-high heat 3 minutes or until vegetables are tender and liquid evaporates.

Combine vegetables, macaroni, cheese cubes, and next 6 ingredients in a large bowl, stirring well. Transfer to a 1½-quart baking dish coated with cooking spray. Bake, uncovered, at 325° for 20 minutes. Sprinkle with breadcrumbs and paprika; bake an additional 10 minutes or until thoroughly heated. Yield: 10 servings.

Per serving: Calories 95 (4% from fat)
Carbohydrate 17.6g   Protein 4.8g   Fat 0.4g (Sat. Fat 0.1g)
Cholesterol 1mg   Sodium 434mg

Macaroni Olive Gratin

1   cup elbow macaroni, uncooked
⅓   cup chopped green pepper
⅓   cup chopped celery
⅓   cup chopped onion
2   tablespoons olive oil
1   cup mayonnaise
½   cup (2 ounces) shredded Cheddar
        cheese
1   (8-ounce) carton sour cream
1   (4-ounce) can sliced mushrooms,
        drained
1   (4-ounce) can sliced ripe olives,
        drained
1   (4-ounce) jar diced pimiento,
        drained
¼   teaspoon black pepper
⅛   teaspoon ground red pepper
¼   cup Italian-seasoned breadcrumbs
2   tablespoons margarine, melted
¼   teaspoon paprika

Cook macaroni according to package directions. Drain and set aside.

Sauté green pepper, celery, and onion in hot olive oil in a medium skillet over medium-high heat 5 minutes or until tender.

Combine vegetables, macaroni, mayonnaise, and next 7 ingredients in a large bowl; stir well. Transfer to a greased 1½-quart baking dish. Bake, uncovered, at 325° for 20 minutes. Combine breadcrumbs and margarine; stir well. Sprinkle breadcrumb mixture and paprika over casserole. Bake an additional 10 minutes or until thoroughly heated. Yield: 10 servings.

Per serving: Calories 348 (80% from fat)
Carbohydrate 14.3g   Protein 4.7g   Fat 30.9g (Sat. Fat 7.9g)
Cholesterol 29mg   Sodium 633mg

Pasta with Mushrooms and Pine Nuts is full of flavorful ingredients that add little or no fat, such as sun-dried tomatoes, shiitake mushrooms, and roasted red peppers. The luscious pasta also has sun-dried tomatoes, mushrooms, and peppers, but it gets extra punch from pesto sauce.

PASTA WITH MUSHROOMS AND PINE NUTS

1½ ounces sun-dried tomatoes
½ cup hot water
6½ ounces linguine, uncooked and broken in half
1 cup canned no-salt-added chicken broth, undiluted
3½ ounces fresh shiitake mushrooms, thinly sliced
½ cup chopped shallots
1 teaspoon minced garlic
2 teaspoons dried whole basil
½ teaspoon freshly ground pepper
½ cup drained roasted red peppers in water, cut into thin strips
¼ cup pine nuts, toasted
2 tablespoons grated Parmesan cheese
2 tablespoons chopped fresh parsley
 Fresh basil sprigs (optional)

Combine tomatoes and water in a small bowl; cover and let stand 15 minutes. Drain tomatoes, and slice thinly; set aside.

Cook pasta according to package directions, omitting salt and fat. Drain and set aside.

Place chicken broth in a large nonstick skillet; bring to a boil. Add mushrooms, shallots, and garlic; cook, uncovered, over medium heat 5 minutes. Add tomato, basil, and ground pepper. Cook, covered, 10 minutes. Add reserved pasta, pepper strips, pine nuts, and cheese; stir well. Cover and cook an additional 5 minutes or until thoroughly heated. Sprinkle with fresh parsley, and serve immediately. Garnish with fresh basil sprigs, if desired. Yield: 10 (½-cup) servings.

Per serving: Calories 119 (21% from fat)
Carbohydrate 19.6g Protein 5.0g Fat 2.8g (Sat. Fat 0.6g)
Cholesterol 1mg Sodium 120mg

Mushroom Pesto Pasta

1½ ounces sun-dried tomatoes
½ cup hot water
6½ ounces linguine, uncooked and broken in half
3½ ounces fresh shiitake mushrooms, thinly sliced
½ cup chopped shallots
3 tablespoons olive oil
½ cup commercial pesto sauce
½ cup canned, drained roasted red peppers, cut into thin strips
⅓ cup chopped fresh parsley

Combine tomatoes and water in a small bowl; cover and let stand 15 minutes. Drain tomatoes, and slice thinly; set aside.

Cook pasta according to package directions, omitting salt and fat. Drain and set aside.

Sauté mushrooms and shallots in hot olive oil until tender. Add tomato and pesto sauce; cook, uncovered, over medium heat 5 minutes. Add reserved pasta and pepper strips; stir well. Cover and cook an additional 5 minutes or until thoroughly heated. Sprinkle with fresh parsley, and serve immediately. Yield: 10 (½-cup) servings.

Per serving: Calories 194 (51% from fat)
Carbohydrate 20.9g Protein 5.1g Fat 10.9g (Sat. Fat 1.7g)
Cholesterol 1mg Sodium 231mg

Left: *Pasta with Mushrooms and Pine Nuts*

Spinach and Noodle Bake stays healthy with low-fat products such as nonfat sour cream, evaporated skimmed milk, egg substitute, and reduced-fat Swiss cheese. Nutty Spinach Noodle Casserole is rich with toasted walnuts, sour cream, half-and-half, and lots of Swiss cheese.

SPINACH AND NOODLE BAKE

8   ounces medium egg noodles, uncooked
½   cup chopped onion
¼   cup canned no-salt-added chicken broth, undiluted
1   teaspoon minced garlic
1   (10-ounce) package frozen chopped spinach, thawed and drained
1   (4-ounce) can sliced mushrooms, drained
1   cup (4 ounces) shredded reduced-fat Swiss cheese
1   (8-ounce) carton nonfat sour cream alternative
½   cup frozen egg substitute, thawed
½   cup evaporated skimmed milk
¼   teaspoon salt
¼   teaspoon sweet Hungarian paprika
¼   teaspoon ground red pepper
¼   teaspoon black pepper
    Vegetable cooking spray

Cook noodles according to package directions, omitting salt and fat. Drain and set aside.

Combine onion, chicken broth, and garlic in a large saucepan; stir well. Cook over medium heat, stirring constantly, until onion is tender. Add noodles, spinach, and mushrooms; stir well.

Combine cheese and next 7 ingredients in a medium bowl; stir well. Add cheese mixture to noodle mixture, stirring well. Spoon into an 11- x 7- x 1½-inch baking dish coated with cooking spray. Cover and bake at 350° for 30 minutes or until thoroughly heated. Yield: 12 servings.

Per serving: Calories 140 (17% from fat)
Carbohydrate 18.7g   Protein 10.0g   Fat 2.7g (Sat. Fat 1.1g)
Cholesterol 24mg   Sodium 145mg

Nutty Spinach Noodle Casserole

8   ounces medium egg noodles, uncooked
¼   cup chopped onion
1   tablespoon olive oil
⅓   cup chopped walnuts, toasted
1   (10-ounce) package frozen chopped spinach, thawed and drained
1   (4-ounce) can sliced mushrooms, drained
2   cups (8 ounces) shredded Swiss cheese
1   (8-ounce) carton sour cream
½   cup half-and-half
2   eggs, lightly beaten
½   teaspoon salt
¼   teaspoon sweet Hungarian paprika
¼   teaspoon ground red pepper
¼   teaspoon black pepper

Cook noodles according to package directions. Drain and set aside.

Sauté onion in hot olive oil in a large saucepan over medium-high heat until tender. Add noodles, walnuts, spinach, and mushrooms; stir well.

Combine cheese and remaining ingredients in a medium bowl; stir well. Add cheese mixture to noodle mixture, stirring well. Spoon into a lightly greased 2½-quart casserole. Cover and bake at 350° for 30 minutes or until thoroughly heated. Yield: 12 servings.

Per serving: Calories 244 (54% from fat)
Carbohydrate 17.4g   Protein 11.5g   Fat 14.7g (Sat. Fat 7.3g)
Cholesterol 84mg   Sodium 210mg

Both recipes produce a delectably creamy risotto containing peas, carrot, onion, and tangy Romano cheese. In the luscious Romano Walnut Risotto, the onions are sautéed in butter and olive oil, and toasted walnuts and extra cheese add even more texture and flavor.

VEGETABLE PIMIENTO RISOTTO

¾ cup frozen English peas
¾ cup chopped carrot
3 cups canned no-salt-added chicken broth, undiluted and divided
½ cup Chablis or other dry white wine
⅓ cup finely chopped onion
⅓ cup chopped green onions
1 cup Arborio rice, uncooked
3 tablespoons freshly grated Romano cheese
1 (2-ounce) jar diced pimiento, drained
2 tablespoons chopped fresh parsley

Arrange peas and carrot in a vegetable steamer over boiling water. Cover and steam 8 minutes or until vegetables are tender. Set aside.

Combine 2½ cups broth and wine in a medium saucepan; place over medium heat. Bring to a simmer; cover, reduce heat, and maintain a very low simmer.

Place remaining ½ cup broth in a medium saucepan; bring to a boil over medium-high heat. Add chopped onion and green onions; cook 4 minutes or until tender. Stir in rice. Add ½ cup simmering broth mixture to rice mixture; stir constantly until most of the liquid is absorbed. Continue adding broth mixture, ½ cup at a time, stirring each time until liquid is absorbed (the entire process should take about 30 minutes). Stir in peas, carrot, cheese, pimiento, and parsley; serve immediately. Yield: 8 (½-cup) servings.

Per serving: Calories 130 (7% from fat)
Carbohydrate 25.1g Protein 3.7g Fat 1.0g (Sat. Fat 0.5g)
Cholesterol 3mg Sodium 56mg

Romano Walnut Risotto

¾ cup frozen English peas
¾ cup chopped carrot
3 cups canned ready-to-serve chicken broth
½ cup Chablis or other dry white wine
⅓ cup finely chopped onion
⅓ cup chopped green onions
2 tablespoons margarine, melted
2 tablespoons olive oil
1 cup Arborio rice, uncooked
¼ cup plus 2 tablespoons freshly grated Romano cheese, divided
¼ cup chopped walnuts, toasted
2 tablespoons chopped fresh parsley

Arrange peas and carrot in a vegetable steamer over boiling water. Cover and steam 8 minutes or until vegetables are tender. Set aside.

Combine broth and wine in a medium saucepan; place over medium heat. Bring to a simmer; cover, reduce heat, and maintain a very low simmer.

Sauté chopped onion and green onions in margarine and hot olive oil in a medium saucepan over medium-high heat until tender. Add rice, and sauté 4 minutes or until rice is translucent. Add ½ cup simmering broth mixture to rice mixture; stir constantly until most of the liquid is absorbed. Continue adding broth mixture, ½ cup at a time, stirring each time until liquid is absorbed (the entire process should take about 30 minutes). Stir in peas, carrot, ¼ cup cheese, walnuts, and parsley. Sprinkle with remaining 2 tablespoons Romano cheese; serve immediately. Yield: 8 (½-cup) servings.

Per serving: Calories 224 (43% from fat)
Carbohydrate 25.0g Protein 7.1g Fat 10.6g (Sat. Fat 2.3g)
Cholesterol 6mg Sodium 409mg

For low-fat flavor, simmer the rice and onions in no-salt-added chicken broth, and sprinkle with a few pine nuts. Add a Mediterranean touch to the luscious version by sautéing the rice in olive oil and stirring in a generous portion of nuts.

WILD RICE WITH PINE NUTS

2 cups canned no-salt-added chicken broth, undiluted
1 cup chopped onion
½ cup wild rice, uncooked
½ cup brown rice, uncooked
3 tablespoons pine nuts, toasted
1 teaspoon pepper
1 teaspoon dried whole basil
⅛ teaspoon salt

Combine first 4 ingredients in a medium saucepan; bring to a boil. Cover, reduce heat, and simmer 30 minutes. Stir in toasted pine nuts and remaining ingredients. Cover and simmer an additional 15 minutes or until rice is tender and liquid is absorbed. Yield: 6 (½-cup) servings.

Per serving: Calories 161 (27% from fat)
Carbohydrate 26.1g Protein 4.5g Fat 4.9g (Sat. Fat 0.8g)
Cholesterol 0mg Sodium 58mg

Mediterranean Wild Rice

½ cup wild rice, uncooked
½ cup brown rice, uncooked
3 tablespoons olive oil, divided
2 cups canned ready-to-serve chicken broth
1 cup chopped onion
½ cup pine nuts, toasted
1 teaspoon pepper
1 teaspoon dried whole basil
½ teaspoon salt

Sauté wild rice and brown rice in 2 tablespoons hot olive oil in a medium saucepan over medium-high heat 2 minutes. Add broth; bring to a boil. Cover, reduce heat, and simmer 30 minutes.

Sauté onion in remaining 1 tablespoon hot olive oil in a medium skillet over medium-high heat until tender. Stir in toasted pine nuts and remaining ingredients. Add onion mixture to rice mixture. Cover and simmer an additional 15 minutes or until rice is tender and liquid is absorbed. Yield: 6 (½-cup) servings.

Per serving: Calories 293 (59% from fat)
Carbohydrate 28.0g Protein 7.3g Fat 19.2g (Sat. Fat 2.9g)
Cholesterol 0mg Sodium 470mg

Parslied Rice Casserole contains more rice, fewer eggs, and less cheese than the other casserole, and it also has nonfat yogurt and low-fat cottage cheese. The cheesy Green Rice Casserole gains richness from whole milk, Cheddar cheese, and eggs.

PARSLIED RICE CASSEROLE

1 (8-ounce) carton plain nonfat yogurt
1 tablespoon all-purpose flour
1½ cups 1% low-fat cottage cheese
1 egg white
½ teaspoon hot sauce
⅛ teaspoon salt
⅛ teaspoon pepper
4 cups cooked long-grain rice (cooked without salt or fat)
¾ cup (3 ounces) reduced-fat Cheddar cheese
½ cup chopped green onions
¼ cup minced fresh parsley, divided
1 tablespoon chopped fresh cilantro
Vegetable cooking spray

Combine yogurt and flour in a large bowl; stir until smooth. Add cottage cheese and next 4 ingredients, stirring well. Stir in rice, Cheddar cheese, green onions, 3 tablespoons parsley, and cilantro.

Spoon mixture into a 2-quart baking dish coated with cooking spray. Bake, uncovered, at 350° for 30 minutes or until thoroughly heated. Sprinkle with remaining 1 tablespoon parsley. Yield: 12 servings.

Per serving: Calories 130 (12% from fat)
Carbohydrate 19.3g Protein 8.5g Fat 1.8g (Sat. Fat 1.0g)
Cholesterol 6mg Sodium 213mg

Green Rice Casserole

2 cups cooked long-grain rice
1 cup (4 ounces) shredded sharp Cheddar cheese
¾ cup whole milk
½ cup chopped fresh parsley
¼ cup margarine, melted
3 eggs, separated
¼ cup chopped green pepper
¼ cup finely chopped onion
½ teaspoon salt
1 (4-ounce) can chopped green chiles, drained

Combine first 5 ingredients in a large bowl; stir well. Stir in egg yolks, green pepper, onion, salt, and green chiles.

Beat egg whites at high speed of an electric mixer until stiff peaks form. Gently fold into rice mixture. Spoon mixture into a lightly greased 2-quart baking dish. Bake, uncovered, at 350° for 30 minutes or until thoroughly heated. Yield: 12 servings.

Per serving: Calories 147 (58% from fat)
Carbohydrate 10.1g Protein 5.4g Fat 9.4g (Sat. Fat 3.6g)
Cholesterol 67mg Sodium 438mg

Parson's Curried Fruit omits the wine and uses fruit in either juice or light syrup instead of fruit in heavy syrup. It also leaves out the margarine and toasted almonds. Sweetened fruit, wine, and almonds make Curried Fruit with Almonds a side dish rich enough to serve as dessert.

PARSON'S CURRIED FRUIT

1   (16-ounce) can apricot halves in light syrup
1   (8-ounce) can pineapple chunks in juice
1   (16-ounce) can peach halves in juice, drained
1   (16-ounce) can pear halves in juice, drained
3   tablespoons brown sugar
2   teaspoons curry powder

Drain apricot halves and pineapple chunks, reserving 1 cup liquid. Set liquid aside.

Combine drained apricots, pineapple, peaches, and pears in an 11- x 7- x 1½-inch baking dish. Combine reserved liquid, brown sugar, and curry powder in a small bowl; stir well. Pour over fruit mixture. Bake, uncovered, at 350° for 25 minutes or until thoroughly heated and bubbly. Serve with a slotted spoon. Yield: 8 (½-cup) servings.

Per serving: Calories 92 (2% from fat)
Carbohydrate 22.9g   Protein 0.7g   Fat 0.2g (Sat. Fat 0.0g)
Cholesterol 0mg   Sodium 5mg

Curried Fruit with Almonds

1   (16-ounce) can pear halves in heavy syrup
1   (16-ounce) can peach halves in heavy syrup
1   (16-ounce) can pitted Royal Anne cherries
1   (15¼-ounce) can pineapple chunks in heavy syrup
½   (16-ounce) can apricot halves in heavy syrup
¼   cup firmly packed brown sugar
3   tablespoons all-purpose flour
3   tablespoons margarine
½   cup golden raisins
½   cup Reisling or other sweet white wine
2   teaspoons curry powder
¼   cup sliced almonds, toasted

Drain fruit, reserving ¾ cup liquid. Set drained fruit and liquid aside.

Combine brown sugar and flour in a saucepan; stir well. Gradually stir in reserved liquid. Add margarine and raisins; cook over medium heat, stirring constantly, until mixture comes to a boil. Boil, stirring constantly, 1 minute. Remove from heat; stir in wine and curry powder.

Spoon drained fruit into an 11- x 7- x 1½-inch baking dish; pour wine mixture over fruit. Sprinkle with sliced almonds. Bake, uncovered, at 350° for 25 to 30 minutes or until thoroughly heated. Yield: 10 (½-cup) servings.

Per serving: Calories 206 (21% from fat)
Carbohydrate 42.3g   Protein 1.5g   Fat 4.9g (Sat. Fat 0.8g)
Cholesterol 0mg   Sodium 52mg

Sautéed Pineapple makes the most of the natural sweetness of pineapple and adds minimal sugar and margarine. Eggs, margarine, and cubes of French bread give Scalloped Pineapple a rich custard base.

SAUTÉED PINEAPPLE

2 (20-ounce) cans pineapple chunks in juice
1 tablespoon reduced-calorie margarine
2 tablespoons brown sugar
1 tablespoon rum
½ teaspoon ground cinnamon

Drain pineapple chunks, reserving ¼ cup juice. Set drained pineapple and juice aside.

Melt margarine in a large nonstick skillet over medium heat; add pineapple chunks, reserved juice, brown sugar, rum, and cinnamon. Bring to a boil; reduce heat, and simmer 5 minutes, stirring frequently. Serve warm. Yield: 6 servings.

Per serving: Calories 103 (10% from fat)
Carbohydrate 23.1g Protein 0.0g Fat 1.2g (Sat. Fat 0.2g)
Cholesterol 0mg Sodium 21mg

Scalloped Pineapple

1 (20-ounce) can crushed pineapple in heavy syrup, undrained
1¼ cups sugar
⅓ cup margarine, melted
4 (1-ounce) slices French bread, cut into 1-inch cubes
3 eggs, well beaten
½ teaspoon ground cinnamon

Combine all ingredients in a medium bowl, stirring well. Spoon mixture into a lightly greased 11- x 7- x 1½-inch baking dish. Bake, uncovered, at 350° for 35 to 40 minutes or until golden and bubbly. Serve warm. Yield: 6 servings.

Per serving: Calories 419 (28% from fat)
Carbohydrate 71.8g Protein 5.4g Fat 13.2g (Sat. Fat 2.9g)
Cholesterol 111mg Sodium 262mg

From left: *Chocolate Torte (page 218), Cocoa Meringue Cookies and Chocolate Filled Meringue Cookies (page 221), Rum Raisin Ice Milk (page 210)*

DESSERTS

You'll do more than satisfy your sweet tooth when you enjoy Honeyed Ambrosia. The honey-drizzled fruit offers familiar flavor with less than one gram of fat. Go beyond the traditional fruit and coconut mixture with Layered Ambrosia, and top fruit with pecans and whipped cream.

Honeyed Ambrosia

½ cup honey
¼ cup chopped fresh mint
¼ cup lemon juice
3 cups fresh grapefruit sections
4 oranges, peeled and thinly sliced
3 tablespoons flaked coconut, toasted

Combine first 3 ingredients in a small bowl; stir well.

Combine grapefruit sections and orange slices in a medium bowl. Drizzle honey mixture over fruit; toss gently to coat. Cover and chill at least 2 hours. Just before serving, sprinkle fruit mixture with coconut. Yield: 12 (½-cup) servings.

Per serving: Calories 91 (6% from fat)
Carbohydrate 22.6g Protein 0.9g Fat 0.6g (Sat. Fat 0.5g)
Cholesterol 0mg Sodium 5mg

Layered Ambrosia

2 medium bananas, peeled and sliced
1 teaspoon lemon juice
1½ cups orange sections
1½ cups fresh strawberries, halved
1½ cups fresh pineapple chunks
¼ cup sour cream
1 tablespoon sugar
2 tablespoons Grand Marnier or other orange-flavored liqueur
½ cup flaked coconut
½ cup whipping cream, whipped
½ cup chopped pecans, toasted

Combine banana and lemon juice in a small bowl; toss gently to coat. Layer orange sections, banana, strawberries, and pineapple in a 1½-quart serving bowl; cover and chill.

Combine sour cream, sugar, and liqueur; fold in coconut and whipped cream. Spoon sour cream mixture over fruit, and sprinkle with pecans. Yield: 12 (½-cup) servings.

Per serving: Calories 156 (56% from fat)
Carbohydrate 16.5g Protein 1.5g Fat 9.8g (Sat. Fat 4.4g)
Cholesterol 16mg Sodium 16mg

End your meal on a sweet and tangy note with one of these pineapple desserts. The light version is glazed with a mixture of orange juice, rum, and honey and topped with nonfat frozen yogurt. The luscious Pineapple Fritters are dipped in a sweetened batter, fried, and crowned with ice cream.

GLAZED PINEAPPLE

6 (¾-inch-thick) slices fresh pineapple
    (about 1 medium)
¼ cup plus 2 tablespoons firmly packed
    brown sugar
    Vegetable cooking spray
1 tablespoon margarine
1 cup unsweetened orange juice
3 tablespoons dark rum
2 tablespoons honey
1½ cups vanilla nonfat frozen yogurt

Sprinkle both sides of pineapple slices evenly with brown sugar.

Coat a large nonstick skillet with cooking spray; add margarine. Place over medium-high heat until margarine melts. Add pineapple slices, and cook 4 minutes on each side or until tender. Transfer pineapple slices to individual serving plates.

Add orange juice, rum, and honey to skillet; bring to a boil. Cook until mixture is reduced to ½ cup. Pour orange juice mixture evenly over pineapple slices; top each slice with ¼ cup frozen yogurt. Serve immediately. Yield: 6 servings.

Per serving: Calories 231 (10% from fat)
Carbohydrate 47.7g Protein 2.5g Fat 2.5g (Sat. Fat 0.4g)
Cholesterol 0mg Sodium 60mg

Pineapple Fritters

¾ cup all-purpose flour
½ teaspoon baking powder
⅛ teaspoon salt
¼ cup sugar
¼ cup plus 1 tablespoon whole milk
1 tablespoon margarine, melted
1 egg, lightly beaten
    Vegetable oil
6 (¾-inch-thick) slices fresh pineapple
    (about 1 medium)
½ cup sifted powdered sugar
¼ teaspoon ground cinnamon
1½ cups Neapolitan ice cream

Combine first 4 ingredients in a medium bowl; add milk, margarine, and egg, stirring with a wire whisk until blended.

Pour oil to a depth of 2 to 3 inches into a Dutch oven; heat to 375°. Dredge pineapple slices in flour mixture. Fry pineapple slices in hot oil, 2 slices at a time, until golden, turning once. Drain well on paper towels.

Combine powdered sugar and cinnamon; sift over warm pineapple slices. Transfer slices to individual serving plates; top each with ¼ cup Neapolitan ice cream. Serve immediately. Yield: 6 servings.

Per serving: Calories 516 (57% from fat)
Carbohydrate 54.3g Protein 5.1g Fat 32.4g (Sat. Fat 7.7g)
Cholesterol 54mg Sodium 142mg

Top the light poached pears with raspberry sherbet and drizzle with melted chocolate for a simple but elegant dessert. Pralines-and-cream ice cream and a rich chocolate sauce contribute to the lusciousness of Poached Pear Sundaes.

POACHED PEARS WITH RASPBERRY SHERBET

3 large ripe pears
2 teaspoons lemon juice
1 cup white Zinfandel or other blush wine
½ cup sugar
½ cup unsweetened apple juice
1 tablespoon lemon juice
1 (1-ounce) square semisweet chocolate, melted
1½ cups raspberry sherbet
  Fresh raspberries (optional)
  Fresh mint sprigs (optional)

Peel and core pears; cut in half lengthwise, and brush with 2 teaspoons lemon juice.

Combine wine and next 3 ingredients in a large saucepan; bring to a boil. Add pears; cover, reduce heat, and simmer 15 minutes or until tender, turning once. Transfer pears and poaching liquid to a bowl; cover and chill thoroughly.

Drizzle half of melted chocolate evenly onto 6 dessert plates. Transfer pears to plates, using a slotted spoon. Discard poaching liquid. Top each pear with ¼ cup sherbet. Drizzle remaining chocolate evenly over sherbet. If desired, garnish with fresh raspberries and mint sprigs. Serve immediately. Yield: 6 servings.

Per serving: Calories 133 (16% from fat)
Carbohydrate 29.9g Protein 1.1g Fat 2.3g (Sat. Fat 1.0g)
Cholesterol 0mg Sodium 34mg

Poached Pear Sundaes

3 large ripe pears
2 teaspoons lemon juice
1 vanilla bean
1 cup plus 1 tablespoon maple syrup, divided
½ cup apple juice
¼ cup sugar
2 tablespoons water
1½ tablespoons whipping cream
1 tablespoon margarine
1 (1-ounce) square semisweet chocolate, chopped
½ (1-ounce) square unsweetened chocolate, chopped
3 cups pralines-and-cream ice cream
2 tablespoons chopped almonds, toasted

Peel and core pears; cut in half lengthwise, and brush with lemon juice.

Cut vanilla bean in half lengthwise. Scrape seeds into a large saucepan. Add vanilla bean halves, 1 cup maple syrup, and apple juice to saucepan; bring to a boil. Add pears; cover, reduce heat, and simmer 15 minutes or until tender, turning once. Remove and discard vanilla bean halves. Transfer pears and poaching liquid to a bowl; cover and chill thoroughly.

Combine sugar and water in a small saucepan; bring to a boil, stirring frequently until sugar dissolves. Add whipping cream; bring to a boil. Remove from heat. Add margarine and chocolates; stir until chocolates melt. Stir in remaining 1 tablespoon maple syrup. Cool completely.

Transfer pears to 6 dessert plates, using a slotted spoon. Discard poaching liquid. Top each pear with ½ cup ice cream. Spoon chocolate sauce evenly over ice cream, and sprinkle evenly with almonds. Serve immediately. Yield: 6 servings.

Per serving: Calories 371 (40% from fat)
Carbohydrate 55.3g Protein 4.4g Fat 16.6g (Sat. Fat 7.4g)
Cholesterol 35mg Sodium 83mg

Left: *Poached Pear with Raspberry Sherbet*

Enjoy the sweetness of fresh melon in these chilled dessert soups. Flavor the light soup with a hint of mint, or heighten the flavor of the luscious version with orange-passion fruit juice. The light soup replaces whipping cream and regular sour cream with low-fat yogurt and nonfat sour cream.

MINTED CANTALOUPE DESSERT SOUP

6   cups cubed cantaloupe (about
    2 large)
¾   cup unsweetened orange juice
3   tablespoons lime juice
¼   teaspoon peppermint extract
1   (8-ounce) carton vanilla low-fat yogurt
2   teaspoons powdered sugar
2   tablespoons nonfat sour cream
    alternative
    Fresh mint sprigs (optional)

Place 3 cups cantaloupe and next 3 ingredients in container of an electric blender; cover and process until smooth, stopping once to scrape down sides. Add remaining 3 cups cantaloupe; cover and process until smooth.

Combine yogurt and powdered sugar in a large bowl; stir in cantaloupe mixture. Cover and chill. To serve, ladle soup into individual bowls. Top each serving with 1 teaspoon sour cream. Garnish with mint sprigs, if desired. Yield: 6 (1-cup) servings.

Per serving: Calories 122 (7% from fat)
Carbohydrate 26.2g   Protein 4.1g   Fat 1.0g (Sat. Fat 0.6g)
Cholesterol 2mg   Sodium 46mg

Creamy Cantaloupe Dessert Soup

6   cups cubed cantaloupe (about
    2 large)
¼   cup orange-passion fruit juice
2   tablespoons Sauterne or other sweet
    white wine
⅓   cup whipping cream
2   tablespoons powdered sugar
1   tablespoon plus 2 teaspoons
    sour cream
    Edible roses (optional)

Place 3 cups cantaloupe, juice, and wine in container of an electric blender; cover and process until smooth, stopping once to scrape down sides. Add remaining 3 cups cantaloupe; cover and process until smooth.

Combine whipping cream and powdered sugar in a large bowl; stir in cantaloupe mixture. Cover and chill. To serve, ladle soup into individual bowls. Top each serving with 1 teaspoon sour cream. Garnish with roses, if desired. Yield: 5 (1-cup) servings.

Per serving: Calories 168 (40% from fat)
Carbohydrate 24.5g   Protein 2.5g   Fat 7.5g (Sat. Fat 4.6g)
Cholesterol 24mg   Sodium 30mg

Give in to your craving for a creamy milkshake and leave most of the fat behind with a Chocolate Wafer Malt. It's made with nonfat frozen yogurt and low-fat chocolate milk. For a richer indulgence, blend ice cream, fudge sauce, and cookies into a Mocha Mud Slide Malt.

CHOCOLATE WAFER MALTS

 2 quarts vanilla nonfat frozen yogurt, softened and divided
 2 cups 1% low-fat chocolate milk, divided
20 chocolate wafer cookies, coarsely crumbled and divided

Combine half each of softened yogurt and chocolate milk in container of an electric blender; cover and process until smooth, stopping once to scrape down sides. Stir in half of crumbled cookies. Pour mixture into glasses.

Repeat procedure with remaining half of frozen yogurt, chocolate milk, and cookies. Serve immediately. Yield: 8 (1-cup) servings.

Per serving: Calories 260 (11% from fat)
Carbohydrate 50.2g Protein 9.7g Fat 3.3g (Sat. Fat 1.1g)
Cholesterol 12mg Sodium 208mg

Mocha Mud Slide Malts

 1 cup whole milk
 1 teaspoon instant coffee granules
 6 cups vanilla ice cream, divided
 ½ cup commercial hot fudge sauce, divided
 ½ cup chocolate-flavored instant malted milk, divided
 ¼ cup Kahlúa or other coffee-flavored liqueur, divided
 6 cream-filled chocolate sandwich cookies, coarsely chopped

Combine milk and coffee granules, stirring until granules dissolve. Pour half of milk mixture into container of an electric blender; add half each of ice cream, fudge sauce, malted milk, and liqueur. Cover and process until smooth, stopping once to scrape down sides.

Add remaining half of milk mixture, ice cream, fudge sauce, malted milk, and liqueur. Cover and process until smooth. Stir in chopped cookies. Serve immediately. Yield: 6 (1-cup) servings.

Per serving: Calories 597 (34% from fat)
Carbohydrate 79.1g Protein 12.4g Fat 22.7g (Sat. Fat 10.9g)
Cholesterol 66mg Sodium 365mg

These cool treats offer double-fruit flavor from fresh raspberries and strawberries. The light recipe is a sorbet, so it contains no milk or cream. Berry Berry Ice Cream is extravagantly rich with whipping cream and buttermilk.

VERY BERRY SORBET

2 cups fresh raspberries
2 cups fresh strawberries, sliced
½ cup sugar
1½ cups sparkling white grape juice
Fresh raspberries (optional)
Fresh mint sprigs (optional)

Place 2 cups raspberries in a wire-mesh strainer; press with back of spoon against the sides of the strainer to squeeze out juice. Discard pulp and seeds remaining in strainer.

Combine raspberry juice, strawberries, and sugar in container of an electric blender; cover and process until smooth, stopping once to scrape down sides. Combine fruit puree and white grape juice; stir well.

Pour mixture into freezer container of a 2-quart hand-turned or electric freezer. Freeze according to manufacturer's instructions. Pack freezer with additional ice and rock salt; let stand 1 hour before serving. If desired, garnish with fresh raspberries and mint sprigs. Yield: 10 (½-cup) servings.

Per serving: Calories 83 (3% from fat)
Carbohydrate 20.6g Protein 0.6g Fat 0.3g (Sat. Fat 0.0g)
Cholesterol 0mg Sodium 2mg

Berry Berry Ice Cream

1½ cups fresh raspberries
1½ cups fresh strawberries
¼ cup water
1⅓ cups sugar
2 cups buttermilk
1 cup whipping cream
½ cup unsweetened orange juice
Fresh raspberries (optional)
Fresh strawberries (optional)

Combine first 3 ingredients in container of an electric blender; cover and process until smooth, stopping once to scrape down sides.

Place berry mixture in a wire-mesh strainer; press with back of spoon against the sides of the strainer to squeeze out juice. Discard pulp and seeds remaining in strainer. Add sugar, buttermilk, cream, and orange juice to strained mixture; stir well.

Pour mixture into freezer container of a 1-gallon hand-turned or electric freezer. Freeze according to manufacturer's instructions. Pack freezer with additional ice and rock salt; let stand 1 hour before serving. Garnish with fresh berries, if desired. Yield: 14 (½-cup) servings.

Per serving: Calories 162 (37% from fat)
Carbohydrate 24.9g Protein 1.7g Fat 6.7g (Sat. Fat 4.1g)
Cholesterol 25mg Sodium 44mg

Left: *Very Berry Sorbet*

Rum Raisin Ice Milk contains skim milk products and uses fewer eggs than the indulgent ice cream.

RUM RAISIN ICE MILK

⅓ cup raisins
⅓ cup dark rum
2 eggs
1 cup sugar
1 teaspoon cornstarch
2 cups skim milk
2 cups evaporated skimmed milk
½ teaspoon vanilla extract

Combine raisins and rum in a small saucepan; bring to a boil. Remove from heat; cover and let stand at room temperature 1 hour. Drain raisins; discard rum. Finely chop raisins, and set aside.

Beat eggs in a medium bowl at high speed of an electric mixer 3 minutes or until thick and pale. Combine sugar and cornstarch; gradually add to beaten eggs, beating constantly.

Transfer mixture to a large saucepan; stir in skim milk. Cook over medium heat, stirring constantly, until mixture thickens and just begins to boil. Remove from heat, and let cool. Stir in evaporated skimmed milk, vanilla, and raisins. Cover and chill thoroughly.

Pour mixture into freezer container of a 1-gallon hand-turned or electric freezer. Freeze according to manufacturer's instructions. Pack freezer with additional ice and rock salt, and let stand 1 hour before serving. Yield: 11 (½-cup) servings.

Per serving: Calories 153 (6% from fat)
Carbohydrate 29.8g Protein 6.4g Fat 1.1g (Sat. Fat 0.4g)
Cholesterol 43mg Sodium 90mg

Rum Raisin Ice Cream

½ cup raisins
½ cup dark rum
4 eggs
1 cup sugar
2 cups whole milk
2 cups whipping cream
½ teaspoon vanilla extract

Combine raisins and rum in a small saucepan; bring to a boil. Remove from heat; cover and let stand at room temperature 1 hour. Drain raisins; discard rum. Finely chop raisins, and set aside.

Beat eggs in a large bowl at high speed of an electric mixer 3 minutes or until thick and pale. Gradually add sugar, beating until blended.

Transfer mixture to a large saucepan; stir in milk. Cook over medium-low heat, stirring constantly, until mixture thickens and coats a metal spoon. Remove from heat, and let cool. Stir in whipping cream, vanilla, and raisins. Cover and chill thoroughly.

Pour mixture into freezer container of a 1-gallon hand-turned or electric freezer. Freeze according to manufacturer's instructions. Pack freezer with additional ice and rock salt, and let stand 1 hour before serving. Yield: 12 (½-cup) servings.

Per serving: Calories 285 (56% from fat)
Carbohydrate 25.5g Protein 4.5g Fat 17.8g (Sat. Fat 10.5g)
Cholesterol 134mg Sodium 58mg

Pecan Cheesecake uses light cheese products and has less than one-fourth the fat of Praline Cheesecake.

PECAN CHEESECAKE

Vegetable cooking spray
⅓ cup vanilla wafer crumbs
1 (12-ounce) carton 1% low-fat cottage cheese
3 (8-ounce) packages light process cream cheese product, softened
½ cup sugar
¼ cup plus 2 tablespoons firmly packed dark brown sugar
2 eggs
1 teaspoon vanilla extract
½ teaspoon butter flavoring
2 egg whites
⅛ teaspoon cream of tartar
½ cup plus 2 tablespoons sugar, divided
3 tablespoons finely chopped toasted pecans, divided
1 (8-ounce) carton nonfat sour cream alternative

Coat bottom of a 9-inch springform pan with cooking spray; sprinkle with vanilla wafer crumbs.

Place cottage cheese in container of an electric blender; cover and process until smooth. Add cream cheese and next 5 ingredients; cover and process until smooth. Transfer mixture to a large bowl.

Beat egg whites and cream of tartar at high speed of an electric mixer until foamy. Gradually add ¼ cup sugar, 1 tablespoon at time, beating until stiff peaks form and sugar dissolves (2 to 4 minutes). Fold egg white mixture and 2 tablespoons pecans into cream cheese mixture. Spoon into pan. Bake at 325° for 50 minutes or until almost set. Remove from oven; increase temperature to 375°.

Combine sour cream and remaining ¼ cup plus 2 tablespoons sugar, stirring until smooth. Spread mixture on top of cheesecake. Bake an additional 5 minutes. Remove from oven, and let cool on a wire rack. Cover and chill thoroughly. Sprinkle with remaining 1 tablespoon pecans. Yield: 16 servings.

Per serving: Calories 223 (38% from fat)
Carbohydrate 25.0g Protein 9.5g Fat 9.4g (Sat. Fat 4.7g)
Cholesterol 53mg Sodium 363mg

Praline Cheesecake

1 cup ground toasted pecans
¼ cup firmly packed brown sugar
¼ cup margarine, melted
3 tablespoons all-purpose flour
3 (8-ounce) packages cream cheese, softened
¾ cup firmly packed dark brown sugar
1 tablespoon cornstarch
1 (5-ounce) can evaporated milk
3 tablespoons praline liqueur or 2 teaspoons vanilla extract
3 eggs
1 (8-ounce) carton sour cream
3 tablespoons sugar
1 egg yolk
½ teaspoon vanilla extract
16 pecan halves, toasted

Combine first 4 ingredients in a medium bowl, stirring well. Press mixture into bottom of a 9-inch springform pan. Bake at 350° for 15 minutes. Let cool completely on a wire rack.

Beat cream cheese at medium speed of an electric mixer until fluffy. Combine ¾ cup brown sugar and cornstarch; add to cream cheese mixture, beating well. Add milk and liqueur, beating at low speed until blended. Add 3 eggs, one at a time, beating just until blended. Spoon cream cheese mixture into prepared crust. Bake at 325° for 50 minutes. Remove from oven; increase temperature to 400°

Combine sour cream, 3 tablespoons sugar, 1 egg yolk, and ½ teaspoon vanilla. Spread mixture on top of cheesecake. Bake an additional 5 minutes. Turn oven off. Partially open oven door, and let cheesecake cool in oven 30 minutes. Remove from oven, and let cool on a wire rack. Cover and chill thoroughly. Arrange pecan halves on top of cheesecake. Yield: 16 servings.

Per serving: Calories 495 (70% from fat)
Carbohydrate 31.1g Protein 8.8g Fat 38.6g (Sat. Fat 17.4g)
Cholesterol 148mg Sodium 259mg

Both cakes have creamy frostings, but the light version contains egg whites and nonfat cream cheese.

LIGHT CARROT CAKE

1	(8-ounce) can crushed pineapple in juice
2½	cups sifted cake flour
2	teaspoons baking soda
⅛	teaspoon salt
1	teaspoon ground cinnamon
½	teaspoon ground allspice
¼	teaspoon ground nutmeg
¾	cup firmly packed brown sugar
3	tablespoons vegetable oil
4	egg whites
⅔	cup skim milk
3	cups shredded carrot
2½	teaspoons vanilla extract, divided
	Vegetable cooking spray
1	egg white
¼	teaspoon cream of tartar
½	cup sugar
1	(8-ounce) package Neufchâtel cheese
½	(8-ounce) package nonfat cream cheese product

Drain pineapple, reserving 2 tablespoons juice.

Combine flour and next 5 ingredients. Combine brown sugar, oil, and 4 egg whites; beat well. Add flour mixture to brown sugar mixture alternately with milk. Mix after each addition. Stir in pineapple, carrot, and 2 teaspoons vanilla. Pour into a 13- x 9- x 2-inch pan coated with cooking spray. Bake at 350° for 30 minutes.

Beat 1 egg white and cream of tartar at high speed of an electric mixer until soft peaks form. Combine ½ cup sugar and reserved juice in a saucepan. Bring to a boil; cook, without stirring, over medium heat 3 minutes or until candy thermometer registers 238°. Pour sugar mixture in a thin stream over egg white while beating constantly at high speed. Continue to beat at high speed 7 minutes. Combine cheeses and remaining ½ teaspoon vanilla; beat at high speed until fluffy. Add one-third of egg white mixture; beat just until blended. Fold in remaining egg white mixture. Spread over cake. Yield: 16 servings.

Per serving: Calories 223 (25% from fat)
Carbohydrate 35.3g Protein 6.5g Fat 6.1g (Sat. Fat 2.6g)
Cholesterol 13mg Sodium 299mg

Rich Carrot Cake

2	cups all-purpose flour
2	teaspoons baking soda
¼	teaspoon salt
2	teaspoons ground cinnamon
⅛	teaspoon ground nutmeg
1½	cups sugar
1	(8-ounce) carton sour cream
½	cup vegetable oil
4	eggs, lightly beaten
1½	teaspoons vanilla extract
2½	cups shredded carrot
1	cup chopped walnuts
½	cup raisins
1	(8-ounce) package cream cheese, softened
½	cup butter, softened
1	(16-ounce) package powdered sugar, sifted
1	teaspoon vanilla extract
⅓	cup flaked coconut
⅓	cup finely shredded carrot

Combine first 5 ingredients in a large bowl, and stir well. Combine 1½ cups sugar, sour cream, oil, eggs, and 1½ teaspoons vanilla; add to flour mixture, and stir with a wire whisk until blended. Stir in 2½ cups carrot, walnuts, and raisins.

Pour batter into 2 greased and floured 9-inch square cakepans. Bake at 350° for 25 to 30 minutes or until a wooden pick inserted in center comes out clean. Cool cakes in pans on wire racks 10 minutes; remove from pans, and let cool completely on wire racks.

Beat cream cheese and butter at medium speed of an electric mixer until smooth. Gradually add powdered sugar, beating until well blended. Stir in 1 teaspoon vanilla. Spread frosting between layers and on top and sides of cake. Combine coconut and ⅓ cup shredded carrot; sprinkle on top of cake. Yield: 16 servings.

Per serving: Calories 539 (46% from fat)
Carbohydrate 68.7g Protein 7.3g Fat 27.5g (Sat. Fat 11.1g)
Cholesterol 93mg Sodium 277mg

Bake a low-fat sponge cake or a butter cake rich with nuts and cream of coconut.

PINEAPPLE GLAZED SPONGE CAKE

1¼ cups sugar, divided
1 cup sifted cake flour
4 egg yolks
½ teaspoon coconut extract
10 egg whites
1 teaspoon cream of tartar
½ teaspoon salt
½ teaspoon vanilla extract
   Vegetable cooking spray
1¼ cups sifted powdered sugar
2 tablespoons unsweetened pineapple
   juice

Sift ½ cup sugar and flour together 3 times; set aside. Beat egg yolks at high speed of an electric mixer 3 minutes or until thick and pale. Add coconut extract; beat at medium speed 3 minutes or until thickened. Set aside.

Beat egg whites, cream of tartar, and salt at high speed of electric mixer until foamy. Gradually add remaining ¾ cup sugar, 2 tablespoons at a time, beating until stiff peaks form and sugar dissolves (2 to 4 minutes).

Sprinkle flour mixture over egg white mixture, ¼ cup at a time; fold in carefully. Fold egg yolk mixture and vanilla into egg white mixture.

Coat the bottom of a 10-inch tube pan with cooking spray. Pour batter into prepared pan, spreading evenly. Bake at 350° for 45 to 50 minutes or until cake springs back when lightly touched. Invert pan; cool 40 minutes. Loosen cake from sides of pan, using a narrow metal spatula; remove from pan. Place cake on a serving plate.

Combine powdered sugar and pineapple juice in a small bowl, stirring until smooth. Drizzle over cooled cake. Yield: 12 servings.

Per serving: Calories 199 (9% from fat)
Carbohydrate 41.2g Protein 4.5g Fat 1.9g (Sat. Fat 0.6g)
Cholesterol 73mg Sodium 161mg

Piña Colada Cake

1¾ cups butter, softened and divided
1½ cups sugar
4 eggs
3 cups sifted cake flour
1 tablespoon baking powder
½ teaspoon salt
1 cup whole milk
2½ teaspoons vanilla extract, divided
½ cup unsweetened pineapple juice
½ cup cream of coconut
2 tablespoons rum
3 cups sifted powdered sugar
¾ cup pineapple preserves
1 cup flaked coconut
1 (3½-ounce) jar macadamia nuts,
   chopped

Beat ¾ cup butter at medium speed of an electric mixer until creamy. Gradually add 1½ cups sugar, beating well. Add eggs, one at a time, beating after each addition. Combine flour, baking powder, and salt; add to butter mixture alternately with milk, beginning and ending with flour mixture. Beat at low speed just until blended after each addition. Stir in 2 teaspoons vanilla.

Pour batter into a greased and floured 13- x 9- x 2-inch pan. Bake at 350° for 30 minutes or until a wooden pick inserted in center comes out clean. Remove from oven. Punch holes in cake with wooden pick.

Combine pineapple juice, cream of coconut, and rum; stir well. Drizzle juice mixture over warm cake. Cool completely in pan on a wire rack.

Beat remaining 1 cup butter at medium speed of electric mixer until creamy; gradually add powdered sugar, beating well. Add preserves and remaining ½ teaspoon vanilla, beating at medium speed of electric mixer until of spreading consistency. Spread frosting on top of cake; sprinkle with coconut and macadamia nuts. Yield: 15 servings.

Per serving: Calories 634 (49% from fat)
Carbohydrate 78.4g Protein 5.4g Fat 34.2g (Sat. Fat 19.7g)
Cholesterol 120mg Sodium 412mg

Almond Roulage is rich with whipped cream; the light cake roll is laced with frozen yogurt and fruit.

Peach Melba Cake Roll

Vegetable cooking spray
4 eggs, separated
1 cup sugar, divided
1 teaspoon vanilla extract
¾ cup plus 2 tablespoons sifted cake flour
¾ teaspoon baking powder
¼ teaspoon salt
2 tablespoons sifted powdered sugar
1 (12-ounce) package frozen raspberries in light syrup, thawed
1 cup diced fresh ripe peaches
1 cup peach nonfat frozen yogurt
1 tablespoon peach schnapps

Coat a 15- x 10- x 1-inch jellyroll pan with cooking spray. Line pan with wax paper; coat with cooking spray. Beat egg yolks until thick and pale. Add ½ cup sugar, beating well. Stir in vanilla.

Beat egg whites at high speed of an electric mixer until foamy. Add remaining ½ cup sugar, 1 tablespoon at a time, beating until stiff peaks form and sugar dissolves. Fold egg white mixture into yolk mixture. Combine flour, baking powder, and salt. Fold flour mixture into egg mixture. Spread into pan. Bake at 375° for 10 minutes or until a wooden pick inserted in center comes out clean.

Sift 2 tablespoons powdered sugar in a 15- x 10-inch rectangle on a towel. When cake is done, immediately loosen from sides of pan, and turn out onto towel. Peel off wax paper. Starting at narrow end, roll up cake and towel together. Place, seam side down, on a wire rack; let cool completely.

Place raspberries in container of an electric blender; cover and process until smooth, stopping twice to scrape down sides. Cover and chill.

Combine peaches, yogurt, and schnapps. Unroll cake, and remove towel. Spread yogurt mixture over cake, leaving a 1-inch margin around edges. Reroll cake; cover and freeze until yogurt mixture is firm. Serve each slice on top of 1 tablespoon plus 2 teaspoons raspberry puree. Yield: 10 servings.

Per serving: Calories 217 (10% from fat)
Carbohydrate 45.0g   Protein 4.5g   Fat 2.3g (Sat. Fat 0.7g)
Cholesterol 88mg   Sodium 120mg

Almond Roulage

4 eggs, separated
1 cup sugar, divided
1 teaspoon vanilla extract, divided
¾ cup plus 2 tablespoons sifted cake flour
¾ teaspoon baking powder
¼ teaspoon salt
½ cup ground toasted almonds
½ cup sifted powdered sugar, divided
1 cup whipping cream
1½ tablespoons amaretto
1 cup slivered almonds, toasted, chopped, and divided
½ cup red currant jelly, melted and divided

Grease a 15 - x 10- x 1-inch jellyroll pan; line with wax paper. Grease and flour wax paper. Beat egg yolks in a large bowl until thick and pale. Add ½ cup sugar, beating well. Stir in ½ teaspoon vanilla.

Beat egg whites at high speed of an electric mixer until foamy. Add remaining ½ cup sugar, 1 tablespoon at a time, beating until stiff peaks form; fold into egg yolk mixture. Combine flour, baking powder, salt, and ground almonds; fold into egg mixture. Spread into pan. Bake at 375° for 10 minutes.

Sift 2 tablespoons powdered sugar in a 15- x 10-inch rectangle on a towel. When cake is done, immediately loosen from sides of pan, and turn out onto towel. Peel off wax paper. Starting at narrow end, roll up cake and towel together. Place, seam side down, on a wire rack; let cool completely.

Beat whipping cream, amaretto, and ½ teaspoon vanilla until foamy; gradually add remaining powdered sugar, beating until soft peaks form. Fold in ½ cup chopped almonds. Unroll cake; remove towel. Brush cake with ⅓ cup jelly. Spread whipped cream mixture on cake, leaving a ¾-inch margin around edges; reroll cake. Place on a serving plate, seam side down. Brush with remaining jelly. Sprinkle with ½ cup almonds. Cover and chill. Yield: 10 servings.

Per serving: Calories 399 (45% from fat)
Carbohydrate 48.7g   Protein 7.6g   Fat 20.1g (Sat. Fat 7.0g)
Cholesterol 121mg   Sodium 128mg

Right: *Almond Roulage*

Top Almond Berry Cakes with whipped cream; use reduced-calorie topping for the light version.

BLUEBERRY SHORTCAKE

4 cups fresh blueberries
½ cup sugar
2 tablespoons lemon juice
2 teaspoons cornstarch
2 tablespoons water
  Vegetable cooking spray
1¾ cups all-purpose flour
1½ teaspoons baking powder
¼ teaspoon salt
¼ cup margarine, softened
⅓ cup plus 2 tablespoons sugar, divided
1 egg, separated
¾ cup skim milk
½ teaspoon vanilla extract
1 egg white
1½ cups reduced-calorie frozen whipped topping, thawed

Combine first 3 ingredients; cook 5 minutes. Transfer berries to a bowl using a slotted spoon. Combine cornstarch and water; add to blueberry liquid, and bring to a boil. Boil 1 minute; stir in blueberries. Chill.

Coat a 9-inch round cakepan with cooking spray. Dust with 1 teaspoon flour. Combine remaining flour, baking powder, and salt. Beat margarine at medium speed of an electric mixer until creamy; add ⅓ cup sugar, beating well. Add egg yolk, beating just until blended. Add flour mixture to creamed mixture alternately with milk. Mix well after each addition. Stir in vanilla.

Beat egg whites at high speed of electric mixer until foamy. Add remaining sugar, 1 tablespoon at a time, beating until stiff peaks form. Stir ½ cup egg white into batter; fold in remaining egg white. Spoon into pan. Bake at 350° for 30 minutes. Cool on a wire rack 10 minutes. Remove from pan; let cool on wire rack. Slice in half horizontally. Drain blueberries, reserving half of juice. Drizzle juice over bottom layer. Spread ¾ cup whipped topping over cake layer; spoon half of blueberries over topping. Top with remaining cake layer. Repeat procedure with remaining ¾ cup topping and blueberries. Yield: 10 servings.

Per serving: Calories 269 (23% from fat)
Carbohydrate 48.3g Protein 4.6g Fat 6.8g (Sat. Fat 3.3g)
Cholesterol 23mg Sodium 189mg

Almond Berry Cakes

3 cups fresh blueberries
1 cup plus 1 tablespoon sugar, divided
1 tablespoon lemon juice
2 teaspoons cornstarch
1 tablespoon water
2 tablespoons amaretto
4 cups all-purpose flour
1 tablespoon baking powder
½ teaspoon salt
⅓ cup ground toasted almonds
½ cup butter
1 egg
1 cup half-and-half
⅛ teaspoon almond extract
1 cup whipping cream
½ cup sifted powdered sugar
¼ cup toasted sliced almonds

Combine blueberries, ¾ cup sugar, and lemon juice; cook 5 minutes. Transfer berries to a bowl using a slotted spoon. Combine cornstarch and water; add to blueberry liquid, and bring to a boil. Boil 1 minute; stir in blueberries and amaretto. Chill.

Combine ¼ cup sugar, flour, and next 3 ingredients. Cut in butter with a pastry blender. Combine egg, half-and-half, and extract; reserve 1 tablespoon. Add remaining half-and-half mixture to flour mixture, stirring until dry ingredients are moistened. Turn out onto a floured surface; knead 6 times. Roll to ½-inch thickness. Cut 8 shortcakes with a 4¼-inch heart-shaped cutter; place on a greased baking sheet. Brush with half-and-half mixture; sprinkle with 1 tablespoon sugar. Bake at 425° for 14 minutes. Let cool.

Beat whipping cream until foamy; add powdered sugar, beating until soft peaks form. Slice each cake in half horizontally. Spoon blueberry sauce over bottom halves; spoon half of whipped cream over berries. Place top half on each. Top with remaining whipped cream; sprinkle with almonds. Yield: 8 servings.

Per serving: Calories 708 (40% from fat)
Carbohydrate 96.0g Protein 10.7g Fat 31.6g (Sat. Fat 17.1g)
Cholesterol 112mg Sodium 419mg

Right: *Almond Berry Cake*

Cocoa and nonfat buttermilk help trim calories yet maintain tenderness in Chocolate Torte.

CHOCOLATE TORTE

½ cup margarine, softened
2 cups sugar, divided
2 egg whites
1 egg
1 cup nonfat buttermilk
½ cup water
2 cups all-purpose flour
1 teaspoon baking soda
¼ teaspoon salt
¼ cup unsweetened cocoa
Vegetable cooking spray
¾ cup no-sugar-added raspberry spread
⅔ cup unsweetened cocoa
¼ cup cornstarch
1 cup 1% low-fat milk
¼ teaspoon vanilla extract
Fresh raspberries (optional)
Fresh mint sprigs (optional)

Beat margarine at medium speed of an electric mixer until creamy; add 1½ cups sugar, beating until fluffy. Add egg whites and egg, one at a time, beating after each addition. Combine buttermilk and water. Combine flour and next 3 ingredients; add to margarine mixture alternately with buttermilk mixture. Mix after each addition.

Pour batter into 2 (8-inch) round cakepans coated with cooking spray. Bake at 350° for 22 minutes or until a wooden pick inserted in center comes out clean. Cool in pans on wire racks 10 minutes; remove from pans. Let cool.

Stir raspberry spread well. Slice each cake layer in half horizontally. Place 1 layer on plate; spread with ¼ cup raspberry spread. Repeat with next 2 layers; top with fourth layer. Cover and chill.

Combine remaining ½ cup sugar, ⅔ cup cocoa, and cornstarch in top of a double boiler. Stir in milk. Bring water to a boil. Reduce heat to low; cook, stirring constantly, 18 minutes or until of spreading consistency. Stir in vanilla. Cover and chill. Spread on top and sides of cake. If desired, garnish with raspberries and mint sprigs. Yield: 12 servings.

Per serving: Calories 349 (24% from fat)
Carbohydrate 60.0g Protein 6.7g Fat 9.5g (Sat. Fat 2.4g)
Cholesterol 20mg Sodium 260mg

Chocolate Cream Torte

2 cups all-purpose flour
1 teaspoon baking soda
½ teaspoon salt
2 cups sugar
½ cup unsweetened cocoa
¾ cup vegetable oil
¼ cup buttermilk
2 teaspoons vanilla extract
2 eggs
1 cup boiling water
2 (1-ounce) squares semisweet chocolate, melted
2 tablespoons raspberry nectar
1½ tablespoons butter, softened
2 tablespoons sifted powdered sugar
¾ cup whipping cream, whipped
¾ cup seedless raspberry preserves
2 cups whipping cream
⅓ cup sifted powdered sugar

Combine first 9 ingredients; beat at medium speed of an electric mixer 2 minutes. Stir in water. Pour batter into 2 greased and floured 8-inch round cakepans. Bake at 350° for 25 minutes or until a wooden pick inserted in center comes out clean. Cool in pans on wire racks 10 minutes; remove from pans. Let cool.

Combine melted chocolate and raspberry nectar. Let cool. Beat butter at medium speed of electric mixer until fluffy. Add 2 tablespoons powdered sugar; beat until blended. Add chocolate mixture, beating well. Fold whipped cream into chocolate mixture.

Stir preserves well. Slice each cake layer in half horizontally. Place 1 layer on plate; spread with ¼ cup preserves. Spread one-third of chocolate mixture over preserves. Repeat with next 2 layers and remaining preserves and chocolate mixture. Top with fourth layer.

Beat 2 cups whipping cream until foamy; add ⅓ cup powdered sugar, beating until soft peaks form. Spread on sides and pipe on top of cake. Yield: 12 servings.

Per serving: Calories 648 (54% from fat)
Carbohydrate 72.6g Protein 6.0g Fat 38.7g (Sat. Fat 17.7g)
Cholesterol 117mg Sodium 231mg

The chocolaty flavor of Peppermint Brownies comes from unsweetened cocoa instead of dark chocolate.

PEPPERMINT BROWNIES

½ cup plus 2 tablespoons reduced-calorie margarine, softened
1⅓ cups sugar
8 egg whites
½ cup nonfat sour cream alternative
⅓ cup evaporated skimmed milk
1 teaspoon vanilla extract
½ teaspoon peppermint extract
1⅓ cups all-purpose flour
1 teaspoon baking powder
¼ teaspoon salt
⅔ cup unsweetened cocoa
Vegetable cooking spray
3 cups sifted powdered sugar
¼ cup unsweetened cocoa
¼ cup plus 1 tablespoon hot water
3 tablespoons finely crushed peppermint candies

Beat margarine at medium speed of an electric mixer until creamy; gradually add 1⅓ cups sugar, beating well. Add egg whites and next 4 ingredients; beat well.

Combine flour, baking powder, salt, and ⅔ cup cocoa; add to margarine mixture, mixing well. Pour batter into a 13- x 9- x 2-inch pan coated with cooking spray. Bake at 350° for 20 to 25 minutes or until a wooden pick inserted in center comes out clean. Cool in pan on a wire rack.

Combine powdered sugar and ¼ cup cocoa; stir well. Add water, 1 tablespoon at a time, stirring until smooth. Pour over brownies, and spread evenly. Sprinkle with crushed peppermint. Let stand 10 minutes before cutting into bars. Yield: 18 brownies.

Per brownie: Calories 185 (18% from fat)
Carbohydrate 35.6 Protein 3.4g Fat 3.6g (Sat. Fat 0.7g)
Cholesterol 0mg Sodium 110mg

Fudgy Brownies

1 (3½-ounce) bar Swiss dark chocolate, chopped
3 (1-ounce) squares unsweetened chocolate, chopped
¼ cup plus 2 tablespoons margarine, softened
½ cup firmly packed dark brown sugar
¼ cup sugar
2 eggs
⅓ cup Grand Marnier or other orange-flavored liqueur
1 teaspoon vanilla extract
½ teaspoon grated orange rind
½ cup plus 2 tablespoons all-purpose flour
¼ teaspoon salt
½ cup finely chopped pecans

Combine chocolates in top of a double boiler; bring water to a boil. Reduce heat to low; cook until chocolates melt, stirring frequently. Remove from heat, and let cool.

Line a buttered 8-inch square pan with a 7-inch-wide strip of aluminum foil, allowing foil to extend 3 inches over 2 sides of pan. Butter foil.

Beat margarine at medium speed of an electric mixer until creamy; gradually add sugars, beating well. Add eggs, one at a time, beating just until yellow disappears. Add liqueur, vanilla, and orange rind; beat well. Add melted chocolate, and beat at low speed until blended. Add flour and salt; beat at low speed until blended. Stir in pecans.

Spoon mixture into pan. Bake at 350° for 18 minutes or until a wooden pick inserted 2 inches from the edge comes out clean. Cool in pan on a wire rack. Cover and chill at least 4 hours. Using aluminum foil handles, lift brownies out of pan. Cut into squares. Yield: 16 brownies.

Per brownie: Calories 196 (58% from fat)
Carbohydrate 20.5g Protein 2.5g Fat 12.7g (Sat. Fat 4.1g)
Cholesterol 28mg Sodium 100mg

Treat your family to homemade ginger cookies—they'll love both versions. Use reduced-calorie margarine and egg substitute for the cakelike Ginger Tea Cake Cookies, and shortening and molasses for the luscious chewy cookies.

GINGER TEA CAKE COOKIES

½ cup firmly packed brown sugar
½ cup reduced-calorie margarine, softened
¼ cup frozen egg substitute, thawed
1 teaspoon vanilla extract
1¾ cups all-purpose flour
½ teaspoon baking soda
½ teaspoon ground allspice
¼ teaspoon ground cinnamon
¼ teaspoon ground ginger
1 ounce crystallized ginger, minced
3 tablespoons sugar, divided
Vegetable cooking spray

Combine brown sugar and margarine in a medium bowl, stirring well. Stir in egg substitute and vanilla.

Combine flour and next 4 ingredients, stirring well. Gradually add flour mixture to sugar mixture, mixing well. Stir in crystallized ginger. Cover and chill 2 to 3 hours.

Shape dough into 1-inch balls, and roll balls in 2 tablespoons sugar. Place 2 inches apart on cookie sheets coated with cooking spray. Dip a fork in remaining 1 tablespoon sugar, and flatten cookies in a crisscross pattern. Bake at 375° for 7 to 8 minutes or until edges are lightly browned. Remove from cookie sheets, and let cool on wire racks. Yield: 2 dozen cookies.

Per cookie: Calories 77 (29% from fat)
Carbohydrate 12.7g Protein 1.2g Fat 2.5g (Sat. Fat 0.3g)
Cholesterol 0mg Sodium 60mg

Chewy Ginger Cookies

¾ cup shortening
1 cup sugar
1 egg, lightly beaten
¼ cup molasses
2 cups all-purpose flour
2 teaspoons baking soda
¼ teaspoon salt
2 teaspoons ground ginger
2 teaspoons ground allspice
¼ cup sugar

Beat shortening at medium speed of an electric mixer until creamy; gradually add 1 cup sugar, beating well. Add egg and molasses, mixing well.

Combine flour and next 4 ingredients, stirring well. Gradually add flour mixture to creamed mixture, mixing well. Cover and chill 1 hour.

Shape dough into 1-inch balls, and roll balls in ¼ cup sugar. Place 2 inches apart on lightly greased cookie sheets. Bake at 375° for 9 minutes. Remove from cookie sheets, and let cool on wire racks. Yield: 3 dozen cookies.

Per cookie: Calories 92 (37% from fat)
Carbohydrate 14.0g Protein 0.9g Fat 3.8g (Sat. Fat 0.9g)
Cholesterol 6mg Sodium 65mg

Meringue cookies are made from beaten egg whites and sugar. Unsweetened cocoa and semisweet chocolate mini-morsels provide the chocolate flavor in the lighter cocoa cookies, while the luscious cookies feature pecans and a creamy chocolate filling.

COCOA MERINGUE COOKIES

½ cup sugar
1 tablespoon unsweetened cocoa
2 egg whites
¼ teaspoon cream of tartar
½ teaspoon vanilla extract
¼ cup semisweet chocolate mini-morsels

Preheat oven to 350°. Combine sugar and cocoa, stirring well. Beat egg whites and cream of tartar at high speed of an electric mixer until foamy. Gradually add sugar mixture, 1 tablespoon at a time, beating until stiff peaks form and sugar dissolves (2 to 4 minutes). Stir in vanilla and chocolate mini-morsels.

Drop by teaspoonfuls onto cookie sheets lined with aluminum foil. Place in oven, and immediately turn oven off. Do not open door for at least 8 hours. Remove from oven, and carefully peel cookies from foil. Yield: 4 dozen cookies.

Per cookie: Calories 14 (19% from fat)
Carbohydrate 2.6g Protein 0.2g Fat 0.3g (Sat. Fat 0.2g)
Cholesterol 0mg Sodium 3mg

Chocolate Filled Meringue Cookies

2 egg whites
¼ teaspoon cream of tartar
½ cup sugar
1 teaspoon vanilla extract, divided
1 cup finely chopped pecans
1 tablespoon sifted powdered sugar
½ cup butter
2 tablespoons cocoa
3 tablespoons half-and-half
2¼ cups sifted powdered sugar

Preheat oven to 350°. Beat egg whites and cream of tartar at high speed of an electric mixer until foamy. Gradually add ½ cup sugar, 1 tablespoon at a time, beating until stiff peaks form and sugar dissolves (2 to 4 minutes). Stir in ½ teaspoon vanilla and chopped pecans.

Drop mixture by teaspoonfuls onto cookie sheets lined with aluminum foil. Dip finger in 1 tablespoon powdered sugar, and make an indentation in center of each cookie. Place in oven, and immediately turn oven off. Do not open door for at least 8 hours. Remove from oven, and carefully peel cookies from foil.

Combine butter, cocoa, and half-and-half in a small saucepan; bring to a boil over medium heat. Remove from heat, and cool to room temperature. Add 2¼ cups powdered sugar, and beat well with an electric mixer. Stir in remaining ½ teaspoon vanilla.

Just before serving, pipe cocoa mixture (using a pastry bag fitted with a star tip) into the indentation of each cookie. Yield: 4 dozen cookies.

Per cookie: Calories 66 (50% from fat)
Carbohydrate 8.4g Protein 0.4g Fat 3.7g (Sat. Fat 1.4g)
Cholesterol 6mg Sodium 23mg

Kids will love piping and spreading frosting on the light sugar cookies or "painting" the butter cookies. The light recipe is low in saturated fat because it contains margarine instead of butter.

FROSTED SUGAR COOKIES

3/4 cup plus 2 tablespoons firmly packed brown sugar
1/2 cup margarine, softened
1 egg
2 tablespoons skim milk
2 teaspoons vanilla extract
3 cups all-purpose flour
1 1/2 teaspoons baking powder
1/2 teaspoon salt
2 teaspoons all-purpose flour, divided
Vegetable cooking spray
1/2 cup sifted powdered sugar
1 1/4 teaspoons water

Beat brown sugar and margarine at medium speed of an electric mixer until light and fluffy. Add egg, milk, and vanilla; beat well.

Combine 3 cups flour, baking powder, and salt, stirring well. Gradually add flour mixture to creamed mixture, mixing well. Cover and chill at least 2 hours.

Divide dough in half. Work with 1 half at a time, storing remainder in refrigerator. Sprinkle 1 teaspoon flour evenly on work surface. Turn dough out onto floured surface, and roll dough to 1/8-inch thickness. Cut with a 2-inch cookie cutter, and place 2 inches apart on cookie sheets coated with cooking spray.

Bake at 350° for 6 to 8 minutes or until edges of cookies are lightly browned. Remove from cookie sheets, and let cool on wire racks. Repeat procedure with remaining flour and remaining half of dough.

Combine powdered sugar and water. Pipe frosting around the edges of half the cookies; spread frosting on the tops of remaining cookies. Yield: 6 dozen cookies.

Per cookie: Calories 46 (27% from fat)
Carbohydrate 7.6g Protein 0.7g Fat 1.4g (Sat. Fat 0.3g)
Cholesterol 3mg Sodium 40mg

Painted Butter Cookies

3/4 cup plus 2 tablespoons sugar
3/4 cup plus 2 tablespoons butter, softened
1 egg
1 teaspoon grated orange rind
1 teaspoon vanilla extract
2 1/4 cups all-purpose flour
1/4 teaspoon salt
4 egg yolks, lightly beaten
Paste food coloring
1 tablespoon all-purpose flour, divided

Beat sugar and butter at medium speed of an electric mixer until light and fluffy. Add 1 egg, orange rind, and vanilla; beat well.

Combine 2 1/4 cups flour and salt, stirring well. Gradually add flour mixture to creamed mixture, mixing well. Cover and chill at least 2 hours.

Divide egg yolks among several custard cups. Add desired food coloring to each cup, stirring well. Set aside.

Divide dough in half. Work with 1 half at a time, storing remainder in refrigerator. Sprinkle 1/2 tablespoon flour evenly on work surface. Turn dough out onto floured surface, and roll dough to 1/8-inch thickness. Cut with a 2-inch cookie cutter, and place 2 inches apart on lightly greased cookie sheets. Brush food-coloring mixtures lightly onto cookies with a small brush.

Bake at 350° for 10 minutes or until edges of cookies are lightly browned. Remove from cookie sheets, and let cool on wire racks. Repeat procedure with remaining flour, dough, and food-coloring mixture. Yield: 6 dozen cookies.

Per cookie: Calories 50 (50% from fat)
Carbohydrate 5.5g Protein 0.7g Fat 2.8g (Sat. Fat 1.6g)
Cholesterol 22mg Sodium 34mg

Left: *Frosted Sugar Cookies*

Slather low-sugar fruit spread between the peanut butter cookies for a light treat. For double-chocolate pleasure, spoon a creamy filling between the chocolate cookies.

PEANUT BUTTER AND JELLY SANDWICH COOKIES

¼ cup margarine, softened
¼ cup creamy peanut butter
¾ cup sugar
2 egg whites
1 teaspoon vanilla extract
1¾ cups all-purpose flour
1 teaspoon baking soda
⅛ teaspoon salt
Vegetable cooking spray
¾ cup low-sugar strawberry spread

Beat margarine and peanut butter at medium speed of an electric mixer until creamy. Gradually add sugar, beating well. Add egg whites and vanilla; beat well. Combine flour, soda, and salt in a small bowl, stirring well. Gradually add flour mixture to creamed mixture, mixing well.

Shape dough into 40 (1-inch) balls. Place balls 2 inches apart on cookie sheets coated with cooking spray. Flatten cookies into 2-inch circles using a flat-bottomed glass. Bake at 350° for 8 minutes or until lightly browned. Cool slightly on cookie sheets; remove from cookie sheets, and let cool completely on wire racks.

Spread about 1½ teaspoons strawberry spread on the bottom of half the cooled cookies; top with remaining cookies. Yield: 20 cookies.

Per cookie: Calories 113 (33% from fat)
Carbohydrate 18.3g Protein 2.4g Fat 4.1g (Sat. Fat 0.8g)
Cholesterol 0mg Sodium 105mg

Chocolate Sandwich Cookies

½ cup margarine, softened
½ cup shortening
2 cups sugar
4 eggs
4 (1-ounce) squares unsweetened chocolate, melted
2 teaspoons vanilla extract
3¼ cups all-purpose flour
¼ teaspoon salt
1 cup peanut butter morsels
⅓ cup evaporated milk
2½ tablespoons water
2 tablespoons sugar
1 tablespoon margarine
1 teaspoon cornstarch
⅛ teaspoon salt
½ cup semisweet chocolate morsels
½ teaspoon vanilla extract

Beat ½ cup margarine and shortening at medium speed of an electric mixer until creamy. Gradually add 2 cups sugar, beating well. Add eggs, one at a time, beating after each addition. Add chocolate and 2 teaspoons vanilla; beat well. Combine flour and ¼ teaspoon salt; gradually add flour mixture to creamed mixture, mixing well. Stir in peanut butter morsels.

Drop dough by tablespoonfuls onto lightly greased cookie sheets. Bake at 350° for 8 minutes. Cool slightly on cookie sheets; remove from cookie sheets, and let cool completely on wire racks.

Combine evaporated milk and next 5 ingredients in a small saucepan. Cook over medium heat, stirring constantly, 3 to 4 minutes or until thickened and bubbly. Remove from heat; stir in chocolate morsels and ½ teaspoon vanilla. Gently stir until chocolate melts. Let cool.

Place about 1 rounded teaspoon chocolate mixture on the bottom of half the cooled cookies; top with remaining cookies. Yield: 34 cookies.

Per cookie: Calories 213 (45% from fat)
Carbohydrate 27.0g Protein 3.8g Fat 10.7g (Sat. Fat 4.3g)
Cholesterol 27mg Sodium 86mg

*A touch of cocoa adds low-fat chocolate flavor to Peanut Butter Balls. Choco-Nut Balls
are flavored with coconut and dipped in rich melted chocolate.*

PEANUT BUTTER
BALLS

1½ cups vanilla wafer crumbs
1 cup sifted powdered sugar
2 tablespoons cocoa
½ cup plus 1 tablespoon light-colored
 corn syrup
¼ cup plus 2 tablespoons creamy peanut
 butter
2 tablespoons sifted powdered sugar

Combine first 3 ingredients in a large bowl, and stir
well. Combine corn syrup and peanut butter, stirring well. Add to crumb mixture; mix well.

Shape mixture into 1-inch balls. Sprinkle evenly
with 2 tablespoons powdered sugar. Store in an airtight container. Yield: 44 candies.

Per candy: Calories 53 (31% from fat)
Carbohydrate 8.5g Protein 0.8g Fat 1.8g (Sat. Fat 0.2g)
Cholesterol 0mg Sodium 28mg

Choco-Nut
Balls

1¼ cups vanilla wafer crumbs
1 cup sifted powdered sugar
⅓ cup flaked coconut
¼ cup plus 2 tablespoons butter, melted
2 tablespoons light-colored corn syrup
1 teaspoon vanilla extract
½ cup chunky honey-roasted peanut
 butter
8 (1-ounce) squares semisweet chocolate

Combine first 3 ingredients in a large bowl, and stir
well. Add butter and next 3 ingredients; stir well.
Cover and chill 30 minutes. Shape into 1-inch balls,
and chill an additional 30 minutes.

Place chocolate in top of a double boiler; bring
water to a boil. Reduce heat to low; cook until chocolate melts, stirring frequently. Dip balls in melted
chocolate, coating well. Place on wax paper to set.
Store in an airtight container in refrigerator. Yield:
35 candies.

Per candy: Calories 111 (58% from fat)
Carbohydrate 11.9g Protein 1.5g Fat 7.2g (Sat. Fat 3.2g)
Cholesterol 5mg Sodium 53mg

Prepare Creamy Napoleons with puff pastry or the light napoleons with phyllo pastry.

PHYLLO NAPOLEONS

2½ tablespoons cornstarch
2⅔ cups skim milk, divided
¾ cup sugar
2 teaspoons vanilla extract
3 eggs, lightly beaten
8 sheets frozen phyllo pastry, thawed
Butter-flavored vegetable cooking spray
10 ounces frozen unsweetened strawberries, thawed
1 tablespoon cornstarch
¼ cup red currant jelly
2 tablespoons Cognac
Fresh strawberries (optional)

Combine 2½ tablespoons cornstarch and ⅓ cup milk in a saucepan, stirring well. Add remaining 2⅓ cups milk, sugar, vanilla, and eggs. Cook over medium heat, stirring constantly, until mixture comes to a boil. Cook, stirring constantly, 2 minutes or until thickened. Cover and chill.

Place 1 sheet of phyllo on a dry surface (keep remaining phyllo covered). Coat with cooking spray. Layer remaining phyllo on first sheet, coating each sheet with cooking spray. Cut stack in half lengthwise; place 1 portion on top of the other, forming 16 layers. Cut stack into 8 squares; transfer to a baking sheet coated with cooking spray. Bake at 375° for 5 minutes.

Separate each phyllo stack, making 6 sheets for bottom layer, 4 sheets for middle layer, and 6 sheets for top. Place bottom layers on individual plates; top each with ¼ cup custard mixture. Top with middle layer and ¼ cup custard. Top with remaining layer.

Position knife blade in food processor bowl; add strawberries, and process until smooth. Pour puree through a wire-mesh strainer into a saucepan, discarding pulp. Add 1 tablespoon cornstarch to strawberry puree; stir well. Add jelly, and cook over medium heat, stirring constantly, until thickened. Cook 1 minute. Remove from heat; stir in Cognac. Drizzle over phyllo stacks. Garnish with berries, if desired. Serve immediately. Yield: 8 servings.

Per serving: Calories 251 (13% from fat)
Carbohydrate 45.2g Protein 6.7g Fat 3.7g (Sat. Fat 0.9g)
Cholesterol 85mg Sodium 163mg

Creamy Napoleons

1½ cups sugar
½ cup plus 1 tablespoon cornstarch, divided
⅛ teaspoon salt
3 cups whole milk
8 egg yolks
1 tablespoon vanilla extract
2 sheets commercial puff pastry, thawed
1 (10-ounce) package frozen sweetened strawberries, thawed
¼ cup red currant jelly
2 tablespoons Cognac
¾ cup whipping cream, whipped
2 tablespoons sifted powdered sugar
2 tablespoons grated semisweet chocolate
Fresh strawberries (optional)

Combine 1½ cups sugar, ½ cup cornstarch, and salt. Add milk, stirring well. Cook over medium heat, stirring constantly, until thick. Beat egg yolks until thick and pale. Stir one-fourth of hot mixture into yolks; add to remaining hot mixture, stirring constantly. Bring to a boil; cook, stirring constantly, 1 minute or until thick. Remove from heat; stir in vanilla. Let stand at room temperature 30 minutes. Cover and chill.

Roll pastry to remove fold lines. Cut into 8 squares. Place on baking sheet; bake at 350° for 15 minutes. Let cool. Cut each square in half horizontally.

Place strawberries in an electric blender; cover and process until smooth. Press through a sieve; discard pulp. Combine strawberry puree and remaining 1 tablespoon cornstarch in a saucepan; stir. Add jelly; cook over medium heat until thick. Cook, stirring constantly, 1 minute. Remove from heat; stir in Cognac.

Place bottom halves of pastry squares on plates. Fold whipped cream into custard; spoon onto pastry squares. Top with remaining halves. Sprinkle with powdered sugar and chocolate. Spoon strawberry sauce in small circles onto plates; pull a wooden pick through circles. Garnish with berries, if desired. Yield: 8 servings.

Per serving: Calories 798 (46% from fat)
Carbohydrate 96.7g Protein 11.1g Fat 40.7g (Sat. Fat 12.5g)
Cholesterol 261mg Sodium 255mg

Right: *Creamy Napoleon*

Blueberry Peach Crumble, with its crunchy macaroon topping, offers a light alternative to cobbler. The luscious cobbler has a sweetened almond pastry crust.

BLUEBERRY PEACH CRUMBLE

6 commercial coconut macaroons
½ cup all-purpose flour
¼ cup sugar, divided
2 tablespoons brown sugar
3 tablespoons reduced-calorie margarine, melted
3 cups sliced fresh peaches
3 cups fresh blueberries
1 tablespoon all-purpose flour
2¼ cups vanilla nonfat frozen yogurt

Place macaroons on a baking sheet. Bake at 275° for 25 minutes.

Position knife blade in food processor bowl; add macaroons, and process until coarsely chopped. Combine chopped macaroons, ½ cup flour, 2 tablespoons sugar, and brown sugar in a medium bowl. Add margarine, and stir well. Set aside.

Combine peaches and blueberries in an 8-inch square baking dish. Combine remaining 2 tablespoons sugar and 1 tablespoon flour; sprinkle over fruit mixture. Top with macaroon mixture. Bake, uncovered, at 350° for 30 minutes. Serve warm, and top each serving with ¼ cup frozen yogurt. Yield: 9 servings.

Per serving: Calories 240 (27% from fat)
Carbohydrate 43.2g Protein 3.8g Fat 7.1g (Sat. Fat 0.4g)
Cholesterol 0mg Sodium 75mg

Blueberry Peach Cobbler

2½ cups all-purpose flour
⅔ cup ground toasted almonds
1 teaspoon salt
⅔ cup butter
¼ cup plus 3 tablespoons whole milk
4 cups fresh blueberries
4 cups coarsely chopped fresh peaches
1½ cups sugar
¼ cup cornstarch
2 tablespoons amaretto
2 tablespoons butter
½ teaspoon ground cinnamon
1 egg white, lightly beaten
2 tablespoons sugar
2 tablespoons chopped almonds
2¼ cups French vanilla ice cream

Combine first 3 ingredients; cut in ⅔ cup butter with a pastry blender until mixture is crumbly. Sprinkle milk, 1 tablespoon at a time, evenly over surface of flour mixture; stir with a fork until dry ingredients are moistened. Knead dough 4 or 5 times. Cover and chill 1 hour.

Combine blueberries and next 6 ingredients in a large saucepan. Cook over medium heat, stirring frequently, 10 minutes or until thickened. Remove from heat; let cool.

Roll half of chilled pastry into a 13-inch square on a floured surface, and place in a greased 8-inch square baking dish. Pour fruit mixture into pastry-lined dish. Roll remaining pastry into a 10-inch square. Place pastry over fruit mixture. Fold edges under, and flute. Brush pastry with egg white; sprinkle with 2 tablespoons sugar and chopped almonds. Cut several slits in top crust. Bake at 375° for 40 minutes or until golden. Serve warm, and top each serving with ¼ cup ice cream. Yield: 9 servings.

Per serving: Calories 636 (36% from fat)
Carbohydrate 97.4g Protein 8.7g Fat 25.5g (Sat. Fat 13.1g)
Cholesterol 61mg Sodium 474mg

Top the light fruit pie with a cheesy streusel mixture. Enclose the rich filling in Spirited Fruit Pie with two sheets of flaky pastry.

Streusel Fruit Pie

1¼ cups plus 2 tablespoons all-purpose flour, divided
⅛ teaspoon salt
3 tablespoons vegetable oil
2 tablespoons ice water
2½ tablespoons lemon juice, divided
    Vegetable cooking spray
¾ cup plus 2 tablespoons sugar, divided
½ teaspoon ground cinnamon
¼ teaspoon ground nutmeg, divided
3 cups peeled, chopped cooking apple
2 cups peeled, chopped pear
⅓ cup quick-cooking oats, uncooked
2 tablespoons margarine
½ cup (2 ounces) finely shredded reduced-fat sharp Cheddar cheese

Combine 1 cup flour, salt, and oil; stir until crumbly. Combine water and 1 teaspoon lemon juice; sprinkle evenly over surface of flour mixture, and toss with a fork until mixture is crumbly. (Do not form a ball.) Press into a 4-inch circle on heavy-duty plastic wrap; cover with additional plastic wrap. Roll into an 11-inch circle.

Remove top sheet of plastic wrap. Invert dough into a 9-inch pieplate coated with cooking spray; remove remaining plastic wrap. Fold edges of pastry under, and flute. Line pastry with wax paper; fill with pie weights. Bake at 400° for 8 minutes. Remove wax paper and weights; prick bottom and sides of pastry with a fork. Bake 6 minutes. Cool on a wire rack.

Combine ½ cup sugar, 2 tablespoons flour, cinnamon, and ⅛ teaspoon nutmeg. Toss fruit with remaining lemon juice; add flour mixture, and stir. Spoon into pastry. Bake at 350° for 25 minutes.

Place oats in container of an electric blender; process until ground. Combine oats, remaining sugar, ¼ cup flour, and ⅛ teaspoon nutmeg; cut in margarine with a pastry blender until mixture is crumbly. Stir in cheese. Sprinkle over fruit, and bake 30 minutes. Let cool completely. Yield: 8 servings.

Per serving: Calories 320 (28% from fat)
Carbohydrate 54.1g   Protein 5.1g   Fat 10.1g (Sat. Fat 2.4g)
Cholesterol 5mg   Sodium 121mg

Spirited Fruit Pie

½ cup raisins
½ cup brandy
1 (15-ounce) package refrigerated piecrusts, divided
4 cups peeled, coarsely chopped Granny Smith apple
2 cups peeled, coarsely chopped pear
1½ tablespoons fresh lemon juice
⅔ cup firmly packed dark brown sugar
¼ cup sugar
¼ cup all-purpose flour
¼ teaspoon salt
1½ teaspoons ground cinnamon
1 vanilla bean, halved
¼ cup butter
1 egg, lightly beaten
1 tablespoon water
1 tablespoon sugar
    Cheddar cheese slices (optional)

Combine raisins and brandy; cover and let stand at room temperature 8 hours. Drain raisins, discarding brandy.

Roll 1 piecrust into a 12-inch circle on a floured surface; fit pastry into a 9½-inch deep-dish pieplate.

Combine apple and pear; add lemon juice, tossing lightly. Combine brown sugar and next 4 ingredients; add to fruit mixture. Scrape seeds from vanilla bean. Melt butter in a large skillet; add fruit mixture, and cook until mixture is slightly softened. Stir in raisins and vanilla seeds. Spoon into pastry shell.

Roll remaining piecrust into a 12-inch circle on a floured surface. Place on top of fruit mixture. Fold edges under, and crimp. Combine egg and water, stirring well. Brush pastry with egg mixture, and sprinkle with 1 tablespoon sugar. Bake at 350° for 50 to 55 minutes or until golden. Top with cheese, if desired. Yield: 8 servings.

Per serving: Calories 497 (37% from fat)
Carbohydrate 72.8g   Protein 5.3g   Fat 20.6g (Sat. Fat 7.3g)
Cholesterol 44mg   Sodium 385mg

Meringue seals the light pie, and sweetened whipped cream tops Banana Pie Spectacular.

LIGHT BANANA CREAM PIE

¾ cup sifted cake flour
2 tablespoons unsweetened grated coconut, toasted
2 tablespoons margarine, melted
1 to 2 tablespoons cold water
   Butter-flavored cooking spray
¾ cup plus 2 tablespoons sugar, divided
2 tablespoons cornstarch
⅛ teaspoon salt
1½ cups skim milk
1 egg
1 egg yolk
½ teaspoon vanilla extract
2 medium bananas, peeled and sliced
3 egg whites
½ teaspoon cream of tartar

Combine flour, coconut, and margarine; sprinkle water over surface of mixture, stirring with a fork until crumbly. (Do not form a ball.) Press into a 4-inch circle on heavy-duty plastic wrap. Cover with another sheet of plastic wrap. Roll into a 12-inch circle. Remove top sheet of plastic. Invert pastry into a 9-inch pieplate coated with cooking spray; remove remaining plastic. Fold edges under, and flute. Prick bottom of pastry. Bake at 325° for 15 minutes; cool on a wire rack.

Combine ½ cup sugar, cornstarch, and salt in a saucepan. Add milk, stirring well. Cook over medium heat, stirring constantly, until thickened. Beat egg and egg yolk until thick. Stir one-fourth of hot mixture into beaten egg; add to remaining hot mixture, stirring constantly. Cook, stirring constantly, 2 minutes or until thick. Remove from heat; stir in vanilla. Place banana in pastry. Top with filling.

Beat egg whites and cream of tartar at high speed of an electric mixer until foamy. Add remaining sugar, 1 tablespoon at a time, beating until stiff peaks form. Spread meringue over filling, sealing to edge of pastry. Bake at 325° for 25 minutes. Cool completely before serving. Yield: 8 servings.

Per serving: Calories 241 (21% from fat)
Carbohydrate 43.4g   Protein 5.4g   Fat 5.6g (Sat. Fat 2.1g)
Cholesterol 56mg   Sodium 137mg

Banana Pie Spectacular

⅔ cup sugar
½ cup cornstarch
⅛ teaspoon salt
3 cups whole milk
3 egg yolks, beaten
2 tablespoons margarine
1 teaspoon vanilla extract
⅛ teaspoon freshly grated nutmeg
2 large bananas, peeled and cut into ¼-inch slices
1½ teaspoons lemon juice
1 baked 9-inch pastry shell
¾ cup whipping cream
2 tablespoons sifted powdered sugar
¼ cup large shreds coconut, toasted

Combine first 3 ingredients in a heavy saucepan. Gradually add milk, stirring well. Bring to a boil over medium heat, stirring constantly.

Stir one-fourth of hot mixture into egg yolks; add to remaining hot mixture, stirring constantly. Cook 2 minutes or until thick. Remove from heat, and transfer to a bowl; stir in margarine, vanilla, and nutmeg. Cool completely.

Sprinkle banana slices with lemon juice; stir into egg mixture. Spoon mixture into baked pastry shell. Cover with plastic wrap; chill thoroughly.

Beat whipping cream until foamy; gradually add powdered sugar, beating until soft peaks form. Spread whipped cream over chilled banana filling. Top with coconut. Yield: 8 servings.

Per serving: Calories 442 (49% from fat)
Carbohydrate 50.7g   Protein 6.7g   Fat 24.1g (Sat. Fat 10.6g)
Cholesterol 125mg   Sodium 256mg

Serve a wedge of brownie pie with nonfat frozen yogurt, or splurge on fudge pie topped with ice cream.

BROWNIE PIE À LA MODE

½ cup reduced-calorie margarine
¼ cup unsweetened cocoa
¾ cup sugar
¾ cup all-purpose flour
1 teaspoon baking powder
1½ teaspoons vanilla extract
2 egg whites
  Vegetable cooking spray
1 (1-ounce) package pre-melted
  unsweetened chocolate
1 quart cookies-and-cream nonfat frozen
  yogurt
4 low-fat cream-filled chocolate sandwich
  cookies, cut in half (optional)

Melt margarine in a small saucepan over medium heat; stir in cocoa. Pour mixture into a large bowl. Add sugar and next 4 ingredients; stir well.

Spread batter in a 9-inch round pan coated with cooking spray. Bake at 350° for 20 minutes or until a wooden pick inserted in center comes out clean. Let cool in pan on a wire rack. Cut into 8 wedges.

Drizzle pre-melted chocolate evenly onto 8 dessert plates. Place a brownie wedge on each plate, and top each wedge with ½ cup frozen yogurt. Garnish each with a cookie half, if desired. Yield: 8 servings.

Per serving: Calories 294 (30% from fat)
Carbohydrate 48.6g Protein 6.7g Fat 9.7g (Sat. Fat 2.3g)
Cholesterol 0mg Sodium 223mg

Gooey Fudge Pie à la Mode

1 unbaked 9-inch pastry shell
1 cup sugar
½ cup all-purpose flour
½ cup margarine, melted
⅓ cup unsweetened cocoa
¼ cup firmly packed brown sugar
¼ cup whole milk
1 teaspoon vanilla extract
⅛ teaspoon salt
2 eggs
2 (1.4-ounce) English toffee-flavored
  candy bars, chopped
4 cups vanilla ice cream
½ cup chocolate syrup
  Fresh raspberries (optional)

Bake pastry shell at 350° for 5 minutes. Set aside.

Combine sugar and next 8 ingredients in a large bowl. Beat at medium speed of an electric mixer 5 minutes or until smooth. Stir in chopped candy. Pour filling into prepared pastry shell. Bake at 350° for 35 minutes or until filling is set and pastry is golden. Let cool completely on a wire rack.

To serve, cut into 8 wedges and top each with ½ cup ice cream and 1 tablespoon chocolate syrup. Garnish with raspberries, if desired. Yield: 8 servings.

Per serving: Calories 695 (42% from fat)
Carbohydrate 89.1g Protein 9.4g Fat 32.8g (Sat. Fat 11.4g)
Cholesterol 89mg Sodium 584mg

Top the tart with hazelnuts and sweetened whipped cream; top the spiced pie with nonfat frozen yogurt.

SPICED PUMPKIN PIE

1 cup all-purpose flour
⅛ teaspoon salt
3 tablespoons vegetable oil
3 tablespoons cold water
1 teaspoon lemon juice
  Vegetable cooking spray
1½ cups canned pumpkin
⅓ cup sugar
¾ cup evaporated skimmed milk
½ cup frozen egg substitute, thawed
¼ cup reduced-calorie maple syrup
½ teaspoon ground cinnamon
¼ teaspoon ground cloves
¼ teaspoon ground allspice
2½ cups vanilla nonfat frozen yogurt

Combine flour and salt in a medium bowl. Add oil, stirring until crumbly. Combine cold water and lemon juice. Sprinkle mixture, 1 tablespoon at a time, over surface of flour mixture. Toss with a fork until dry ingredients are moistened. Press dough into a 4-inch circle on plastic wrap. Cover with another sheet of plastic wrap, and chill 5 minutes.

Roll dough into an 11-inch circle. Place in freezer 5 minutes or until top sheet of wrap can be easily removed. Invert dough into a 9-inch pieplate coated with cooking spray, and remove remaining sheet of plastic wrap. Fold edges under and flute, if desired.

Combine pumpkin and next 7 ingredients in a large bowl; stir well. Pour mixture into pastry shell. Bake at 350° for 1 hour or until a knife inserted in center comes out clean. Cool completely on a wire rack. To serve, cut into 10 slices, and top each with ¼ cup frozen yogurt. Yield: 10 servings.

Per serving: Calories 187 (26% from fat)
Carbohydrate 30.3g Protein 5.6g Fat 5.3g (Sat. Fat 1.4g)
Cholesterol 5mg Sodium 88mg

Hazelnut Pumpkin Tart

1 (15-ounce) package refrigerated
    piecrusts, divided
1 cup hazelnuts, toasted, skinned, and
    finely chopped
3 eggs
1 (16-ounce) can pumpkin
½ cup firmly packed brown sugar
⅓ cup sugar
1 cup half-and-half
¾ teaspoon ground ginger
¾ teaspoon ground cinnamon
⅛ teaspoon salt
  Dash of ground nutmeg
  Dash of ground allspice
  Dash of ground cloves
1 cup whipping cream
½ cup sifted powdered sugar
1 tablespoon minced crystallized ginger
30 whole hazelnuts, toasted and skinned

Roll 1 piecrust into a 12-inch circle on a floured surface. Fit into an 11-inch tart pan with removable bottom. Prick bottom and sides of pastry shell. Bake at 375° for 5 minutes. Let cool in pan on a wire rack. Sprinkle with chopped hazelnuts.

Beat eggs at high speed of an electric mixer. Add pumpkin and next 9 ingredients; beat well. Pour into pastry. Bake at 375° for 35 minutes. Cool in pan on wire rack. Cover and chill at least 2 hours.

Cut 30 shapes from remaining piecrust using a small leaf cookie cutter. Place on an ungreased baking sheet. Bake at 450° for 6 minutes. Remove to a wire rack; let cool.

Beat whipping cream until foamy; gradually add powdered sugar, beating until soft peaks form. Fold in crystallized ginger. Cover and chill 1 hour.

Arrange whole hazelnuts and pastry leaves on tart. Serve with whipped cream mixture. Yield: 10 servings.

Per serving: Calories 480 (59% from fat)
Carbohydrate 45.2g Protein 7.8g Fat 31.5g (Sat. Fat 10.3g)
Cholesterol 108mg Sodium 190mg

Right: *Hazelnut Pumpkin Tart*

INDEX

*Page numbers for all light recipes are
preceded by an asterisk (*).*

*Page numbers for all light recipes are
preceded by an asterisk (*).*

Page numbers for all light recipes are preceded by an asterisk (*).

ACKNOWLEDGMENTS & CREDITS

Oxmoor House wishes to thank the following
individuals and merchants:

Annieglass, Santa Cruz, CA
Barbara Eigen Arts, Jersey City, NJ
Biot, New York, NY
Birmingham Antique Mall, Inc., Birmingham, AL
Bridgewater/Boston International, Newton, MA
Bromberg's, Birmingham, AL
Cassis & Co., New York, NY
Christine's, Birmingham, AL
Goldsmith/Corot, Inc., New York, NY
Gorham, Providence, RI
Izabel Lam, Long Island City, NY
Martin & Son Wholesale Florist, Birmingham, AL
Pillivuyt, Salinas, CA
Swid Powell, New York, NY
Aletha Soulé, New York, NY
Table Matters, Birmingham, AL
Union Street Glass, Oakland, CA
Vietri, Hillsborough, NC

Source of Nutritional Analysis Data:

Computrition, Inc., Chatsworth, California.
Primarily comprised of *Composition of Foods: Raw,
Processed, Prepared.* Agriculture Handbook No. 8
Series. United States Department of Agriculture,
Human Nutrition Information Service, 1976-1991.